FIX IT AND SAIL

FIX IT AND SAIL

Everything You Need to Know to Buy and Restore a Small Sailboat on a Shoestring

BRIAN GILBERT

International Marine / McGraw-Hill

Camden, Maine ■ New York ■ Chicago ■ San Francisco
Lisbon ■ London ■ Madrid ■ Mexico City ■ Milan
New Delhi ■ San Juan ■ Seoul ■ Singapore ■ Sydney ■ Toronto

The McGraw-Hill Companies

1 2 3 4 5 6 7 8 9 DOC DOC 9 8 7 6 5

Library of Congress Cataloging-in-Publication Data

Gilbert, Brian, 1960–

Fix it and sail : everything you need to know to buy and restore a small sailboat on a shoestring / Brian Gilbert.

   p. cm.

Includes bibliographical references and index.

ISBN 0-07-145809-3 (pbk. : alk. paper)

1. Sailboats—Maintenance and repair. 2. Sailboats—Purchasing. I. Title.

VM351.G55 2006

623.8220288—dc22

2005026411

Questions regarding the content of this book should be addressed to

International Marine
P.O. Box 220
Camden, ME 04843
www.internationalmarine.com

Questions regarding the ordering of this book should be addressed to

The McGraw-Hill Companies
Customer Service Department
P.O. Box 547
Blacklick, OH 43004
Retail customers: 1-800-262-4729
Bookstores: 1-800-722-4726

Photographs and illustrations by Brian Gilbert.

Disclaimer

Boat restoration and repair naturally involves working with hazardous substances, potentially dangerous tools, and a host of other risks and dangers. The information contained in this book is anecdotal; the author and publisher make no guarantee of the fitness or accuracy of any information contained in this book, and specifically disclaim any liability resulting from the use of this material. Use of the information contained in this book is at the reader's own risk. You are responsible for your own safety, and should take every precaution to protect yourself from accident or injury.

CONTENTS

ACKNOWLEDGMENTS

I am deeply grateful for the support of many people, during both the reconstruction of my little sailboat and the writing and production of this book. I received many suggestions, tips, and notes of support from the members of the MacGregor e-mail list, sponsored by SailNet. John Acton, Bert Ward, and Jeff Lackey, whom I'd never really met other than through e-mail, all drove several hours to help me celebrate my inaugural sail, which was a really nice gesture.

Bill Van Allen, another individual whom I've only known through e-mails, has been a phenomenal help by proofreading and correcting the early text, suggesting improvements, and so on. He has spent many hours reviewing material, and this book is vastly improved because of his input. Tom Stockwell has also reviewed later versions of this book and made good suggestions, and I'm grateful for his effort.

Bob White graciously posted restoration images and comments on his website, www.macgregor-boats.com, and has donated much programming time and Web space. His website gave me the idea to expand that information into this form.

I am also greatly indebted to the folks at International Marine, whose time and efforts transformed this manuscript into a real book. While I appreciate all who worked on it, I need to especially recognize Bob Holtzman, my editor, whose suggestions have made this book much more readable, and Jonathan Eaton, who had the faith to take this job on in the first place.

I'd also like to thank a few close friends, Mark Kennedy and Suzanne Boisvert, for sailing with me and putting up with my constant chatter about all things sailing so many years ago. And my slipmate, Larry Lee, who was always ready to lend a tool, or a hand, or a sense of humor whenever anyone was working on a boat.

And naturally, I owe a tremendous debt of thanks to my wife Karen, who never once laughed at me or questioned my judgment when I brought a floating trash pile home to decorate her side yard for two years, nor as I continued to throw money into this project. Her continual support has been extremely gratifying. It reminds me of a toast that I read about in Mathew Wilson's *Cruising Guide to the Bahamas*—a toast to:

The wind that blows,
The ship that goes,
And the lass that loved a sailor.

This book was written with the hope that more people can experience the joy and freedom that sailing in your own boat allows. I've always been hooked on the idea that sailing is for everyone, and that voyaging in your own little boat can be done for a lot less money than many people believe.

This book is ultimately about dispelling some of the myths of sailing. Big, showy boats have been used for ages to demonstrate wealth. In my local library, there's even a sailing book with the subtitle *The Beautiful People and Their Beautiful Boats*. *Fix It and Sail* has nothing to do with that type of boating.

The idea of saving money and sailing may sometimes seem to be mutually exclusive, but my intent is to reconcile these two thoughts as much as possible. A sailboat is a big investment, but it's well within the means of just about anyone as long as you have the desire. Owning a boat and sailing it well are some of life's great pleasures, and they can be enjoyed by you.

CHAPTER 1

Why Restore a Small Boat?

Economics, Practical Considerations, and Having It Your Way

Once upon a time—a long, long time ago—I owned and lived aboard a Catalina 27. For roughly four years, I lived aboard my boat. Then I decided it was time to go back to school. I sold the boat, moved inland, and used the money to get married and earn my master's degree.

I had always heard it said that the two greatest days in a sailor's life are the day he buys his boat and the day he sells it. Pardon me for saying so, but that's a boatload of manure. I was grateful to sell my boat, but it took all of two weeks before I started feeling like I had made a mistake. Almost immediately I started thinking about another boat to buy.

Eight years and one baby later, I still had no boat. The money for a sailboat always seemed to be urgently needed for one bill or another, so my wife and I had very little to work with. I decided to sit down and define the parameters for a boat that would fit my family's lifestyle.

Part of the problem was me: Having lived aboard a boat, I had definite ideas about what I wanted: a large, high-quality yacht. But my dream boat was totally unrealistic, at least at this stage of my life—newly married, fresh from grad school, unable to find work that capitalized on my degree, with a baby thrown into the mix. We didn't go too crazy buying stuff for our son, but we did want one of us to stay home with our son, and the lost income became significant. As our son Kyle got older, my wife was able to land a good job, I found a part-time editing contract (with flexible hours so I could homeschool Kyle), and we moved into a new house (with the accompanying mortgage and expenses). There was a little money left over after we paid the bills, but not much. I soon understood that there would never be enough to go out and buy that Island Packet 32.

That's when I finally settled on the idea of a trailerable sailboat—something that I could use to dash away for quick day sails, the occasional overnight or weekend cruise, and maybe a little longer trip once or twice a year. So I sat down and tried to turn my rather amorphous daydreams into concrete plans. Our sailboat would have to be:

1. Affordable. Although this can mean widely different things to different people, with us it meant really, really affordable—as in, not a lot of money at all. Like many young families, we had numerous priorities (our young son, for example) that ate up what little cash we had left over at the end of the month.

2. Small. A smaller boat would be a great deal cheaper and would suit the lake sailing that we'd be doing. Oh, sure, I'll cruise the Caribbean someday, but in the meantime, I could sail this boat. Then, when the tropical breezes start to blow my way, I can use the equity in the small boat to move up to something larger. I did want a boat that was large enough to sleep on in relative comfort, meaning some form of cabin (a Catalina 22, for example).

3. Trailerable. A boat on wheels can be vastly more flexible to use than one that's stuck in the water. Trailerability also reduces maintenance expenses and improves affordability, as I describe in more detail in the next section.

4. Quick. The boat had to be quick to fix, quick to rig, quick to launch, and quick to sail. It seems that time is a rare commodity these days, and we needed a boat that didn't take up all our spare minutes.

The only thing that seemed to fill all these requirements was an older, small sailboat (18–23 feet), with a trailer, in need of some repairs and maintenance. I eventually found one that came close, though it ended up needing a lot more repairs than I planned on. More about my particular choice later.

Reducing the Costs of Sailing

Our boat would have to be cheap—both to buy and to maintain. I figured I could come up with about $1,500 to buy the boat, which is not a lot of money. Realistically, the only boats in this range are trailerable.

A trailerable boat gives you options for storing it in the off season that larger boats don't have. You can keep it in your backyard and work on it over the winter if you like, or store it on the trailer in a rental yard or marina. Stick it in a slip during the summer months, and you'll be sailing at the drop of a hat. Some marinas will rent a parking space near their boat ramp where the boat can be kept fully rigged. As long as there aren't any overhead power lines, you can load up the car, drive to the marina, hook up the trailer, and slide it into the water. This can be a lot easier than trailering from house to the water every time you want to sail (although you still have that option), and it can be a lot cheaper than keeping the boat in a slip.

A trailerable boat kept at home is accessible for work without the haulout, yard fees, and trucking expenses that larger boats require. This reduces the cost of maintenance. Parking the boat in the backyard over the winter enables you to dash out and do a quick job whenever you have a free moment, instead of having to pack up the tools, drive to the yard or storage facility, discover you've forgotten something, and spend the rest of the day cursing your absentmindedness.

Cash Value

Generally speaking, sailboats are very poor investments. We've all heard the "hole-in-the-water-into-which-you-pour-money" bit. However, I've never heard this phrase from someone who actually owns and uses a boat. Oversimplifications like this are usually pronounced gleefully by landlubbers.

But there is a grain of truth there. Sailboats in top condition can bring a price that's vastly different from the price of a boat that's been neglected. What some people fail to realize is that the difference is often less than the restoration cost, especially if you do all the work yourself.

That said, a sailboat is not like a car, where the value drops every year until it effectively reaches zero and you haul the thing to the dump. As long as the hull is basically sound, nearly any fiberglass boat can be restored. The restored boat, in good condition, can be sold for a reasonable amount of money—its value is preserved, up to a point. A boat doesn't appreciate in value the way real estate does, but its worth doesn't evaporate like a car either. I like to think of a boat like a bank account that doesn't earn any interest—the money is always there and can be recovered to some degree when it's time to sell. But a boat is a whole lot more fun than a bank account.

Emotional Reasons

Buying a sailboat isn't like buying a toaster. You can't really weigh features against price, then pick the best value;

there are too many variables involved. One of those variables involves your feelings. Don't ignore them. Sailing is mainly an aesthetic activity; it's not essential for our survival. So the aesthetics of the boat, and your feelings about sailing, need considering, too.

I like the idea of fixing up a boat. It preserves the resources that went into creating it, and in all cases those resources are considerable. Thousands of pounds of fiberglass and resin have been kept out of a landfill because of my efforts. Some boats (not mine) have teak in them, and with the replacement price of teak reaching $15 per board foot, you'd be crazy to throw it away. With my boat, I took an ugly, useless eyesore and made it into something functional and, to my mind at least, fairly good-looking. I get a tremendous amount of satisfaction from that. You can, too.

You've probably heard this old adage from the world of real estate: "What are the three most important things to consider when buying a house? Location, location, and location." Well, the equivalent adage with boats could be "Condition, condition, and condition." Neither phrase is an absolute truth, but it's valid to say that condition is one of the single most important determinants of a boat's value. And while this book is about buying a junker cheap and fixing her up, you'd be nuts not to consider paying a little more for a boat in markedly better condition. Sometimes a boat that is a little dated, but relatively clean and ready-to-use, can be purchased for perhaps $1,000 more than a similar boat in dismal condition. This is especially true with smaller, trailerable-sized boats. If you have the cash, spending it up front, making a few upgrades as time and cash allow, and sailing sooner will usually (but not always) make more sense. This may not be the case if you're really tight on disposable cash, or if you have definite ideas about sailing and how you want to set up your boat.

Which Boat?

On any given day, there are thousands of different boats in your size and price range for sale in the United States. How do you decide which one is the best choice?

First off, don't try to find the best choice. Concentrate instead on making a good choice. So many people get hung up on finding the "perfect" boat, but this boat doesn't exist. All boats are compromises, so develop a flexible attitude. Think about the type of sailing you want to do. Are you a racer at heart, or does the thought of a hot cup of coffee in the morning mist get your heart thumping? Maybe you'd like a little of both? Where will you be sailing? San Francisco Bay commonly has 35-knot winds, while the lakes where I sail are often dead calm. Each area has boat types that are better suited to it. Will

you be sailing alone or with a crew? With your husband or wife? With kids? (These last two are especially important, because in my house at least, if they ain't happy, *nobody's* happy. So try to include them in the process.)

Physical Location of the Boat

An important factor to consider when buying a boat is its physical location. Depending on where you live and plan to sail, the cost of the boat you choose can go up—sometimes significantly. For example, let's say you live outside of the major sailing areas (as I do) and you find a great deal on a Cal 25. Trouble is, it's in California, you're not, and it doesn't come with a trailer. You could have the boat trucked to you at a cost of about $3,000. Add the cost of getting the boat on and off the truck, and suddenly your great deal isn't so great. If you have a vehicle capable of towing it, you might get lucky and find a boat with a trailer—but the trailer will likely need some work to make it roadworthy. If you *don't* have a vehicle capable of towing, one option might be to rent an empty U-Haul truck

WHAT'S A BUC?

BUC International Corporation is a marine industry service corporation that has been around for 40 years. It began by publishing the BUC Used Boat Price Guides in 1961 with only 5,000 entries. Today, the "BUC books" are an industry standard, containing values for over 700,000 used boats. You can purchase BUC's printed price guides, or look up values online at www.bucvalu.com.

A word about the BUC values: BUC defines "average condition" this way: "Average condition means that the vessel is ready for sale, requiring no additional work and normally equipped for its size." So a boat that "needs some cleaning" is below average or poor, depending on the work required. Likewise, incomplete boats (boats without a mast) are not considered "normally equipped," so they command a lower price as well.

Note that the BUC value does not include the trailer or motor.

NADA also publishes a boat price guide. Its website is www.nadaguides.com. ∎

and use that to tow the boat. The bottom line: The closer to home your prospective purchase is, the better.

As you think about these issues, get familiar with boat values. I'm not referring to a sales term, but the published book values for used sailboats. I used the BUC values (see sidebar) while looking for my boat, but other guides exist, including NADA's. You'll notice that there are patterns in the prices for older boats; some, like MacGregors, are relatively inexpensive, while others aren't. Some prices drop over time; others don't seem to change that much. Whatever you do, avoid being an impulse buyer. There will always be more neglected boats available than people willing to fix them up, so in a sense, this is a buyer's market. The first thing you need to do when you see a boat for sale is look up the BUC value. This gives you a baseline idea of how much the boat is worth.

Remember that this is a baseline idea, not an absolute value. The real value of any boat is what a buyer will pay for it. In some areas, particular boats sell well above the book value, while others are at or even below the given figure. Outboard motors usually aren't part of the BUC value, and the replacement cost of an outboard can go as high as $1,200 to $1,400 for a new 9.9 hp. I bought a used 5 hp for $450. Keep in mind that a good or repairable trailer can have a big impact on the selling price as well.

The Self-Survey

Professional marine surveys are almost always a good idea, but for a small, inexpensive, trailerable sailboat, you may not need one. I make this claim for several reasons:

- The cost. A competent surveyor will charge at least $300, and that's over half of what I paid for my boat.
- The type of boat we're talking about. Any neglected sailboat will have a plethora of problems, and

most surveyors will tell you to pass on just the sort of boat that you're after.

An exception to this would be if you can find a surveyor who is sympathetic to your idea of fixing up an old boat. Another exception might be if you don't have much experience in boat work, and you really have no idea of the extent of a vessel's problems. Or perhaps the boat is a long distance away, and a survey would be less than a plane ticket. In this case, getting a surveyor to work for you becomes a viable option.

If you do choose to do your own survey, you should become familiar with the art of fault-finding in boats. Ian Nicholson has written one of the few books available on the subject called *Surveying Small Craft*. Other books on boat repair and maintenance will give you an idea of the magnitude of work required for various jobs. One of my favorites is *This Old Boat* by Don Casey. Another good writer on this subject is Ferenc Maté, who wrote *From a Bare Hull* and *The Finely Fitted Yacht*. Though both these books deal with newer boats, they offer a wealth of information. I'm a big fan of boatbuilding, sailing, and cruising books; in the following chapter, we'll look at some additional titles you may find helpful.

With this background information in mind, I've come up with a list of potential "boat-killer" problems to watch out for. Remember when I said that nearly any fiberglass boat can be brought back? This is true in theory, but some of the following problems can result in a boat that takes far more effort than it's worth.

"Boat-Killers"

Structural Cracks or Holes in the Hull. Unless the boat is free—and even then—consider that this type of problem involves a major repair that may never look right. If it isn't fixed perfectly, you may never be able to sell your boat later. There are so many available boats without this sort of problem that it rarely makes sense to tackle this unless the boat is worth a great deal of money repaired (for example, a Bristol Channel Cutter or a Flicka). An article in the July 2002 issue of *Good Old Boat* magazine describes the replacing of a ten-foot section of hull from a sunken Hinckley. When completed, this boat will be worth hundreds of thousands of dollars, thus justifying some very extreme repair measures. But for most boats, you don't want to go there.

Missing Major Equipment. The replacement cost of a mast and standing rigging, for example, will often be higher than the value of the entire boat. Rudders—possibly even a keel—can be replaced. But it's almost always better to repair an existing part than to fabricate one from scratch, especially of you don't have a pattern. Likewise, a boat with a brand-new motor, trailer, or sails may turn out to be a bargain, despite the higher initial purchase price.

Extensive Wood Rot. While a small amount of rot isn't too big a deal, large rotten areas or water-delaminated plywood bulkheads mean a pretty major repair job. A telltale sign to watch for is a mud line near the cabin sole, where standing water has sat in the boat for a while. If this mud line gets

---

SAILING TERMS

The *cabin sole* is the boat's floor. The walls (the flat ones that divide the boat into front and back compartments) are called *bulkheads,* while the ceiling is called the *overhead.* In boatspeak, *ceiling* refers to strips of finished wood that are screwed to the inside surfaces of the hull.

Go figure. ∎

---

as high as the bulkheads, they may be starting to delaminate. In an inconspicuous area, poke the wood with an ice pick or pocketknife. If the tip goes in easily, there's trouble, and that area needs attention.

A "Partially Restored" Boat.

You'll need to know how things went together before you can put them back. If the boat has been taken apart, then it has a huge strike against it. Plus, you'll need to use the rotten pieces to make patterns (see Chapter 4)—this is hard to do if the rotten pieces have been thrown away. Very often, someone buys a boat, realizes the project is just too much, and decides to cut his losses. A situation like this might be worth investigating closer, but it will be harder to put the boat right. The seller should expect to deeply discount a boat like this; after all, you're doing him a favor by bailing him out. Remember: Arm yourself with knowledge before you take on someone else's nightmare. Sometimes, a knowledgeable restorer has unusual reasons for stopping a project and selling (a death in the family, for example), and you can pick up on a great deal. But cases like this are rare, so be careful of partial restorations.

Tools to Bring

Tools for the small boat surveyor are fairly simple: a notebook and pen, a finely-tipped awl or pocketknife (to check for rotten wood), and a flashlight or work light. A camera can really help refresh your memory later, but interior shots are hard to get correctly exposed. Inexpensive autoflash cameras aren't made for tight interiors and dark close-ups, so use the best camera you can. A digital camera is the best choice, because you have the luxury of viewing the pictures right after you've taken them. Some people have used video cameras with great results; you can add a running commentary to refresh your mind later. After you look at a few boats, the details start to run together.

Where Do I Begin?

When I look at a boat, I like to start at the bilge and work my way up. There isn't much of a bilge on most small boats, so this means looking at the keel/centerboard area. Repairs here aren't necessarily all that difficult, but the weight of the keel plus the problem of limited access make repairs a big job. On my MacGregor, for example, the keel was made up of three plates of ½-inch-thick steel, welded together and

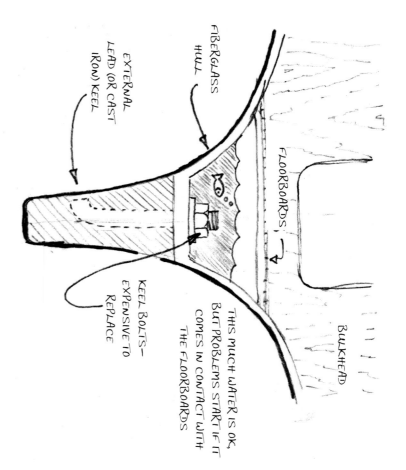

FIBERGLASS HULL

EXTERNAL LEAD (OR CAST IRON) KEEL

FLOORBOARDS

THIS MUCH WATER IS OK, BUT PROBLEMS START IF IT COMES IN CONTACT WITH THE FLOORBOARDS

KEEL BOLTS— EXPENSIVE TO REPLACE

BULKHEAD

A fixed keel bilge. There's room here to hold the water that will find its way aboard, though the keel makes launching and trailering difficult.

encapsulated in polyester resin and fiberglass. The polyester failed over the years, and the plates began to rust. Rust expands metal, and the fiberglass skin had swollen the keel until it stuck inside the keel trunk. A previous owner had sliced away large sections of the offending areas, leaving the metal exposed when the boat was in the water. The only fix was to rebuild the keel from the metal plates up. The repair itself wasn't that complex in theory, but the reality of lowering the keel out of the boat and maneuvering it around was a royal pain. Some boats have cast-iron keels, making repairs much easier. If I had been able to find one, I

would have replaced this keel with a cast version.

Blisters are a common problem with boats that are left in the water. Experts disagree on the exact cause, but water migrates into the fiberglass resin and collects in pockets that can be as small as a pinhead, just under the gelcoat, or as large as a quarter, forming deep within the laminate. They can even lift apart the layers of fiberglass in the hull, causing significant structural damage. Gelcoat blisters are mainly cosmetic but could indicate future problems if you're planning on keeping the boat at a marina. Large, deep blisters need to be dug out, thoroughly dried, filled with epoxy,

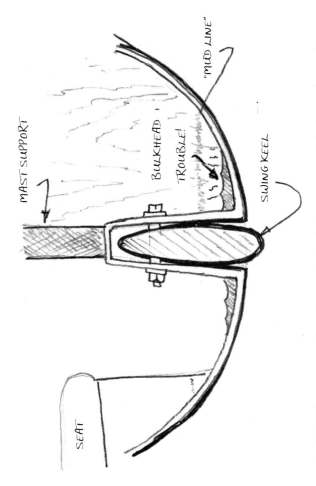

MAST SUPPORT

"MUD LINE"

BULKHEAD
TROUBLE!

SWING KEEL

SEAT

A swing keel bilge. Water collects by gravity in the lowest part of the boat. There's a far higher likelihood that any standing water will cause damage compared to a boat with a traditional bilge. This is one of the "trailerability tradeoffs."

and sanded. Then the whole hull needs to be barrier-coated with a special paint containing coal-tar solids or epoxies (such as Interlux's Interprotect 2000, which is epoxy-based, or VC-Tar Barrier Coat, which contains coal tar). Earlier repair practices of coating the entire hull with epoxy have in some cases made the problem worse. At any rate, the amount of work required to fix a badly blistered hull can be considerable. But if the boat is otherwise in good shape, this can be used as leverage to lower the purchase price. Trailerable boats seem to be less afflicted with blisters, as they are often stored on the trailer.

When you look at the interior, think low and inside: low down in the hull where the water collects, and inside all the lockers, covers, and hiding places. One of the things you're looking for is

standing water, because it can cause a surprising amount of damage in a fiberglass boat. Standing water greatly accelerates rot in wood, delaminates plywood bulkheads, corrodes wiring and fasteners—it's generally bad news. If the boat has deep standing water in it, that's a sign of a careless owner, and you can expect to find much preventable damage caused by neglect. The selling price on this type of boat should be very, very low. Don't believe the often-chanted sales mantra, "All she needs is a good cleaning." In my opinion, no boat can survive an appreciable amount of time with water in it without suffering significant damage.

Now I'm not talking about a little water in the bilge. Boats with fixed keels or keel centerboards sometimes have a bilge beneath the floorboards. The bilge

WHAT ABOUT THE SAILS?

When you look at a potential boat to restore, pay particular attention to the condition of the sails. Get all of them out of the bag and spread them out on the lawn. I'm of the opinion that folded sails can indicate a conscientious owner. There's an argument that sails are better stored by simply stuffing them in the bag, because the wrinkles are never in the same place, but the sails are never folded exactly the same way each time, are they? Points off if you find the boat stored for the winter with the sails wrapped around the boom. More points off if the sail cover is in tatters or missing. Sailcloth is sensitive to UV rays, so a rotten sail follows soon after the cover goes.

Try to find out when the sails were made. If they're the original sails, you can count on replacing them unless they look really good. You want the cloth to be somewhat stiff and the stitching tight. The stitches are usually the first to deteriorate, so examine them closely. ■

is designed to be able to cope with a certain amount of water that will inevitably find its way aboard. Leaving standing water in the bilge might accelerate blistering, but, other than that, a small amount of water doesn't hurt.

Many trailerables with retractable centerboards or daggerboards don't have a bilge in the traditional sense. Instead, you stand on the lowest part of the boat and walk through any puddles that collect. A boat like this can only cope with a small amount of water before it comes into contact something that isn't supposed to be wet, like wood or wiring. So watch out for any water that'll get your feet wet as you look at the interior.

If you don't see any standing water down below, that's better, but you're not out of the woods. Now you're looking for evidence that the boat has flooded in the past. Usually, in lower-priced boats, a seller will pump out his neglected boat, but he won't take the time to clean away the evidence. What you're looking for is

a mud line, a small dark band that forms at the top of the flood. Think, "ring around the bathtub." Look inside all the lockers, especially the ones under the quarter berths; these lockers are rarely cleaned out, even if the rest of the cabin is spotless and shiny.

If you find evidence of flooding, ask the owner about it. Show him the line if he denies it, and begin searching for water damage and rot below the line. Here's another chance to use your handy fine awl or a pocketknife. With the owner's permission, probe the wood parts to see if you can find any rot, but do it in areas that won't show. You may see marks where other potential buyers have done the same. Be especially suspicious if wiring was submerged, and doubly so if there are splices in the wiring that have been submerged. This can lead to mysterious intermittent shorts that are difficult to trace.

Now seems like a good time to talk about liners. Starting about 1973 or so, boat builders figured out that they could save a lot of time by installing molded fiberglass cabinetry inside a boat, rather than building the interiors piece-by-piece. These hull liners or hull socks, as they were sometimes called, fit inside the hull and cut completion time and material costs dramatically. This method of construction has some drawbacks, mainly the loss of access to important parts of the hull and centerboard. It can also be an inherently weaker form of construction, because the liners are bonded to the hull in fewer places than a piece-built plywood interior where each bond would add stiffness to the hull. But one of the big advantages is that less plywood and lumber are used down low in the boat. Thus, flooding isn't as serious a problem as it is in boats built without liners. Less wood means that the boat may do all right with a very thorough cleaning in cases of neglect (in other words, standing water). Even so, you still need to be careful; some liners are attached using plywood "tabs" that are bonded to the hull, and then the liner is screwed to the tabs to secure it. There's no way to inspect wood that's buried behind a liner in this way. If the tabbing is severely rotted, it could allow portions of the interior to come adrift in a seaway—not a pleasant thought. If the boat looks badly neglected, you should suspect this sort of problem, but otherwise a boat with a liner might be a good deal easier to restore than one without.

CHAPTER 2

Resources and Choices for the Small Boat Sailor

Books, Websites, Magazines, and a Look at a Few Boats

Sailboats are a lot like dogs. There are a lot of good dogs out there, but there are a lot of bad ones, too. Some of those bad dogs were born that way—poorly bred and troublesome right from the start. Others started out sound and, through accident or owner neglect, turned bad. You'll want to do some research to find a boat that, even if it's not good as it stands, at least has the potential to become good with some effort.

Where to Get Good Information

A number of resources can help you find a restorable small boat at the right price. I've already mentioned a few good books, but I'll summarize a few more that you might consider.

- *Upgrading Your Small Sailboat for Cruising*, by Paul and Myra Butler. This is one of my favorite books (other than *Fix It and Sail*, of course). It's the only title I've

seen that deals exclusively with boats of the size we're talking about. From the same authors is *Fine Yacht Finishes*, which concentrates on painting and varnishing.

- *This Old Boat*, by Don Casey. This is a good, easy-to-read book that covers all aspects of refinishing a sailboat, right down to making your own sails. While mainly geared toward larger yachts (with appropriately larger sections on engines and plumbing), the book still has a wealth of information that applies to smaller, simpler trailer sailers. Mr. Casey is one of my favorite writers on the subject. I have some of his other books—*Dragged Aboard and Sensible Cruising: The Thoreau Approach*—and I've enjoyed these very much. He has written several additional titles, which deal with specific restoration subjects (*Sailboat Electrics Simplified*,

Canvaswork and Sail Repair, *Sailboat Hull and Deck Repair*, and the omnibus Don Casey's *Complete Illustrated Sailboat Maintenance Manual*). I don't yet have all his restoration books in my personal library, but I've looked them over in bookstores, and they're a great resource to the boat restorer.

■ *From a Bare Hull* by Ferenc Maté. By now this book is quite old, though it was recently republished in paperback. It's about finishing a new boat from a purchased hull. Though it's a little off-topic, it has a lot of information that can help you learn about seaworthy boat construction and, with this knowledge, make better repairs. The book concentrates on larger boats, though, as do his other titles: *The Finely Fitted Yacht* (two volumes of boat-improvement projects) and *Shipshape: The Art of Sailboat Maintenance.*

■ *Boat Joinery and Cabinetmaking Simplified* by Fred Bingham. This is a good, no-nonsense book about making the joinery required for boat interiors. Mr. Bingham is the father of Bruce Bingham, designer of the legendary Flicka (arguably the ultimate small boat). This book offers a lot of useful information regarding woodworking techniques and joinery methods, though its focus is on new boat construction and not restoration and repair. The author's discussions on tools are especially useful. The joinery practices Mr. Bingham teaches would have

been more commonly seen in boats from the early days of fiberglass and are especially applicable to boats without liners. It's solid, no-frills construction, and one of very few books of its kind.

■ *Upgrading the Cruising Sailboat*, 2nd edition, by Daniel Spurr. This book is very well written and beautifully illustrated, but the subject matter—preparing a larger boat for liveaboard, bluewater cruising—is quite different from what we're talking about. Even so, it's well worth reading, and you'll learn sound construction practices and joinery, but you can skip over the sections on wheel steering and autopilots.

I haven't read every book on boat restoration, but I seem to find something of value in every one that I read. More information about these and other useful titles can be found in Appendix 7.

Other print resources for small boat restoration include magazines, but these aren't as useful as they could be. The two major magazines, *Sail* and *Cruising World*, are fun to read, but their editorial focus remains primarily on newer, larger, expensive yachts in exotic locations. Many of their readers are armchair dreamers of the South Seas, and getting there takes a fairly sizeable boat. These magazines have to consider their advertisers, too. After all, boat manufacturers, boat dealers, and charter companies are responsible for a significant amount of their revenue. The subscription price doesn't cover the cost of the printing and distribution, and advertising dollars are the major source of revenues. Naturally, they can't afford to publish articles that say things like, "You don't need to spend a fortune—just fix an old, small boat at a fraction of the cost and start having fun!" This is the sort of problem that killed a really great magazine called *Small Boat Journal* in the mid-1980s. (The back issues are excellent, if you can find them.)

The same problem exists when looking at the brokerage ads in these magazines. The ad space costs too much to list a Seaward 17 for $2,000 (commission to the broker, perhaps $200) when you can put a listing for an Island Packet 37 for $150,000 in the same space (commission to the broker, $15,000). So which would you spend your money advertising if you were a broker? Those little ads cost a bundle, so they naturally go for the big bucks. My personal theory is that cheap boats are listed where the ads are cheap. Community shopper–type publications (where ads are free until an item sells) will sometimes list smaller sailboats in coastal communities. The larger cities are usually better, but this is still somewhat of a long shot.

A few other print magazines (some that I haven't seen, but might be worth checking out) are:

- *Good Old Boat* magazine, dedicated to smaller yacht restoration.

A friend just loaned me a copy, and this is a great bimonthly magazine, though it is expensive at $40 for six issues. It costs more because it has more articles and less advertising, and the articles are well done. 7340 Niagara Lane North, Maple Grove, MN 55311-2655. www.goodoldboat.com.

- *The Small Craft Advisor*, is edited and published by Craig Wagner and Joshua Colvin. Some have said that it's as good as the out-of-print *Small Boat Journal*. That's a pretty tall order, but it's a good magazine in itself, and it concentrates on smaller boats, like the sailboats in this book. PO Box 676, Morro Bay, CA 93442. www.smallcraftadvisor.com.

- *Practical Sailor* is a good *Consumer Reports*–type magazine that might be useful once you become a boat owner. There is no advertising, so the magazine is expensive, but one article might save you the $35 subscription price. Often reviewed are big boats and big-ticket items, so it isn't always directly useful. Still, I've been a subscriber for years (off and on) and have always

BOAT DESIGN RESOURCES

The classic reference on production boat designs is *Maunch's Sailboat Guide* by Ian Maunch—three volumes filled with data on just about every production sailboat ever made, including line drawings. Possibly a better resource would be *Practical Boat Buying*, though some of my favorite smaller boats aren't reviewed and many that are I could never afford. Those boats that are reviewed (and in my imaginary price range) are examined in great depth and detail. ∎

HOT OFF THE WEB

Here are a few Web addresses that list sailboats for sale. There's no shortage of neglected sailboats out there:

http://boats.com/content/sailing.jsp

www.boatmall.com

www.geocities.com/perfectpocketyacht/index.html

www.onlyboatclassifieds.com

www.pocketcruisers.com

www.sailboatowners.com

www.sailingmatters.com/classifieds/

www.sailnet.com/boatsearch/

www.whatboat.com

been satisfied overall. PO Box 420235, Palm Coast, FL 32142-0235.

Online newspaper classifieds are another source that's sometimes more accessible. Most newspaper classifieds are searchable on the Internet (for example, I found a Capri 17, better than new, for $4,000 by searching TampaTribune.com).

Not to be ignored, though, is the old-fashioned library search. Many larger libraries still keep subscriptions to the major newspapers in print form. Just taking a trip to your local library and browsing through the Sunday editions of major papers, especially those from coastal cities, is a simple solution.

Some other resources on the Internet are highly useful. For finding boats, there's Boat Trader (www.boattraderonline.com), which lists over 80,000 boats. A recent search resulted in over 86 sailboats from 17 to 22 feet, all under $2,000. While Boat Trader is big, only a small percentage of the listings have photos.

Soundings has had a good print classified section, but its online version yields the same results as Boat Trader.

Yacht World is another Internet-based boat search (www.yachtworld.com) that can be more useful. Using the same search terms as Boat Trader, I recently found 14 boats, but all had photographs with them. Sometimes you can rule out a boat based on a single picture (a total basket case or a boat that's exceedingly ugly).

There may be other websites that I don't know about and likely some that have appeared (or disappeared) between this writing and your reading of this book. Naturally, the Internet is an ever-changing medium.

And, of course, there's eBay's sail auctions (http://listings.eBaymotors.com/aw/plistings/all/category26433/index.html). This can be the place to find a great deal, but I've also heard some horror stories. For example, a successful bidder paid for a boat only to find out the "owner" had no registration papers. I think asking a seller to provide lots of pictures and a scan of the boat's documentation before you bid is reasonable. I've bought lots of sailing equipment through eBay. In general, I've been quite satisfied, though sometimes eBay has been a poor choice on my part. Know your prices before you bid; you can sometimes find equipment for less money through normal retail suppliers.

Also, www.trailersailor.com has lots of resources for owners of trailerable sailboats. There are dozens of class-specific websites, like www.macgregor owners.com for MacGregor sailboats or www.cal25.com for Cal sailboats. Your best bet is to do an Internet search for the specific boat that you're interested in.

My Short List of Commonly Available Boats to Restore

What follows are some quick descriptions of boats that I was considering when I bought my boat. This list is by no means comprehensive; there are literally hundreds of boats in this size range. These boats were the ones I was able to

find. Also, I needed a boat that could be pulled by an average car. (I had purchased a used 6-cylinder Voyager with the intention of using it to pull a boat, only to discover that it was rated to pull just 2,200 pounds. A transmission specialist told me that I shouldn't pull anything with this car. I sold it and bought a Nissan Frontier pickup that can pull 3,750 pounds, which is pretty average, though with its standard transmission it cannot pull my boat up a steep ramp.) A boat's beam is usually restricted to 8 feet wide by highway laws, though some states allow 8 feet 6 inches.

I don't make any claim of knowing these boats' particular sailing characteristics, as I've never sailed on any of them. Some are *tender* (also known by the nervous nonsailor as "tippy"), some are *stiff* (the opposite of "tippy"), some have better windward ability than others, and so on. The main criteria for my little list was "commonly available." For example, the West Wight Potter 19 is a great little boat that fits all of my parameters, but these

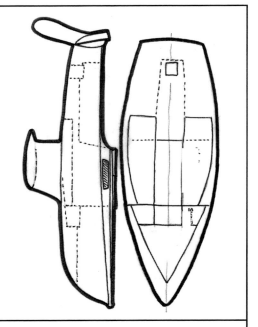

Cal 20
LENGTH: 20' 0"

BEAM: 7' 0"

DRAFT: 3' 4"

DISPLACEMENT: 1,950 lbs

BALLAST: 900 lbs

SAIL AREA: 196 sq. ft.

SAMPLE BOAT: A 1964 model in San Pedro, California. No trailer or motor. Lien sale, asking $750. BUC value for this boat (poor condition, West Coast) $1,200–$1,400 retail.

boats are rarely offered for sale used, and when they are, they're usually well maintained and expensive. You'll see twenty Catalinas, Odays, or MacGregors to every one Potter 19. Also, many of these boats have had various changes made to them over the years, so later models look vastly different than newer ones.

I needed a boat that was inexpensive, reasonably available, safe in a seaway (at least as safe as possible for such little boats), and not hopelessly ugly. The boats I list here more or less follow those criteria. I finally ended up with a MacGregor Venture 222 (more info about that particular boat will follow).

Note: Sample prices were found on the Internet and are the asking price, not the selling price. They were current in 2005.

Cal 20. When I lived on my boat, some friends of mine owned a Cal 20. It was a tiny boat, but Marion and Mike seemed to do more sailing on their little ship than the rest of the marina combined. Cal 20s

are reportedly very seaworthy, and *Practical Sailor* gave this boat a good review.

One of the advantages/disadvantages of this boat is its fixed keel. It makes trailering and launching the boat quite difficult, but once the boat is in the water, it has the stability of a much larger vessel. The book value of this boat is $1,200. I've seen them for as low as $900 (spring 2000), but this was for a boat that was in pretty sad shape, with no trailer or motor.

Cal 25. Similar in general concept to the Cal 20, the Cal 25 is also a flush-deck, fixed-keel boat. With an 8-foot beam, it's trailerable in theory, but the curb weight of the boat loaded with supplies, trailer, and engine approaches 5,000 pounds. A diesel Suburban or industrial-strength pickup might be able to pull it, but not much else. Still, Cal 25s have a reputation as strong, seaworthy vessels. A few of these boats have circumnavigated.

The Cal 25's main disadvantage, other than its age (most of these are 1975

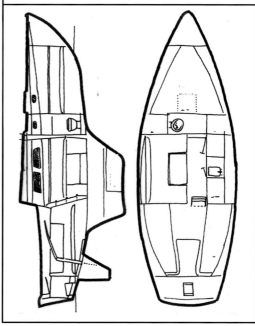

Cal 25

LENGTH: 25'0"

BEAM: 8'0"

DRAFT: 4'0"

DISPLACEMENT: 4,500 lbs

BALLAST: 2,000 lbs

SAIL AREA: 314.5 sq.ft.

SAMPLE BOAT: A 1970 model, located in Hilton Head, South Carolina, with a Johnson 10-hp outboard, no trailer, recently listed for $1,500.

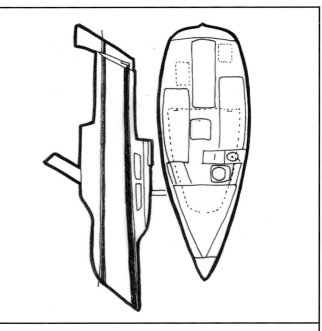

Oday 22
LENGTH: 21'8"
BEAM: 7'2"
DRAFT: 1'3" (board up)/4'3" (board down)
DISPLACEMENT: 2,183 lbs (curb weight approaches 2,500 lbs with the trailer)
BALLAST: 700 lbs
SAIL AREA: 190 sq. ft.
SAMPLE BOAT: A 1976 model in Bridgeton, Missouri, with trailer, four sails, and a 7.5-hp Mercury outboard, asking $2,950. BUC value for the same boat was $2,500 to $2,900.

or earlier, and are likely to have some wear and structural weaknesses, especially in the bulkheads and deck cores), is that it doesn't have standing headroom. A small pop-top helps somewhat.

Currently, prices for Cal 25s range from $1,500 for an "as-is, where-is lien sale, needs a motor" to roughly $6,000 for a nice one. Average asking prices hover around $4,500 to $5,500. The BUC value for a 1973 model is between $5,050 to $5,800.

Oday 22. These are reportedly nice little boats, good-looking, with a serviceable interior. A touch on the heavy side, they're reported to have good stability and mediocre sailing qualities, probably because of their rather smallish keel/centerboard. Note that O'Day also made a "222," which was a similar, though slightly different, model built from 1983 to 1988.

Catalina 22. Catalina 22s look good and are still quite popular. In fact, the asking price on these boats is often much higher than the BUC value. (Then again, asking price and selling price can be very different.) Sailing abilities are reportedly average.

Com-Pac 16. These boats aren't terribly practical (for my preferred style of cruising, that is—I like boats with a little more cabin). They're super for daysailing. The cabins are tiny and dark, and it's been said that they don't really perform well upwind. But they look great. The Com-Pac 23 is a lot more practical below decks, but it's so expensive that it's way out of my range.

Pearson 22. The fixed keel on this boat would likely cause some launching difficulties, but Pearson has a reputation for producing quality yachts. They weren't

Catalina 22

LENGTH: 21'6"

BEAM: 7'8"

DRAFT: 1'8" (board up)/5'0" (board down)

DISPLACEMENT: 2,250 lbs

BALLAST: 550 lbs

SAIL AREA: 212 sq. ft.

SAMPLE BOAT: A 1974 model in Sturgeon Bay, Wisconsin, with trailer, 6-hp Evinrude, main, jib, and 150 genoa. "Needs some TLC." (This term can mean almost anything. At best, the seller is saying "The boat is a mildew farm." At worst, the boat is sitting on the bottom of the lake.) Asking $2,800. BUC value for this boat (below average condition, Midwest) $2,300 to $2,650 retail.

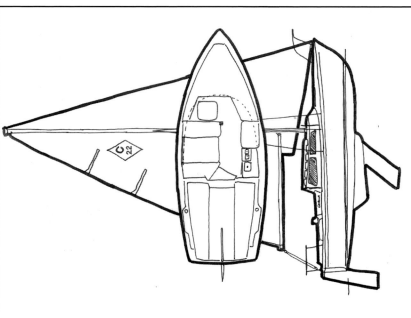

1. Introduced in 1969, the Catalina 22's low cost and good looks made it a popular boat. This one is a typical sample of a neglected boat. 2. Interior of the Catalina 22. Replacing the cushions is a big job, and the table will need some modifications to get rid of the sag, or the table could be replaced. On the plus side, the interior liner will respond to a good cleaning rather than a full paint job. 3. A Catalina 25 in need of some attention. Only 3 feet longer than a 22, it probably represents a tenfold increase in the amount of work required to bring it back to top condition. 4. The payoff in a larger boat, though, is the much more livable interior. Where the 22 is like camping in a fiberglass pup tent, the 25 lends itself to more extended cruises.

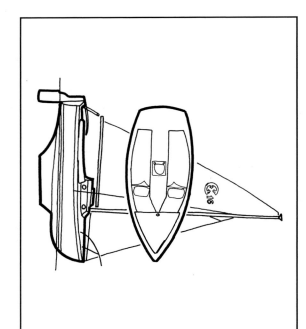

Com-Pac 16

LENGTH: 16'0"
BEAM: 7'0"
DRAFT: 1'6"
DISPLACEMENT: 1,950 lbs
BALLAST: 450 lbs
SAIL AREA: 115 sq. ft.
SAMPLE BOAT: A 1984 model in Bridgeton, Missouri, with trailer and 3.3-hp Mercury outboard. Asking $3,200. BUC value for this boat (average condition, Midwest) $1,750 to $2,100 retail.

produced in large numbers, so finding one may be tricky, but it would be a great candidate for restoration. Pearson also produced a 26-footer called an Ariel that had a full keel. It wasn't a trailerable sailboat, but it's a very rugged and sea-friendly design that would be a fine boat if brought up-to-date.

Tanzer 22. Tanzer was an active factory in Canada, producing many models of popular and well-built yachts. Then in 1987, the Royal Bank of Canada abruptly called their loan—C&C, another Canadian boat manufacturer financed by the Royal Bank, had just declared bankruptcy a month earlier—and forced the company into receivership. There is still an active class association for smaller Tanzers (www.tanzer22.com), and these boats can still be found in varying conditions. Trailers are more difficult to

MODIFIED BOATS

Every now and again, you come across a boat that has been extensively modified. Usually, these boats sound like a good deal—until you get a look at them. Sometimes a major modification is an improvement, but often this hurts a boat's value. Boats like this are best avoided, unless the previous owner's attempt at amateur marine architecture can be rectified at a reasonable expense. For example, my boat came with three large ports cut into the hull below the sheer. Ugly, useless, and a potential boat sinker if one were ever stove in. (They do brighten the interior a little, though.) I figured that I could epoxy the holes after a season or two, but I've yet to do it. ■

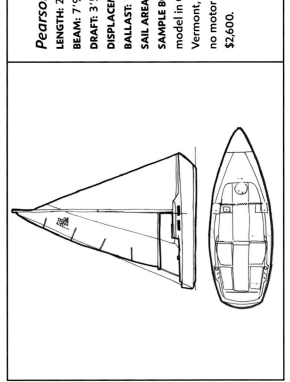

Pearson 22

LENGTH: 22'3"

BEAM: 7'9"

DRAFT: 3'5" (fixed keel)

DISPLACEMENT: 2,600 lbs

BALLAST: 1,000 lbs

SAIL AREA: 217 sq. ft.

SAMPLE BOAT: A 1968 model in Colchester, Vermont, with four sails and no motor or trailer, asking $2,600.

come by. Generally speaking, Tanzers were roomy for their size because of their generous beam and flush deck.

Bristol 24. While this boat could be considered "trailerable" in terms of its size, it's really much too heavy to be a practical over-the-road boat. At nearly 6,000 pounds displacement, she's a very small version of a heavy cruiser. Add the difficulty of ramp-launching a boat with a 3½-foot keel, and you can quickly see that this isn't the quick family getaway boat that some of the others are.

On the other hand, she has full standing headroom and was built like a tank. In light winds, she might sail like one, too, but if you have your sights set on some heavy-weather ocean cruising, it may be worth a look. Over 725 were built, and as tough as these things look, quite a few should still be around. Their owners tend to hang on to them, though.

Irwin 23. The Irwin 23 was considered a lightweight when it was originally introduced, though now it isn't generally regarded as such. According to owners, she sails well with the centerboard up. Irwins have a reputation for being poorly constructed, and because the factory made so many different boats at the same time, this reputation may be partially deserved. But as with any boat, Irwin 23s may be turned into able sailers with some time and care. According to some, neglected 23s can be found for as little as $1,500, but the 25s are a little more common. Built from 1969 until 1975, these boats are reported to have 5 feet 2 inches of headroom in the main cabin.

MacGregors

If you go out looking at older boats, you'll probably run across at least one MacGregor. These boats range in size from 19 to 25 feet in six models, with some models having different versions from year

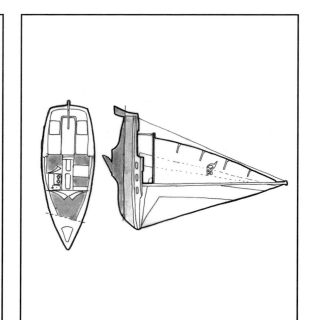

Tanzer 22

LENGTH: 22'
BEAM: 7'10"
DRAFT: 3'5" (fixed keel model); 2'0"/4'0" (keel/centerboard model)
DISPLACEMENT: 2,900 lbs
BALLAST: 1,250 lbs (fixed keel model); 1,500 lbs (centerboard model)
SAMPLE BOAT: A 1982 model in the Northeast with a 99-hp Tohatsu outboard, asking $3,995.

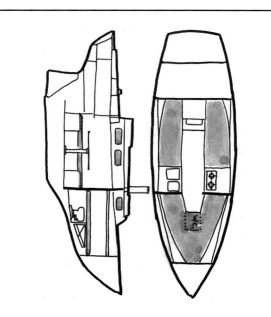

Bristol 24

LENGTH: 24'7"
BEAM: 8'
DRAFT: 3'5"
BALLAST: 3,000 lbs
DISPLACEMENT: 5,920 lbs
SAIL AREA: 296 sq. ft.
SAMPLE BOAT: a 1969 model in good shape, 99-hp Johnson Sailmaster motor, no trailer, located in the Northeast, listed for $4,900.

to year. They were inexpensive when they were new, and they sold by the dozens. The Mac 25s were especially popular. They're lightly built and, as a result, most are reported to be lively sailers.

Boat junkyards are full of MacGregors. You'll find quite a few that are neglected

and/or heavily modified. You're just as likely to find Mac owners who are actively sailing their boats and who are happy as clams with them. (I've heard lots of negative comments about Macs over the years, like "They're cheap and cheaply made," or "Too light to be a real boat," but these

24

Irwin 23

LENGTH: 23'
BEAM: 8'
DRAFT: 2'5"/5'9"
DISPLACEMENT: 3,200 lbs
BALLAST: 1,500 lbs
SAIL AREA: 256 sq. ft.
SAMPLE BOAT: A 1973 Irwin 23 recently listed for $1,700 in Georgetown, Texas. "Needs bottom job and minor repairs." Includes a tandem-axle trailer, mast and sails, but no motor.

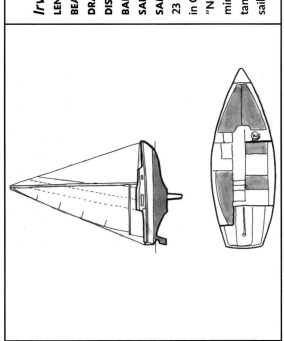

Venture 21

LENGTH: 21'0"
BEAM: 6'10"
DRAFT: 12"/5'6"
DISPLACEMENT: 1,175 lbs
BALLAST: 400 lbs
SAIL AREA: 175 sq. ft.
SAMPLE BOAT: A 1980 model located in California, in good shape, no motor, asking price is $2,400.

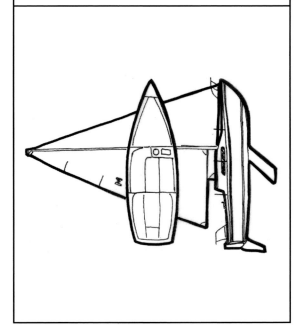

never came from someone who actually owned one.) If you talk to Mac owners, most are generally happy with their boats.

Venture 21. MacGregor used the Venture model name for a number of years. The Venture 21, while not the smallest Mac made, is the smallest that I considered because I wanted to spend at least a few days cruising. Originally designed as a ¼-ton race boat, the accommodations below are spartan.

On any MacGregor, you can count on replacing the electrical system at the very least. It was very cheaply executed at the factory and, by now, it either doesn't work or is a rat's nest of owner patches and repairs. On the plus side, all MacGregors had positive foam flotation installed, and would float even if holed—provided the previous owner hasn't removed the foam to gain storage space. (A bad move, since these boats are easily overloaded and don't sail well if down on their lines. Luckily, there is a fix. See Chapter 5 to see how you can replace foam.)

Venture 22. Only a foot longer than the Venture 21, these boats have a bit more room below. Still, they're on the small side, but they're a practical size for trailering. Note that the Venture 22 was a slightly different, earlier version of the 222 that I restored. The main differences are the lack of a pop-top and absence of a motor cutout on the transom.

MacGregor 23 (Venture of Newport). MacGregor 23s were very similar to the 25s in the hull shape and interior, but

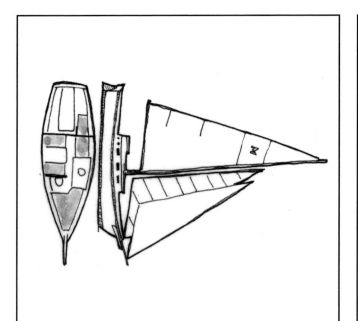

Venture 22
LENGTH: 22'0"
BEAM: 7'4"
DRAFT: 12"/5'6"
DISPLACEMENT: 1,800 lbs
BALLAST: 450 lbs
SAIL AREA: 170 sq. ft.
SAMPLE BOAT: A 1981 model in New York, trailer, but no motor, $2,900.

Note: Venture 22s are nearly identical to the Venture 222.

MacGregor 23 (Venture of Newport)
LENGTH: 22'7"
BEAM: 7'2"
DRAFT: 1'6"/5'6"
DISPLACEMENT: 2,000 lbs
BALLAST: 600 lbs
SAIL AREA: 195 sq. ft.
SAMPLE BOAT: Venture of Newport 23s are rather scarce in the used market, but occasionally turn up. A 1980 model in San Diego recently sold for $4,000. It included a motor, but no trailer, and needed electrical and upholstery work.

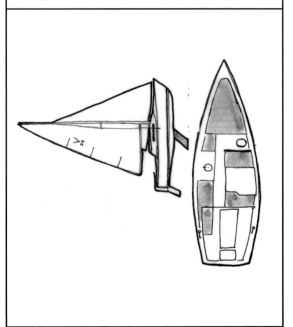

MacGregor 24
(Venture 24/
Venture 224)

LENGTH: 24'7"

BEAM: 7'11"

DRAFT: 1'6"/5'0"

DISPLACEMENT: 2,100 lbs

BALLAST: 525 lbs

SAIL AREA: 231 sq. ft.

SAMPLE BOAT: A 1973 model in Idaho, with a trailer, but no motor, described as a "project boat," asking $2,900.

MacGregor 25 (Venture 25)

LENGTH: 24'11"

BEAM: 7'11"

DRAFT: 1'10"/5'8"

DISPLACEMENT: 2,100 lbs

BALLAST: 625 lbs

SAIL AREA: 231 sq. ft.

SAMPLE BOAT: A 1980 model in Atlanta, Georgia, with a trailer and 8hp Evinrude outboard, listed for $1,500.

Note: The MacGregor 25 layout is very similar to the V24 (above).

the big difference was the deck and rig. It had a traditional look topsides and was cutter-rigged, with a bowsprit and more pronounced sheerline. These are much harder to find, and in terms of their looks, they've aged better than the other MacGregors.

MacGregor 24 (Venture 24/Venture 224). MacGregor 24s were nearly identical to the MacGregor 25, but they had a smaller deckhouse. They aren't as common as the 25, and they're only 4 inches shorter.

MacGregor 25 (Venture 25). Though these boats are known by different names,

they're nearly identical. (A Mac 25 owner may disagree, but the differences in the two boats are hard for me to detect.) The interior layout is similar to the MacGregor 22 but larger overall. These boats are very light for 25-footers, and this is what makes them trailerable. A similar-sized boat by Catalina, for example, has a curb weight of nearly 6,000 pounds, requiring a serious tow vehicle.

Later MacGregor models include the 26D (daggerboard), 26S (swing keel), and the 26X ("Powersailer," supposedly able to take up to a 90-hp outboard motor—why someone would want to do this to a sailboat, I'll never understand).

My boat, a 1972 Venture 222 as it originally appeared on the seller's property. Initially, I wasn't interested, but I reconsidered. It might have been smarter to stay uninterested.

There was even a Mac 36 catamaran, as well as a Mac 65 ULDB (Ultra-Light Displacement Boat).

There are literally dozens of other small boats that could be restored, but the ones above (with some exceptions) are the ones you'll see advertised again and again. I believe that the sheer number of these boats on the market helps keep their price down. If you can find them, some of the micro-cruisers, like the Sovereign 17, or some of the old classics like a Pearson Ariel or O'Day Tempest, would make a really nice boat. Anything will work, really, as long as it hasn't been too heavily modified.

What I Finally Chose

I bought a 1972 MacGregor Venture 222, because it was cheap, located nearby, and came with a trailer. The engine was not working (it was missing the lower foot) so I sold that for $50. The boat was in terrible condition, having been basically abandoned in the woods for five years. Uncovered, the deck leaked and the boat's interior filled with rainwater, and much of the interior was ruined. It was a total basket case.

The owner wanted $1,800 for the boat. I had to explain to him that, for his boat, that was a completely unrealistic price. The BUC value for this boat in ready-to-sail condition was about $2,200,

Another view of "the old boat in the woods."

and this boat would need lots of money and time to get it to that point. I offered $400, he countered with $500, and, in a moment of weakness, I agreed. In retrospect, buying a boat in this condition for $500 may not have been the smartest thing I've ever done, but at least I had a boat.

To be brutally honest, I bought this boat for nearly all the wrong reasons. It had nothing to do with seeking a challenge or rescuing a damsel in distress. I had been looking at boats for years and doing little—my own inaction was bothering me to no end. A recent attempt to

buy a Cal 20 had fallen through, and I didn't want to miss this one. I convinced myself that if I didn't buy this sailboat, I might be without a boat for a long time to come. Besides, this boat was nearby and it had a trailer, so delivery wouldn't be a problem. These plusses were enough for me to rationalize away the boat's many serious flaws, so I signed the check. Of course, since then I've seen boats in much better shape, for not a lot more money. But this one was an excellent guinea pig (with emphasis on the "pig" part).

CHAPTER 3

Getting Ready

Safety, Tooling, and Setting Up Shop

What follows is a play-by-play account of the steps I took to restore this boat.

Every boat is different, but this information can benefit every potential small boat restorer in several ways:

1. It illustrates the correction of some common real-world problems found in old, neglected sailboats.

2. It gives you an idea of the economics of restoring a small sailboat.

3. It helps you understand the time and effort involved in restoring a boat to nearly new condition.

Safety 1: Getting the Boat Home and Getting It Ready

Your first concern when restoring a boat has to be safety. This starts sooner than you may think. Before you do anything else, you'll have to get the boat home without killing someone. Then, once you get it there, you'll have to stabilize and secure it so you don't kill yourself.

Transporting

With any luck, the boat will come with a trailer, so the first thing you'll probably have to do is fix the lights. I can almost guarantee they won't work. You might even make this a condition of the sale. In my case, the trailer had no lights at all, so I made the deal contingent upon delivery to my house. The seller had the responsibility of bringing it to me. If the wheels flew off the trailer while delivering the boat (which was a very real possibility given the trailer's condition), I was not liable for damages nor obligated to complete the sale. This deal allowed me to delay the expense of installing a trailer hitch on my van—an added bonus.

If you have to tow the boat yourself, make sure you have enough tongue weight. Most trailer manufacturers recommend that the tongue weight of the trailer be between five and fifteen percent of the total weight. With my MacGregor, this meant the trailer should have been balanced with about 200 pounds on the hitch—less weight can cause the trailer to fishtail. I wasn't aware of this at the time, and the seller proudly pointed out how his trailer was balanced so that you could lift it up with one arm. This was a dangerous condition for towing; more weight should have been present at the trailer tongue.

Check the bearings for grease; if they're dry or rusty, you could be in for catastrophic results. Drive a few blocks, then stop. Get out and feel the hubs. If they're hot, that's not good. If you continue to drive, the bearings will overheat, break, and off come the wheels. The first job on your newly-purchased project will be new bearings, and it's best to do this before you drive it home.

My seller hitched up his boat, and we began the 20-mile journey to Chattanooga, Tennessee. Because there were no lights on the trailer, I followed closely with my emergency flashers on. A quick

"hub check" revealed no problems—they were just barely warm to the touch—so the remainder of the boat's trip was uneventful, barring my constant maneuvering to dodge the twigs and leaves that kept blowing off the boat. As soon as we backed it into my side yard and unhitched the boat from his pickup, we completed the deal and, for better or worse, it was mine.

Blocking and Leveling

Once you get the boat home, the first thing you'll need to do is block and level the boat. Raise the trailer tongue until the waterline is level; then keep it in position with concrete blocks. I placed a pair of concrete blocks under each aft corner of the trailer; this kept the bow from tipping skyward when I climbed into the cockpit. I figured this out the hard way, of course: I climbed into the cockpit, and the bow slowly rose up, but no damage occurred because, luckily, I

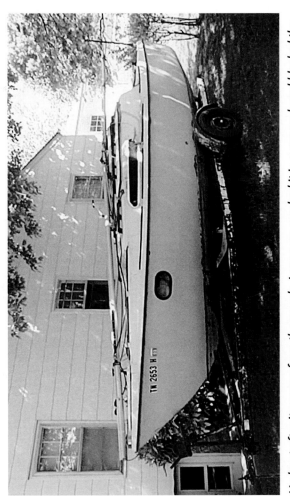

My boat after its rescue from the woods. I pressure-washed it in a carwash and blocked the trailer into position beside the house. It wouldn't move again for nearly two years.

31

had thought to block the wheels as well. (If I hadn't, I'd have been land surfing my 2,000 pound boat down the slight incline of my side yard.) One crafty MacGregor owner installed a pair of screw jacks at each aft corner of the trailer. The screw jacks—the kind used to lift the tongue up-stabilize the boat and they can be used to fine tune the level.

If you have a choice, parking the boat on a level concrete pad is preferable. I didn't have that option, and it would have made lifting the boat and moving the keel much simpler. I also had to buy a plastic tarp carport frame. At first, I tried to get by with a plastic cover that I removed and replaced as needed, but the boat was constantly filling with rainwater, and my carefully applied paint job got stained with organic material constantly dropping from our maple tree. If I had bitten the bullet and bought one in the beginning, I would have saved myself quite a bit of grief. It was $150, and worth every penny. I recommend making or buying some sort of shelter for your boat.

Safety 2: Boat Restoration without Restorative Surgery

There is some basic safety equipment that, if you don't have, you'll need to buy:

Safety Glasses

I prefer glasses over goggles. Goggles seal your eyes better, but they're heavier, bulky, hot, and a little harder to see through. I've gotten so used to safety glasses that I put them on automatically whenever I enter the shop, and they're much less of a bother. Buy yourself several pairs and make a little hanger or pocket in the shop or boat and they'll always be easy to find.

Earplugs

I keep several sets of the disposable foam types in yogurt cups near the safety glasses. Most of the power tools that you'll use can cause hearing damage over the long term. Earplugs are cheap, easy insurance. I don't use the ear muffs for the same reasons I don't like goggles, though they block more sound and are harder to misplace because they're bigger.

Leather Work Gloves

These are especially useful when handling rusty metal, tearing out rotten/splintery wood, and when using an angle grinder. I'm always losing mine, so I buy them three or four pairs at a time. They also help to keep your hands a little cleaner. Cheaper ones are thinner and more flexible.

Rubber Exam Gloves

These are critical for epoxy work, because they allow you to smooth glass with your fingers. They're also the only thing that'll keep your hands clean when working with polyurethane or silicone caulk.

Organic Vapor Mask

Polyurethane paints are toxic, and high vapor concentrations can build up when painting or glassing the boat's interior. An organic vapor mask is also useful when cutting wood on the table saw. I used some Ipe, or Brazilian walnut, and the fine sawdust was very irritating to my lungs. Any form of wood dust is bad news, so you should wear this a lot. Spend a little money and get one that fits well.

While an inexpensive paper nuisance mask is often deemed sufficient and certainly better than nothing, I don't recommend or use them myself. They just don't do a good enough job of filtering very fine particles or smoke, both of which you'll likely encounter when working with tropical hardwoods. I have a very strong reaction to sawdust and smoke from Ipe—it's nearly impossible to breathe if I work it without protection. I've always thought that this is an area where it doesn't hurt to be overly cautious. So whenever I'm in a mildly toxic environment, I suit up like a spaceman.

Tyvek Protective Sleeves/Suits

I tried to make do with old long-sleeved shirts, but I should've worn these instead. Because I didn't, I spent a few itchy nights after sanding fiberglass. The dust irritates the skin, and some people are allergic to it.

Steps

One other safety item I overlooked was a proper set of boarding steps. I was using a concrete block as a step to get into and out of the boat. One night after a rain, I was getting in the boat to check the bilge. The ground was soft, and the block rolled out from under me. I fell on my side, breaking my wrist. I was out of work for nearly four months as a result. If this had happened on a paved driveway, it could have been much worse—as it was, I whacked my head pretty hard in the dirt. If I had taken the time to make myself a proper boarding ladder or steps, I'd have saved myself a great deal of pain, expense, time, and aggravation.

Fire Extinguisher

Heaven forbid you should ever need this, but you should always have one close

by—you'll be working with some volatile and flammable materials. By the way, when the air is thick with acetone fumes, it isn't a good time to light up. In fact, just quit smoking altogether—you won't have the money for cigarettes anyway. Oh, and if your boat comes with a working motor, be sure to remove the gas tank and store it somewhere far away from the boat. This goes double for propane stoves. Propane is heavier than air, and gas from leaky old propane bottles can collect in the bilge in high enough concentrations to explode.

Fans

You'll need at least one old box fan to remove paint vapors from the interior while you're belowdeck. Don't depend on the vapor mask to save you. Fans can be tough to find in stores in the winter, but you can easily find one in the summer months. I have pulled more than one old fan from trash piles, oiled the motors, and had them run for years.

There are probably some other aspects of safety that I've missed, but my intent is to tell you to be very careful. If you're working alone and are away from home, keep your cell phone in your pocket. Be especially careful if you have to lift the boat to do keelwork. I'll cover that in more detail later (Chapter 4), but suffice it to say that working under a poorly supported boat can be dangerous. Hopefully, all you'll get are the usual scrapes, cuts, and bruises, which are plenty irritating in their own right. Treat them immediately with soap and antibiotic ointment, cover with a bandage, and seal with a couple of extra wraps of tape.

Getting Tooled Up

The tools required to restore a boat can vary widely. Some people can do yacht work with little more than a hand saw and a claw hammer, while others need $20,000 in a warehouse-sized shop to get started. I'm somewhere in between. Like most men, I love tools—it's some sort of evolutionary, Cro-Magnon, hunter-gatherer holdover thing. (The theory goes that cavemen who had or could make better tools could kill bigger mammoths and raise better crops. A cavewoman wanted a caveman who could be a good provider, so our interest in tools is somehow connected with sex. But I digress . . .)

You need a basic set of tools to start with. Most of these you'll probably have already, like wrenches, a decent socket set, some screwdrivers, and so on. Generally speaking, it's worth it to buy good hand tools. A Craftsman screwdriver set, for example, is easier to use than a set of cheapo screwdrivers from the dollar store, because the handles are more comfortable and the tips are less likely to bung up screw heads. Same thing with a socket set, though Craftsman sockets can get pretty steep. I've heard that Snap-On sockets and wrenches have the best grip, but I can't afford to test this theory. There are several other good brands available: Husky, SK, Ridgid, and some Stanley (especially the "professional" and "Proto" lines, not their low-cost "homeowner" tools). Just avoid cheap knockoffs like the plague, and you'll be OK.

I had a pretty fair collection of woodworking tools before I started. Probably the most useful large tool is my table saw. If you don't have one, you can work around it, but I've found it helps to make clean, accurate cuts and joints in smaller pieces. My table saw is an ancient 8-inch Craftsman that belonged to my father. Old saws like mine are often available used at good prices, and most were high quality tools. It doesn't have to look fancy, but a decent rip fence and miter gauge are important. (The rip fence is my saw's Achilles Heel—the one weak point on an otherwise great old tool.) If you don't have any experience with one, pick up a table-saw handbook at the library; you'll learn all sorts of neat things to do with it. If you want to buy something new, Rockwell and Craftsman are good brands, though often the older tools were higher quality. Other good brands include Bosch, Ryobi, Makita, Dewalt, Ridgid, and Grizzly. When buying new tools, resist the impulse to get the best bargain you can find. The joy of saving a buck fades quickly, but the frustration returns every time you use it. I've often cursed my frugal nature when trying to make a marginal tool function as it should, and conversely, I've been grateful I spent the extra bucks when a tool did a good job. With a few exceptions, you'll do a better job with a few really good tools than with a whole pile of inexpensive ones.

A ⅜-inch drill is a must, along with a set of decent bits. Watch out for used drills; they often have worn-out chucks, which are expensive to replace. The ¼-inch sizes just don't have the torque to get through stainless steel, but they might be OK if you only need a few small holes through fiberglass. A good battery-operated drill is really handy, but a cheap one isn't worth the aggravation. Some restorers have suggested that a ½-inch drill is better, but I have a bench-

A close look at the business end of the scraper.

top drill press that helps me with the larger holes. Also, a ½-inch hand drill usually has enough torque to injure your wrist if a large bit grabs and you aren't holding the tool firmly, so use caution.

You'll also need a circular saw. I had a new one that burned out after a couple of years. Then I got an old one from the 1950s that still works. I just needed to replace a few parts, like the deteriorated power cord. In general, older tools are heavier and run with much less vibration. It's often very worthwhile to re-build older tools instead of buying new.

Other Miscellaneous Tools

The following is a list of additional tools that I never thought I'd need as much as I did.

Shop Vacuum. While not exactly a tool, I discovered that I used this almost daily to clean up chips and shavings, and occasionally to suck up stray puddles. The thing I absolutely hate about mine is the amount of noise it makes. I've heard that Fen makes a low-noise shop vacuum, but they're expensive. When my old metal shop vacuum expired, I bought a newer all-plastic one. The new vacuum is considerably quieter. Since you'll be using this in the close confines of a boat hull, the amount of noise becomes more than just a nuisance, but a long-term noise-exposure issue.

Scraper. I spent a lot of hours on the business end of these things. I've found the one that works best for me has a heavy-duty replaceable razor edge. Mine had a hard plastic grip that rubbed blisters in my hands, so be sure to use gloves or buy a soft grip from a bicycle shop.

There are several different kinds of scrapers, but not all work well for scraping paint off of a fiberglass boat. Your results may vary, so don't be afraid to try other types and use what works best for you.

Angle Grinder. Also known by my good friend and slip neighbor, Larry Lee, as a "boat eater," I used my angle grinders a lot. Fiberglass dust is super-hard on the motors, and it burns them out, so, in this instance, I recommend buying a cheaper version. I have two cheap ones that I got for $12 at the flea market. Harbor Freight has them as well. (See Appendix 7 for a list of suppliers.) Buy two when you get them, so that they'll both have the same size spindle. I have one small and one large, which is a pain. You can also buy sanding discs for these now, and I used them for grinding fiberglass and old paint off the interior. I did finally get a DeWalt angle grinder, and after eons behind cheap ones, it's a joy to use. It's more powerful, runs cooler, and is quieter than its cheapo counterpart. But since fiberglass work is so hard on an angle grinder, I use it sparingly.

x

4-Inch Resin Bonded Sanding Discs. I had to make a backing pad for my angle grinder, which worked OK but wobbled slightly. Just as I was finishing up the interior cleanup, our local hardware supplier started carrying sanding kits for angle grinders. These include a backing pad and a couple of discs. The discs aren't inexpensive, and they hold up really well considering the abuse I subject them to. I bought one, and use it for lots of things—cleaning up old paint, prepping old fiberglass for epoxy, shaping teak (a notoriously difficult wood to work), roughing wood to prepare it for gluing, and so on.

Chip Brushes. These are disposable brushes with natural bristles (not nylon or foam). Buy a case of these from an in-

dustrial supplier—they're much cheaper that way. I got mine from Harbor Freight. I used them for almost everything except for expensive paint and varnish work. They're especially handy for applying epoxy.

Vise-Grip Pliers. These things saved the day several times. I used them to hold a nut belowdecks while I screwed it tight topside. They're essential if you're going to work without a helper, and super-handy otherwise. They can chew up bolts and nuts, though, so be careful. Get genuine Vise-Grip brand; knockoffs are inexpensive, but their performance is sadly lacking, and it's no economy if you tear up an expensive part because you were too cheap to buy the real thing. One of those sets with several different types and sizes would make a great early-birthday present for yourself. You'll thank yourself every time you use them.

Stationary Wire Wheel/Buffer. Years ago, I bought an inexpensive 6-inch 1,750 rpm grinder. I took the wheels off and replaced them with a 6-inch wire brush wheel, and a sewn felt buff. If you can find one at a yard sale or flea market, get one, but make sure it doesn't turn at high speed (3,400 rpm). That's too fast for most wire brushes.

Wire wheels are good for hardware restoration. It cleans rust stains off of stainless and buffs to a great shine when used with white rouge compound (a fine abrasive that's mixed with wax and molded into a stick). Melt a little on the felt wheel, and then polish your stainless. The resulting shine can look better than new.

The angle grinder box. These things are used so often that they get their own tote, which only costs a few dollars at the hardware store and greatly saves time tracking down the parts. In it are a dedicated pair of safety glasses (never use an angle grinder without safety glasses on), earplugs, sanding and grinding disks, wire brushes, spindle nuts, and pin wrenches.

Hole Saw. I bought a high-quality 1½-inch bimetal hole saw for a job years ago. It was expensive, as I recall, but I have since found myself using it several times for various jobs on the boat. (For instance, cutting locker access openings with radiused edges—the results are stronger and look more professional.)

Disposable Screwdriver Bits. These are commonly used with cordless drills/screwdrivers. I chuck them into my drill, and I can run screws and bolts a zillion times faster than doing it by hand. They're especially handy for disassembly and can also be set into a small ratchet for an instant offset screwdriver. Careless use will damage both the bit and the screw, though, so you shouldn't go too fast.

Clamps. No one has ever complained of having too many clamps. I got by with a pair of 6-inch C-clamps, a few 4-inchers, three 36-inch bar clamps, and had to make up a pair of 5-foot pipe clamps when gluing up the table. Double that amount wouldn't have been unwelcome, except for the pipe clamps, which were only used once.

An inexpensive bench grinder. WARNING: This is one of the most dangerous tools in the shop. It seems harmless, but it isn't. You must have safety glasses and gloves on when you use this thing. As the wire wheel wears out, it starts to throw little wire "needles," which can easily penetrate your skin or go straight through your corneas. It also has a tendency to grab parts from your hands and sling them around the shop, so keep a firm grip. I like low-horsepower motors for this reason.

Setting up Shop

You're going to need some kind of space to work on things. How much space you need depends on your personality. I've heard stories of people restoring boats while living in VW vans, while others feel they can't do a thing without a 2,000-square-foot workshop. The truth is that either approach is "best," depending on your finances, experience, and work habits. Set up your shop the way that feels right to you.

Also, it's a good idea to spend a little time organizing your shop and keeping it relatively clean. See *The Workshop Book*, by Scott Landis, or *The Small Workshop* from *Fine Woodworking*. You'll spend less time hunting down tools if they all have a place to live. Admittedly, I have trouble following my own advice.

I set up shop in the basement of my house. We had a long, rather narrowish space, about 10 feet by 30 feet, punctuated by the occasional support column. In this area I squeezed in a table saw and small jointer. There was a bench-like surface at the far end that mainly got used for storage. I didn't have an actual workbench; instead, I improvised by using sawhorses and working on the floor. Naturally, long pieces whacked the columns every now and again, but I was able to work around them.

My "metal shop" was farther away, in a one-car garage. (I'm a blacksmith by profession, so I had some extra tools that were useful.) Some of our garage is given over to storage, but I'm slowly converting it into a proper shop. I do a lot of benchwork there. There's a vise, an 8-inch grinder, a 6-inch buffer/wire wheel, and a cheap benchtop drill press. I also have a small AC arc welder that I used on two occasions during the restoration—once to add a trailing edge to the keel, and again to fabricate a centerboard winch bracket from stainless.

Having a work space that is physically close to the boat is a great asset, though it isn't always possible. Sometimes, you can bring the shop to the boat. I did a lot of work using a pair of stout sawhorses right next to the hull. A lightweight table saw can be moved to the boat, even used inside the boat if necessary. (Here's a case where smaller—which often translates to cheaper—is better.)

CHAPTER 4

Getting Started

Restoration Strategies, Cleaning, and More

So back to my boat. Our side yard was now decorated with a 22-foot wreck on a trailer.

The Plan

I needed a strategy for the most effective way to handle the thousand or so jobs that needed to be done. Don Casey addresses this subject in his book, *This Old Boat*, and for some of you, his method of organizing your restoration will be more useful. (He breaks projects down into structure, feature, and finish, and further divides those jobs into immediate, less urgent, and someday.) I organized my project somewhat differently, though, because I'm a very right-brained sort of person. I'm not very organized, and I'm sometimes unable to stay on a single project for a long period of time. Instead, I focus intently on a job for a while, but then I find myself involved in another, whether the first job is finished or not. Though this might not be the best way to do things, it's the way

I am. So I needed a planning method that maximized flexibility.

At the heart of it all was a simple spiral-bound composition book. This became my restoration log. The first thing I did was to formulate a loose order of work to be done on the boat—in other words, what gets done in which order. Generally, I decided that it would be best to first paint the exterior during the

Our new yard decoration, the day after it arrived at our house.

39

summer, then do the interior over the winter months, and then re-rig and as-semble in the spring and go sailing. (This was about how it happened, though I ended up taking much longer than I ex-pected.) I recorded these thoughts at the beginning of my comp book and made lists of materials and equipment that I thought I would need. These lists were continually revised as I found I would need more of some things and could do without others.

One section of the book became my expense record, where I recorded ex-actly how much money I spent on the boat. Another section became my work record. I recorded just about every job that I did on the boat and how long it took, rounded to the nearest fifteen minutes. I discovered that even the sim-plest job could take much longer than I expected. As I completed jobs, I discov-ered other areas that needed attention, so my plan was continually under revi-sion. The general plan (fix the boat as best you can, and then go sailing) never changed, but the fine points of my plan (the best time to do a certain job, the scope of the rebuild, the list of salvage-able parts, and so on) did. My log be-came filled with side notes, like the location of original hardware and design ideas that might work.

I also took lots of pictures, both digi-tal and film. I very rarely found myself saying, "Gee, I wish I'd shot fewer pic-tures." Usually the opposite was true. I especially wish I'd shot more of the boat as it was originally found.

Strip Search

The first thing that I did on my boat was strip it down to the bare hull. There was much on the boat that needed to be removed and discarded, especially all the custom exterior woodwork. Almost all of this was rotten to the point that it came off with a gentle tug. Since I wasn't planning on copying any of this for re-placement, most of it went directly into the trash. But before it was tossed, each piece was examined for reusable hard-ware. Any hardware that was stainless or bronze—even small fender washers and screws—was removed and tossed into a box set aside for this purpose. Later, as I was assembling the boat, there were countless times when I needed just one small screw or washer. The "stainless hell box," as I like to call it, saved me several trips to the hardware store for one little screw or bolt. As it was, I'm sure I tossed out quite a bit of useful hardware that I wish I'd taken the time to save. Be anal and save those screws.

If there is even the slightest chance that you might recondition and reuse a part, a different strategy is required. The best method for keeping those bolts and screws where you need them is to re-move the part, put the hardware back into the holes (on the part, not in the boat), and loosely spin on the nuts. This is less secure if you've removed a wood screw, but a piece of tape will keep the hardware in place.

Most boat restorers develop the habit of thinking out loud (otherwise known as talking to themselves). If you find yourself saying, "There's no way I'll be reusing this thing," and you're heading to the trash, stop for a moment. If the part's problems are cosmetic, don't throw the part away! Put it in a box, squirrel it away in the corner of the times called the *doghouse* on old wooden boats, or just plain *house.*) Eyebrows are designed to visually lower the appearance of the topsides, and to channel drips of water away from the portholes. I removed these and tossed them (they're a bear to properly varnish). All of the sailing hardware was marked for location (PORT or STARBOARD, FWD, STERN, and so on) on the underside with a permanent marker and kept in a crate. I also did a detailed drawing of original hardware locations in my restoration log. Even so, I still ended up with a few pieces of mystery hardware. I had no idea where they went.

Although I knew that I was jumping ahead of myself, I started doing the same thing down below—dismantling, assessing, cataloging, and cleaning. (As I mentioned before, you'll have more success if you can stick to one or two specific projects; parts will have less time to get lost, and the way things come apart and go back together will be fresh in your mind. But I'm not like that, so I went for it.)

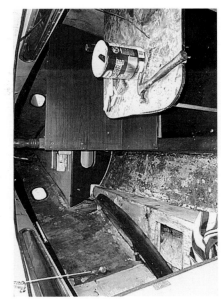

Stripping of the interior. Most of the water-soaked fabrics have been discarded, revealing a difficult surface beneath. It smells a little better, though.

The interior as the boat was found—it's the picture of neglect. I wish that I'd taken more "before" shots, but I think I subconsciously wanted to deny that I'd actually paid money for this mess.

garage, or stick it under the bushes behind the house. It could come in handy later as a pattern, or you could use it as a hole-drilling template. You could very possibly run out of money and have to refinish the piece and replace it a few seasons down the road. The economics of small boat restoration demand that you restore and reuse anything that you can. A quick look through a boating catalog will show you that the cost of the parts can easily exceed the value of the boat, so, when you're talking to yourself, be sure to ask, "Do I have to buy a new one, or can I fix this?"

On my boat, there were many situations in which I obviously had no choice: many parts simply *had* to be either removed or replaced. All of the exterior woodwork was made of walnut, and it turned to compost in my hands. The boat had *eyebrows*—thin battens of wood screwed to the deckhouse just below its upper edge. (The *deckhouse* is the part of the boat that's above deck level, some-

Removing a covering panel revealed this view of the keel winch. Here are a host of problems, including rot, faulty repairs to the winch support, and a concealed "electrical system" that was humorous at best, dangerous at worst. Note the location of the fire extinguisher bracket—totally inaccessible in an emergency.

As I removed interior parts, a bit less found its way into the trash can. The front-loading icebox went, as did the (hopelessly rusted, and subsequently *dangerous*) propane camping stove. Other parts, especially plywood panels, were saved for patterns.

One of the particularly disgusting aspects of my boat was the overuse of fabrics onboard. Practically everything was covered in some sort of fabric—indoor/outdoor carpeting on the cabin sole, some sort of canvas-like material glued to the ceiling (see Sailing Terms on page 9), and vinyl backed by foam rubber

Rot in a plywood berth top. This was a result of a poorly located front-opening icebox. It also shows how an ice pick or small screwdriver can easily locate rotten sections.

ABOUT ICEBOXES

Front-loading iceboxes are not a good idea. Cold air sinks, and every time the door opens, you lose precious cold air. Top loaders, though less convenient to organize, keep ice better. Insulation is paramount, and on stock boats, always inadequate. Four inches of space on all sides isn't too much. A conventional cooler can be modified by adding extra foam, but if it's not carefully sealed you'll grow a mildew farm. Dropping a soft cooler inside a larger rigid one might be a workable solution, if you can find a tight-fitting pair. ■

on the overhead. Once mildew grows on these surfaces—and they nearly always do on a boat—it is difficult, if not impossible, to eradicate. In my case, I had to contend with mildew *and* rot. I ripped out and threw away nearly all of this stuff, with no attempt to make patterns. I didn't want that much cloth on my boat anyway. The exceptions, of course, are the cabin cushion covers. They were the original cushions that were sold with the boat nearly 30 years ago. Considering their age, these weren't all that bad, and I placed them low on my priority list. I did eventually replace them all, though, since some were missing. This is a good job to tackle in the winter months, when it's freezing cold in the boat.

Hopefully, your boat won't have interior problems that are this extensive, especially if you can find a boat with an interior liner that's in fairly good shape. Being protected from the elements, the gelcoat on the liner is usually in much better condition than the exterior gelcoat and will respond very well to hard scrubbing and waxing. The drawback is that the liner can hide structural defects, and often sections must be cut away in order to make an effective repair.

Sometimes this situation can be used to your advantage. Depending on where you need to cut the liner, you might be able to conceal the hole with a nice teak covering board, hinged to provide access to stowage. Net or canvas bags can be used to restrain items in irregularly shaped areas. Move the bags out of the way, and you can inspect critical areas of your hull, gain access to wiring, and so on. It isn't always possible, but it isn't a bad idea. Of course, you can always use the commonly available plastic inspection port covers. Beckson Marine makes several different shapes and sizes.

The 1972 Venture didn't have a liner. Older boats such as mine had an interior that was pieced together from individual plywood panels and bonded to the hull. This method of construction can result in a stronger structure, but more plywood means more chances for rot. Fortunately, it appeared that MacGregor had used either some form of marine-grade plywood or at least a good grade of exterior plywood, since I found remarkably little rot in the basic structure of the boat. The front-loading icebox that the previous owner installed had leaked over the years, and the constant

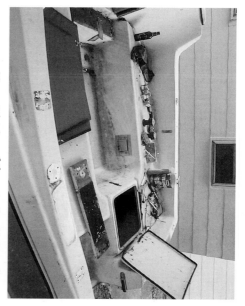

More stripping of the exterior. Notice the mud line that formed when the cockpit was left full of rainwater. Note also the evidence of minor alcohol consumption, a necessary by-product of the work's magnitude.

in some places, but in others it was lifting up in large bubbles. Even though I didn't care for the color, I considered trying to patch the bad areas of the paint. Unfortunately, this option had little chance of success. The paint was some kind of three-part automotive paint that isn't available to consumers; plus, an exact color match would have been difficult. Finally, there was no guarantee that, once repaired, the paint wouldn't lift up in some other area, requiring the job to be done again.

So I decided to strip everything down to bare fiberglass and repaint using a marine-grade polyurethane. Stripping it down took a long time. I tried chemical strippers but, while they did work, the results were lukewarm. I tried several different types of scrapers, but what finally worked best was a razor-type scraper with a replaceable blade. It's kind of like a little single-edged window scraper on steroids. Some of the hull scraped easily, but some of the paint was stuck tight. I

Scraping the Exterior

The goal was to get the boat down to a nearly bare hull and deck. Since the boat obviously leaked badly, all the fittings needed to be rebedded. I planned to strip off all the old paint, apply new paint, and then reattach all the parts with new bedding compound. This always looks better than trying to paint around fittings and wooden parts, and most of the fittings needed reconditioning anyway.

Once everything was removed, what remained was still pretty ugly. The exterior had been repainted by an auto-body shop. The paint finish was good and hard

cycle of dampness and drying (and dripping condensation) had rotted out the panel directly beneath it, with the worst areas near the bolt holes. (This area was repaired later by enlarging a locker lid; a discussion of this process is under Structural Woodworking in Chapter 5.)

Starting to scrape the hull. The yellow automotive paint came up easily in some places, but stuck tight in others. The green layer was probably an earlier paint job, and the original factory gelcoat was probably a thin layer of light blue that was underneath the green.

discovered later that the easy places had a brown spray primer underneath. Places that weren't primed were still well-bonded to the hull and took a lot of work to remove. I'd even speculate that, had this brown stuff not been used, the hull would still be yellow today.

One of the concerns with scraping the hull was how to keep up with the paint chips. Since this was automotive paint, I was fairly sure that there was some amount of lead in it, and contaminating my yard wasn't something I wanted to do. The problem was compounded by the fact that I had to work over a dirt space instead of concrete, so I couldn't just vacuum up stray chips. I put an old canvas awning under the hull and taped sheets of plastic to the hull. One end was taped to the sheer, and the other end was taped to the waterline. The ends were left open, and I reached inside to scrape. I was able to catch the majority of the chips this way. Escapees that made it to the canvas were vacuumed up with a shop-vac.

There were still a few that got into the ground, but I used the shop-vac to get these, along with some dirt. In the end, the site stayed relatively clean. Cleanliness was the main reason that I didn't remove the old finish with a sander; the resulting dust is nearly impossible to control. I tried using the shop-vac connected to the sander, but it didn't work. After the scraping was complete, I finish-sanded the hull with a ¼-sheet pad sander. Scraping and sanding the entire exterior took about three months of part-time work.

Now that I had the paint off, I could better assess the repairs that were needed. In some places, auto-body filler

Collecting the chips. I reached into the folds of the plastic to scrape, and this kept the chips from flying into my face and hair. If I were working over a solid surface, I could have vacuumed them up later.

had been used to fill gouges and scrapes. After all these years, it was still relatively soft—you could dig it out easily with a pocketknife, and dent it with a fingernail. A wire brush mounted on an angle grinder removed this pretty easily while leaving the base fiberglass nicely roughened and prepared for a proper repair.

The scraped hull.

About Epoxy and Fiberglass

The only way to properly repair fiberglass laminate that's fully cured is to use epoxy. This stuff is nothing less than a modern chemical miracle, and it's saved countless old boats. Epoxy is somewhat more expensive than polyester, but its adhesive strength is far greater—so much so that repairs made with epoxy and fiberglass can be considered an integral part of the boat's structure. Epoxy's weakness is its sensitivity to heat. Some epoxies begin to lose their bonding strength at temperatures as low as 120 degrees F.

If you've never used epoxy before, you'll have to learn. Fortunately, it isn't very difficult to become quite skilled in epoxy and fiberglass, with a little practice. It's a good idea to do your first repairs in an area that isn't too conspicuous.

There are a number of good resources available from the epoxy manufacturers that you should read up on before you start mixing up these chemicals. Try the West System (*Fiberglass Boat Repair and Maintenance*, $3; West

System User's Manual, free) or MAS (*MAS Technical Manual*, free). Interlux also has a line of epoxies available. All of these manufacturers produce a fine product, and it's best to pick one and stick with it. (Insert Popeye-the-Sailor laugh here. Arg, arg, arg. Boatwork somehow lends itself to bad puns.) I used epoxy from a small distributor in Florida called Raka, and they gave me a fine product, great service, and an excellent price. That's why I often recommend seeking out and supporting small businesses as you buy your supplies. Other good sources of epoxy and fiberglassing information are Ken Hankinson's *Fiberglass Boatbuilding for Amateurs*, and Allan Vaitses's *The Fiberglass Boat Repair Manual*. My favorite general work, though, is *Upgrading and Repairing your Small Sailboat for Cruising*, by Paul and Myra Butler. They use a lot of epoxy in their work.

It's important to be aware of the dangers associated with epoxy and polyester fumes. Some people have developed a sensitivity to epoxy by using it without

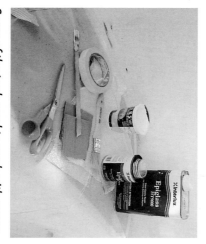

Some of the tools used to work with epoxy can be quite simple. I bought a quart to get myself started, then moved up to a full gallon kit once it ran out.

protection, and they report being unable to be anywhere near the stuff. Avoid contact with your skin, and be sure to wear a vapor mask when mixing epoxy in an enclosed space, like a sailboat hull. Epoxy vapors aren't nearly as strong as the styrene vapors given off polyester resins. These vapors can cause brain damage and, in high enough concentrations, can be lethal. The MEK catalyst can cause blindness—of course, any of these chemical in the eyes is very bad news. Wear safety glasses.

One of the properties of epoxy work that you'll read about is called "amine blush." As the epoxy cures, a by-product of the chemical reaction is an amine acid that forms on the cured surface of the epoxy. It needs to be wiped off with soap and water, because it will prevent other layers of epoxy from bonding to the first surface. Certain formulations are more prone to blushing than others, though, and I had very little blushing with the epoxy that I used—a low-blushing formula from Raka Epoxy.

When you buy epoxy, you'll save yourself hours of grief and frustration if you buy the pumps to go with it.

Accurate mixing is essential with epoxy, and the pumps make it a snap. Epoxy doesn't work like polyester, and too much hardener will cause the batch to not harden at all. Pumps prevent this from happening, and they're quite inexpensive—I paid about $3 each. Besides, you'll kick yourself for days if you have to scrape off an uncured batch because you were too cheap to spring for pumps.

The thing to remember about epoxy (and polyester, too) is that it cures through an "exothermic" reaction. In other words, when resin and hardener combine, they give off heat as they cure. If you're working on a hot day, the ambient temperature can cause overheating problems or reduced "pot time." In other words, it hardens in the pot, before you get a chance to put the stuff where you want it. If the forecast is for temperatures in the nineties, then it might be best to do your epoxy work in the early morning or late afternoon.

The epoxy resin is only part of the story, though. It's much more useful and cost-effective when used with the proper materials and additives. These are most

---

EASY EPOXY?

While I had no problems with my epoxy batches, this experience isn't universal. A friend of mine, Bill Van Allen, mixed up a batch of epoxy that overreacted—it actually began boiling and smoking in the mixing pot.

Epoxy and polyester cure through an exothermic reaction. In other words, when resin and hardener combine, they give off heat as they cure. In fact, the reaction can even start fires, so be careful! Mix small batches whenever possible, and use the manufacturer's metered pumps to ensure proper resin-to-hardener ratios. If you must mix a larger batch, do it in a shallow pan: the larger surface area will minimize the heat buildup, compared to mixing in a deep can or cup. ■

FIBERGLASS CLOTH

A wide variety of fiberglass cloth is available, but for the work we're talking about, you don't need anything fancy. Regular E-glass from a resin supplier will work best. Three to five yards of anything from 6- to 10-ounce cloth should do it. Be sure to shop around—fiberglass cloth from marine stores tends to be overpriced. Buy it off the roll and you'll save a ton. It can be cut with scissors into strips, or you can get fiberglass tape, available in 4- to 6-inch widths. It's very handy, but a little more expensive. And remember that fiberglass cloth and roving are measured by weight per square yard, while fiberglass mat is measured by weight per square foot. So 1½-ounce mat will weigh the same as 13½-ounce cloth. ∎

It's sized by weight per square foot rather than weight per square yard; weights commonly range from ¾ ounce to 3 ounces. It's a little more useful than roving for adding bulk to repairs, but I never needed to use it to do my repairs. (Once I decide to fill in the ports in the hull, though, I'll use mat and cloth.) It's important to remember that if you do use mat, you should alternate the layers of mat with layers of cloth. If two layers of mat are laminated together, they tend to separate, especially when used with polyester.

Epoxy's inherent strength gives it another advantage. Fillers or, more appropriately, additives can be used to make it more effective in certain applications. These usually are various powders that serve to make the epoxy thicker—more like a paste, glue, or foam. There are lots of different powders that you can use. They're readily available from epoxy suppliers. I ended up using two different types of additives: fumed silica, and white-glass microballoons. Fumed silica, when mixed with epoxy, makes a strong, sticky, glue-like compound that cures

commonly fiberglass cloth, roving, mat, and filler powders.

Fiberglass cloth is most often used for repair jobs; 7- to 10-ounce cloth is most common (it's sized by weight per square yard). Lots of different types of weaves are available—such as high-strength, bi-axial, or tri-axial weaves—but these aren't as useful as plain old E-glass. (The E stands for "electrical.") I got a good deal on some high-strength 6-ounce glass cloth through eBay, but while it was a high-quality product, it was very tightly woven, difficult to properly saturate, and stiff—it didn't want to lay into curves. It worked, but not nearly as well as standard cloth would have.

Woven roving, weighing 14 to 36 ounces per square yard, is most commonly used to lay up hulls. You won't have much need for roving, unless you're trying to repair a big hole in the hull and need a thick laminate. It leaves a fairly coarse and unfinished-looking surface, and it's commonly alternated with fiberglass mat.

Fiberglass mat is made of lengths of chopped glass fibers going in random directions and held in place by a binder.

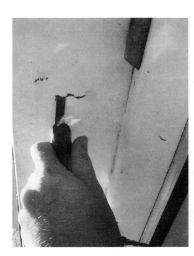

very hard. Microballoons make a light, almost foamlike compound that is easy to sand, but not very strong. I'll talk more about using each later in this chapter.

My boat's previous owner wasn't aware of the benefits of epoxy. Several repairs and modifications were done with polyester resin and fiberglass over a plywood core. In almost all cases, these repairs were failing and had to either be replaced completely, or patched. The biggest example was the boat's foredeck. On the original 72 Venture, the foredeck had a ridge around the edge that followed the sheerline of the boat. (The "sheer" is the very highest edge of the hull.) The deck was lower than the sheer by a few inches, giving it an integral toe rail that might keep you from sliding off the deck. These boats had a reputation for decks that flexed as well. Someone thought that the forepeak would be better with a few inches of headroom and cut the entire thing up with a circular saw. A network of wooden stringers was laid into place, a plywood subfloor was laid down, and the deck was laid on top of that. Everything was wrapped in polyester and glass, sanded fair, and painted.

A bad repair. Gently probing a bubble with a pocketknife, it sank all the way to the hilt. This was an area that was repaired with polyester and painted over. The paint held up, but the repair didn't.

This "improvement" probably worked well for a few years, but after some time and neglect, the polyester lost its bond to the wood. Moisture worked in through the tiniest void or crack, followed by more expansion and contraction of the wood, which led to larger cracks. Rot followed. And then along came a sucker with $500.

To rip the whole thing out and start over was obviously more work than the boat was worth. If it was a Flicka or a Bristol Channel Cutter, maybe, but not a

---

EPOXY VS. POLYESTER

Working with epoxy is similar to working with polyester, but there are significant differences. With polyester, you add drops of MEK (methyl-ethyl ketone) peroxide hardener to a batch of resin. More hardener makes a faster-curing, brittle batch of resin. Epoxy doesn't work this way, and the mixing ratios are much more critical for proper curing. It's often mixed 1:1 or 2:1. If you add too much hardener, the batch might not cure at all. You can thin epoxy with acetone, toluene, or MEK, but this can screw up the hardener ratios. See the *West System User Manual and Product Guide* for more-specific information. (The only time I had a batch go bad is when I tried to thin it with acetone.) ∎

Picking out a rotten core. The area wasn't completely rotted, but the seams where the deck was raised were cracked. This left a band of rot that went nearly around the entire foredeck.

Mac. I decided to effect a repair rather than replace the deck.

The first thing I did was identify the weakest areas. This was done by removing the interior covering panel. This was a sheet of plywood, covered with (mildewed) fabric, which was screwed to the underside of the deck. This panel helped to pretty up the boat, and probably added some insulation and prevented condensation on the overhead—but it also hid the damage as it progressed. I probed the entire area with a pocketknife, both inside and outside. Damage on the exterior was obvious in the form of a network of gaps and cracks where the old deck was raised and filled in. These areas were marked with chalk, to be dug out later. I found two places on the sheer that looked a little odd, and with a few cursory pokes managed to sink my knife in to the hilt. I marked these spots, too. On the inside, some of the fiberglass sheathing was peeling away from the framework as well.

I attacked the damaged areas with a "boat eater" (4½-inch angle grinder) and ground a deep groove where the cracks were. Underneath I found rotten plywood, which was dug out as much as possible. In some areas, it extended under the old deck, and I couldn't get it all. I saturated the whole area with acetone.

Acetone is a solvent that is stronger than paint thinner, evaporates very quickly (and as such, has very strong vapors), and mixes easily with water. It accelerates the evaporation of water on damp surfaces and provides a better bonding surface for epoxy. But it's dangerous stuff to use on a boat's interior, where the ventilation is poor. The vapors can cause dizziness, nausea, vomiting, narcosis, and unconsciousness, and it's highly flammable. Before you fool around with this stuff (or any solvent or compound that you're not familiar with), do yourself a favor, and read the back of the can. Or even better, read the MSDS (*Materials Safety Data Sheet*). You can get the MSDS from your supplier, or type "Acetone MSDS" into a Web search engine to get this information. Please be careful!

Inside, I ground away all the flaking fiberglass that I could.

After the area had a week or so to dry, I stuffed the groove with new fiberglass, trying to make sure the glass went well under the old deck. Then I mixed some epoxy and poured it into the groove. It wicked into the plywood, which was what I wanted. I weighted down the deck with concrete blocks, pressing the old deck into the new epoxy and glass. After three applications, the groove was filled. I sanded this flush and was repair the new cracks, just as I did the old ones. Eventually, all of the polyester that the previous owner used will be ground away and the repairs will be solid epoxy, but it will probably require several years and repair sessions to get to this point. It's an irritation that illustrates the importance of starting with a good, unmodified boat.

Another common exterior repair that I made was filling old holes left by hardware. Lots of these were plugged with silicone caulk or God-knows-what-else, and if they weren't leaking then, they would have been shortly. I assumed that every hole drilled through the boat was a leak, and decided to fill them all and redrill as necessary. This was easily done by taping the underside with masking tape and pouring epoxy into the little well. A two-part hardware-store variety works well for this application; it cures quickly, and it's a little thicker, too.

When the holes were horizontal, a different strategy was required. A thicker-than-normal epoxy is essential, so I would either use a filled epoxy product that is already thick (JB Weld is a good example), or I would mix each batch with a little silica powder until it was thick enough.

When applied to a hole on a vertical surface—an unwanted hole through an interior bulkhead, for example—the epoxy would creep out of the hole before it was cured. To hold it in place, I taped one side, troweled in the epoxy with a putty knife, and covered the other side with another piece of masking tape.

I used a variation to fill holes in my mast, which in places was peppered with old hardware holes. Since I couldn't reach very far into the mast, many of

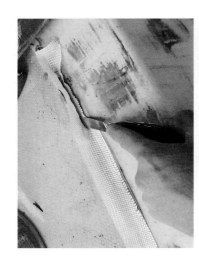

(from top) After I dug out as much rotten wood as possible, I flooded the gap with acetone and then stuffed the gap with narrow strips of fiberglass. Several batches of epoxy were poured into the groove, and then the old foredeck skin was pressed into the epoxy with concrete blocks for weight.

primed the whole area with a sandable undercoater that was compatible with the polyurethane paint that I would be using to paint the deck. There is a commercial product called Git-Rot that is basically a thinned epoxy resin; it would have worked well here, but since I didn't have any and it was about 75 miles to the nearest chandlery, I went with what I had.

Three years later, the repairs I made worked fine, but a whole new series of cracks appeared nearby. All I could do

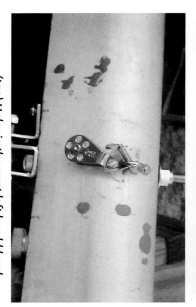
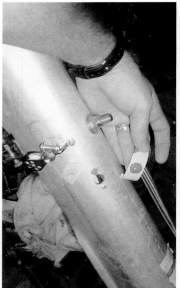

(top) Holes in the mast left by old hardware. Not exactly pretty, and a potential weak spot, but replacing the entire spar is an expensive proposition. (middle) Using masking tape to bridge a large hole. The masking tape will keep the epoxy from running out of the hole until it cures. (bottom) The repaired holes. Still looks pretty ugly, though maybe not quite as bad. The epoxy probably doesn't make any difference in strength, but you never know.

these holes weren't backed by masking tape. Some holes were quite large—about the size of a quarter. And to further complicate things, I wanted to avoid sanding the mast to prevent removing the layer of anodizing. The technique I developed that worked fairly well was to mix up a batch of JB Weld (which was a close, but not perfect, color match) and using a popsicle stick, form a small "button" of epoxy on the sticky side of a piece of masking tape. Then I carefully placed the epoxy over the center of the hole, making sure that the epoxy button touched the edges of the hole. Then I smoothed the surface of the masking tape and let the epoxy cure. The result looks pretty good—about the best that can be expected with this type of repair.

Rebuilding the Keel

Without a doubt, the most difficult and stressful part of the entire restoration (apart from paying for it) was restoring the keel. Early Ventures had a keel that was made from three layers of ½-inch steel, set into a female mold that was poured full of resin. Over time, water found its way into my keel's core, and it started to rust. Rust expands. A lot. It expanded enough to push the keel tight against the keel trunk, wedging it into place. Since repairing it properly takes a lot of work, some misguided boat owner had the idea that the fiberglass was the culprit, and he sawed it away with a circular saw. The keel had to be repaired properly, and in order to do that, it had to come out.

The keel was resting on the trailer's crossbar, so there was no way to get it out without lifting the boat. On a completely flat, concrete driveway, this

WHY CAN'T I SAND MY MAST?

Aluminum is a very useful metal aboard boats, especially in marine-grade, high-strength alloys. Aluminum can corrode, though; a layer of white powder forms on the surface (aluminum oxide). It protects the base metal from further corrosion, but it looks pretty awful. To prevent this from happening, masts are anodized by passing a current through the mast in a chemical solution, leaving a harder, more corrosion-resistant surface. But the surface is thin, and the anodizing is easily removed by sanding. If you sand it, more corrosion will shortly follow.

If you want to paint your mast, it can be done. Remove all fittings and sand with a medium emery cloth. Wipe the spar with a special wash. Interlux makes a two-part primewash for aluminum (#353 zinc chromate, vinyl butyral self-etching primer) for painting aluminum. Follow up with two coats of two-part polyurethane.

Stainless steel fastenings aren't completely compatible with aluminum, and will corrode over time. Using LocTite on the threads of self-tapping screws will help minimize corrosion, as well as keep them from vibrating loose. You can find more about this is in the Marine Metalwork chapter, starting on page 96. ■

wouldn't be so bad, but my boat was on dirt with a gentle slope. I used a half-sheet of ¾-inch plywood under the blocks so that they wouldn't sink unevenly into the soft soil. I lifted the boat a little at a time, using a scissors jack, supporting it with concrete blocks and timbers. It worked. I eventually got the boat high enough to clear the width of

the keel, but it was very unstable and wobbly. I clamped legs to the side to support it, put up extra jackstands, but it still was precarious. (In fact, when I was lowering it back down, it started to fall sideways, and I saved it by bracing it with two-by-fours. Generally, going up was more straightforward, but each time I lowered it, the boat started to

(left) The boat going up. You can just start to see the keel underneath. (right) This is as high as I had to lift the boat to remove the swing keel.

drift to the side. The whole process took years off my life.)

The keel was lowered with the boat's keel winch until the bottom edge was resting on the trailer and secured there. Whatever you do, don't disconnect the keel winch cable until the end. (You'll need a properly functioning keel winch to lower your keel. If yours needs work, fix it before you attempt to lower the keel out of the boat.) I lifted the forward end of the keel with a jack—just enough to take the pressure off the keel pivot bolt—and removed the keel bolt, which I dis-covered was bent nearly 45 degrees. I had to drive it out with a hammer. Once it was removed, I lowered the jack, but nothing happened. The keel was wedged tightly into the trunk. I went inside the boat, drilled a hole in the top of the trunk (actually I enlarged an existing hole), and started to drive the forward end of the keel out by hammering on a steel rod that passed through the hole. I lowered the jack by about ½ inch, went inside and hammered for a while, and then came out and checked the jack. After a few trips back and forth, the keel was touch-ing the jack, so I lowered it another ½ inch. This time, the keel went down a little easier. After lowering the jack a third time, the keel slid free of the trunk

HOSE BARBS FOR DRAINAGE PROBLEMS

Most sailboats are designed so that they will drain well. Puddles that don't drain over-board on the boat will lead to stains, poor footing, and wet sneakers. On wooden boats, they cause rot, so designers and builders of wooden boats take great pains to avoid them. Some fiberglass designs are less carefully executed, and puddles will need to be dealt with.

Fortunately, a solution is as close as your hardware store. It's called a "hose barb," and it's a small piece of brass with threads on one end and a fluted nipple on the other for attaching a piece of hose. You want large hose barbs, with an inside diameter of $3/8$" or bigger. Smaller ones will easily clog with dirt. Mark the spot where the puddle is deepest, and drill a hole, slightly smaller than the threaded end of the hose barb. Coat the threads well with thickened epoxy, and screw the hose barb into place from the inside, until its surface is just flush with the deck or cockpit sole (or whatever surface needs drainage). If you drilled the right size hole, the threads should grip the fiberglass well. Build up the area around the hose barb with thickened epoxy and glass to give it plenty of support. Using the same procedures, install another hose barb on the boat's "topsides" (the sides of the hull above the waterline). It should be fairly high above the waterline but lower than the first one, and the two should be lined up so that a clean run of hose will connect them. Press on the hose, and use two hose clamps on each end to make sure the hose stays put. Note that since hose barbs are commonly brass, they should never be used near or below the waterline. The zinc in the brass will rapidly corrode, causing the fitting to fail and quite possibly sink your boat. ∎

IMPORTANT SAFETY NOTE

While I lifted my boat off of the trailer myself, I don't recommend that you do this with your boat. I got away with it, but despite taking what I thought was every precaution, I took a significant risk, and the boat nearly fell. I'll never do it again. The slightest mistake or miscalculation could easily kill you if you happen to be between the boat and the ground. If you're lucky, a mistake will only cause massive amounts of damage. If you need to do keel work, please, spend the extra money and get a professional to help you. Haul the boat to a yard and ask them to quote a price for removing and replacing the keel. Do this early in your restoration, while the boat looks cruddy, and the yard manager might feel sorry enough for you to discount the price. ∎

and could be lowered by its own weight. Once clear of the hull, the keel cable held the keel upright and prevented it from falling over. Since the keel weight is about 400 pounds, this wouldn't be an insignificant event. I went back into the boat and gently lowered the winch cable, and the keel slowly laid over.

Some of the old Ventures reportedly had solid cast iron keels, and I wish I had been able to find one. Repairing a cast iron keel involves sandblasting and painting, while composite keels, like mine, must be re-laminated with fiberglass.

Maneuvering the keel to work on it was extremely difficult, but I was able to do it with a "keel fork" that I welded together out of scrap rebar (concrete reinforcing steel). I kept the keel on a wooden loading pallet so that I could get the fork under it to turn it or work on its edge. I had endless visions of this thing falling on my leg and breaking it, since it was about this time that I fell getting into the boat and broke my wrist. It wasn't fun. If you need to do this with your boat, I suggest you seek profes-

sional help if at all possible. When you get back from the psychiatrist, maybe you can find someone with an engine hoist to help you move this thing around while you work on it.

The first thing I did was to strip off the old fiberglass. Since much of it was already cut away, this was easy. I did save the leading and trailing edge pieces for a while—just long enough to make sure I had the correct profile for the part of the keel that extended beyond the core.

The keel after it was removed from the boat. Large sections of fiberglass had been cut away, exposing the core.

LIFTING OPTIONS

You will likely need to get the boat off the trailer at some point for keel work or painting the hull. If not done carefully, this can be disastrous, resulting in a wrecked boat and/or serious injury. One option is to pony up the bucks and take the boat to a boatyard with a Travelift. They'll raise and block the boat and return it to the trailer when the work is done. Expect to pay about $200 plus a daily yard fee.

Another option is lifting from above. An example of this can be seen at http://jeffrey.denard.staff.noctrl.edu/boatpage/. To build his lifting gallows, Jeff used a pair of two-by-fours nailed together for the uprights, and a pair of 12-foot 2x8 boards for the horizontal piece that connects the two uprights. If the uprights are well-braced and strong, this would be an easier and safer way to lift the boat—it's a method I'll employ next time. Assembled with bolts, a gallows can be disassembled and stored for later use. Whatever you do, make sure everything is doubly strong and well-braced. Make sure you completely support the boat from below before you work under it. To say this can be dangerous is an understatement—sloppy work here can be fatal. If you have any reservations about removing your keel, hire a professional.

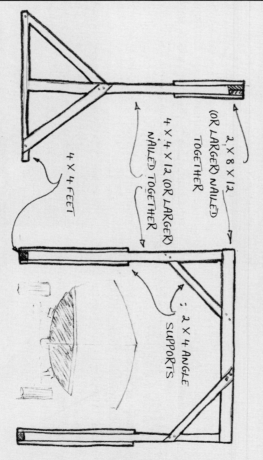

Jeff Denerd's boat gallows.

A second alternative is lifting from below, as I did. It requires a less elaborate setup, but it's much less stable and requires you to be too close to the underside of the boat as it is raised. (There is another description of this process at http://home.usaa.net/~spiritof sailing. Click the link for "Restoration Project.")

Lifting from below is complicated by the fact that the Mac sits low on the trailer, and once you get the boat up, you can't remove the trailer. ∎

Since the center keel core plate was 1 inch thick, I welded on a 1½-by-¼-inch strip along the trailing edge to support the filler that I'd be adding. Here's where the chunk of keel skin that I'd saved came in handy, since I could check the keel for the correct profile.

If you aren't fortunate enough to have access to a welder, or you lack the ability, you could have the job welded for you by a shop. Getting the strip welded on would be simple, but transporting it to and from the shop would not be so easy. Alternatively, you could try to epoxy a thin wedge of shaped foam to the back edge of the keel, but you'd need to support it with many layers of fiberglass cloth for strength. If you can swing it, welding is the better choice.

Next, the keel was sandblasted and primed. I used a high-zinc spray primer and hoped it wouldn't react with the resin I was about to put on.

Here's where I made a big mistake: I filled one side of the keel using polyester resin, thinking that since this was basically a new construction, I wouldn't need to use the expensive epoxy. I mixed up some filler, troweled it and sanded it to shape, and laminated with three layers of glass. That's when I noticed the tini-

est gaps near the core and filler, where the polyester must have slightly shrunk. I had already used up a good amount of my materials that I'd bought for the keel, and I was essentially committed, so I gave the cracks a coat of epoxy, and then laminated another layer of glass with epoxy and turned it over. The other side was done in all epoxy. So far, it appears that the epoxy has sealed it up, but I wish I hadn't used any polyester at all. I ended up throwing away half a gallon.

Moving Right Along: The Interior

While I was working on the keel, I started some of the work inside. I had a fairly empty, but still gross-looking shell. All the rotten fabric had been torn out, and it left a horrible surface—a mix of peeling paint and some sort of adhesive. Worse, in some areas, the paint was holding solid; in others it was peeling. In some places, the adhesive was thick and sticky; in others, dried and flaking. The surface would need lots of preparation if the paint had a prayer of holding up.

Stripping

After experiments with various chemical removers were unsuccessful, I had to resort to mechanical methods. The 4½-inch

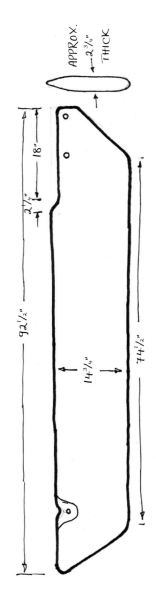

Dimensions for a 1972 Venture keel.

(top) Drilling out the pivot hole for a larger-size bolt. (bottom) Here I've applied filler (resin and microballoons); sanding is next.

the overhead, the areas around the companionway opening, and the quarter berths. After a good deal of thinking about the problem, I decided that this job required a heavy industrial-strength tool—like a sandblaster.

I had used a sandblaster while I was working during college, and I was familiar with what they can do. They'll clean the most complex surface and leave a nicely roughened surface for painting. The big sandblaster that I used, though, required a huge tow-behind diesel compressor and could easily blow a hole through a wooden surface if not kept moving. Smaller pressurized sandblasters are available from companies like Harbor Freight, and I went ahead and bought one. It cost around $110. Still smaller suction-type sandblasters are much cheaper, but in general they don't have nearly enough power to do the job that I needed.

After I learned that my sandblaster would clog on anything other than fine, screened sandblasting sand, I hit the hull. The sandblasting took about two days, though it would have gone much faster and worked better with a larger compressor. I had a small one, which I hooked together with a larger borrowed compressor. Even together, these couldn't keep up with the demand of the sandblaster, and I was constantly waiting around while the compressors built up enough pressure. Renting a big unit would have been more expensive, but it also would have been better in terms of performance. In the end, I had made a huge mess, but the interior was finally clear of most of the loose flakes and ready for a coat of paint.

angle grinder with a very coarse sanding disc worked about as well as anything, so I sanded everything I could get to. It was tedious, dirty work. Ear, eye, and lung protection was absolutely essential, and I set up a box fan over one of the hatches to pull as much fresh air into the cabin as possible.

But after more hours at this than I care to recall, the job still wasn't done. While the angle grinder worked great on broad, flat surfaces, it was too big and bulky to get into some places—namely,

Epoxy Work

Once it was clean, I could do some more work on the interior with the epoxy. I mentioned the elevated foredeck earlier, and this area needed some attention from the underside as well. The previous owner had built a web of stringers to strengthen the deck, since Ventures are known to flex a bit as you walk on them. These stringers were made from wood that was sheathed in fiberglass cloth, but as usual, the polyester couldn't stick to the expanding and contracting wood. It did do a nice job of holding the dampness next to the wood so it could rot.

I probed the stringers with a pocketknife to find areas that had the worst rot. These were heavily sanded with an angle grinder, which was, as usual, a difficult chore. Complex curves and tight spaces combined with itchy fiberglass dust sprinkling all over me left an

(top) Hard to believe, but to get to this point took quite a bit of work. Simply painting this surface wouldn't work. Sanding with an angle grinder helped a great deal, but a sandblaster was needed for the corners and overhead. (bottom) Sandblasting the interior. The pop-top was removed, which made access a good bit easier. A waterblaster, which mixes sand with water and works like a pressure washer, might be another alternative. I tried a plain pressure washer, which did remove some of the loose flakes but didn't go far enough.

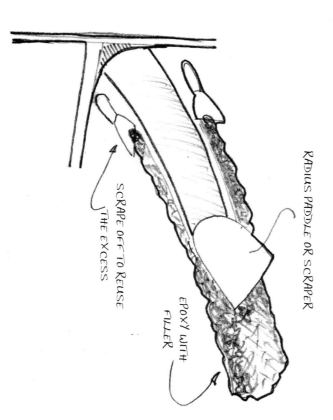

Making a fillet.

SCRAPE OFF TO REUSE THE EXCESS

RADIUS PADDLE OR SCRAPER

EPOXY WITH FILLER

impression of a job that I don't want to repeat anytime soon. And that was just the beginning. Trying to epoxy upside-down was lots of fun—manipulating strips of sticky glass cloth that didn't want to stay up, thanks to gravity. In the end, I gave some of the stringers new glass, but some just received a coat or two of epoxy resin.

This was when I started experimenting with one of epoxy's niftiest tricks: fillets. One of the basic tenets of building with fiberglass-reinforced plastics is that the gentler the curves, the stronger the laminate. Fiberglass doesn't like to be forced around sharp corners. Sharp corners concentrate stresses, and these areas are much more likely to fracture. If an inside corner (for example, where a bulkhead joins a hull) is radiused rather than simply butted to the hull, then the resulting joint is much stronger. Stresses

from the hull are more broadly distributed, and the bulkhead is less likely to form hard spots on the exterior of the hull.

This little detail is time-consuming, and it's often neglected in cheaper yachts. It was certainly the case in mine, where the solution to most problems seemed to be to "slap an extra layer of glass on it and get it out of here." I think the basic laminate is strong enough on my boat, but it could have been better.

That's where the epoxy fillet comes in. You can apply fillets anywhere on the boat where two surfaces come together. The epoxy's adhesive strength is so great that the fillet becomes a permanent part of the boat's structure. I put fillets in the joints of the stringers above the V-berth, where it strengthened and supported the stringers, as well as helped the job look a little more professional.

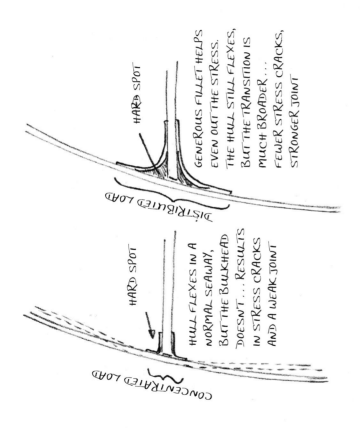

HARD SPOT

GENEROUS FILLET HELPS
EVEN OUT THE STRESS.
THE HULL STILL FLEXES,
BUT THE TRANSITION IS
MUCH BROADER...
FEWER STRESS CRACKS,
STRONGER JOINT

DISTRIBUTED LOAD

HARD SPOT

HULL FLEXES IN A
NORMAL SEAWAY,
BUT THE BULKHEAD
DOESN'T... RESULTS
IN STRESS CRACKS
AND A WEAK JOINT

CONCENTRATED LOAD

To make a fillet, you need some epoxy and some fillers. Fumed silica, sometimes known by the trade name Cab-O-Sil, is an epoxy additive that makes epoxy thick and very sticky. It's sold by Interlux as an "epoxy glue powder." When you mix epoxy with silica, you get a compound that looks and handles very much like Vaseline. It cures rock-hard, and it's almost impossible to sand.

Glass microballoons are the other epoxy additive that you need to know about. It's a very fine white or red powder that, when mixed with epoxy, gives an almost foam-like compound. There is a slightly coarser grade available that's red, and it cures to a burgundy color. It's easy to sand when cured, but it will run off of vertical surfaces when wet.

I used these two additives for my entire boat. What works best is a blend—

microballoons for lightness and ease of sanding, and silica for strength. It also makes your epoxy compound sticky, and it will cling to vertical and overhead surfaces.

So how do you make a fillet? First, grind the joint back to clean, sound fiberglass (or plywood—whatever you're joining). Hand-sanding probably won't be enough unless your boat is very clean and sound to start with. Neglect this step and you might as well be using polyester; because you'll be doing it over later. Next, get your tools ready. You'll need a radius paddle that's shaped to the desired curve. Flexible plastic is best and can be reused, but cardboard will do if you don't mind making new ones each time. It needs to be able to bend a little, so don't use corrugated. Also popular are tongue depressors or light bulbs, but my

(left) Smooth the area with a radius paddle. You can't see it well, but I'm using a piece of cardboard. (right) Before the compound cures, gently place a strip of fiberglass over the joint.

Apply epoxy compound with a stirring stick after sanding away the loose paint and crud from the corner.

very favorite radius paddles are credit cards. Most Americans have a pile of them in their wallets. While they may seem useful for buying boat supplies, they'll only get you in trouble in the long run, so use them for epoxy work. OK, I'm only kidding here—you should carefully guard your credit cards and their numbers. But I do use all those little sample cards that say "Your Name Here" that I keep getting in the mail. Fill out one application, and you'll soon receive enough solicitations to do a dozen boats.

You'll also need putty knives—a narrow one to spread the thickened epoxy into the joint, and a wider one to scrape up the excess left by the radius paddle. Get an empty yogurt cup and some mixing sticks. Wear surgical gloves, a respirator, and eye protection (especially if you're working overhead—this stuff will bond to your sclera as well as the bulkhead).

Mix up a batch of 50-50 silica and microballoons and set aside. Then catalyze the epoxy, mixing well. Then add a spoonful

of filler until the consistency seems right. You'll know when you've added enough silica if the mix whips into stiff peaks, like a good lemon meringue pie.

Trowel the concoction into the joint you want to fillet with a narrow putty knife. Make sure there is plenty of compound in your joint, and don't worry about using too much; you'll scrape off the excess and use it further on down the joint. Then follow up by dragging the

(left) After the compound cures, brush on a coat of epoxy to saturate the fiberglass. (right) The finished fillet before painting. The joint is much stronger and easier to clean.

radius paddle, holding it at an angle to both press the compound into the joint and scrape the surface of the joint. Don't worry—you'll quickly develop a feel for it. Scrape off the excess compound that squeezes past the radius paddle onto the hull, then leave it alone! Extra passes with the paddle will almost always make it worse.

When I put fillets in my hull, I added one extra step. I gently pressed strips of fiberglass into the sticky surface of the fillet. You have to use the lightest of touches, and fingers (protected by surgical gloves) are the best tools for this. When the epoxy in the fillet "kicked" (in other words, when it reacted and began to harden), part of the fiberglass was nicely saturated, and part was not. I brushed on a topcoat of epoxy to bond the fiberglass to the boat and to fill the weave of the glass. The finished result is super-strong, looks good, and was easy to achieve. Using fiberglass strips has the added benefit of holding the compound in place in case you didn't get enough silica into your mix.

I used fillets all over the boat—around the transom, around the motor well, around both sides of the keel trunk, and along the lower edges of the seat/hull joints. I was hesitant to use them too much up high in the cabin, but down low the weight wouldn't be a problem. And the smooth curves would make the surfaces much easier to keep clean, too.

The other main application for the epoxy in my boat was repairing the keel lockdown hole, which had somehow been transformed from a hole to an arc-shaped slot. I've theorized that someone routed the keel lockdown bolt hole into an arc—but why someone would do this is a mystery. Maybe it occurred during a very hard grounding, but the edges of the slot were cut clean. The slot was filled with epoxy compound, several layers of fiberglass were laminated over, and a new hole was drilled in the approximate location of the old hole. Several layers were added to the keel pivot bolt area for good measure.

The Ports

The original ports for the boat were pretty badly crazed and brittle, and they needed replacing. I decided to make a small change for vanity's sake, and divide the long portlight opening into two smaller ones. If this had been done at the factory, it would have made the cabin stronger, but since this was an after-the-fact modification, it probably isn't a great improvement in anything other than looks. The ports were pieces of Plexiglas offcuts from a plastics supplier. They were surface mounted, bedded in silicone, and through-bolted. Lexan is a much stronger alternative, though it's more expensive and not readily available in tints. When mounting ports this way, it's important to remember to drill the holes through the Plexiglas oversize. The Plexiglas and cabin side will expand and contract at different rates in the heat of the summer. If the holes are too closely matched, each will develop a small crack in a short period of time.

In order to divide the single long opening into two smaller ones, I needed to install a filler piece. The very best way to do this would be to use a solid fiberglass laminate, well-bonded and feathered into the original cabin side. I did it the second-best way: I found a few small pieces of very-high-quality thin plywood in the trash pile of a furniture store. It was part of some kind of crate. I'm embarrassed to admit this, but I regularly prowl these places looking for crates, because they're sometimes made from furniture scraps. I've found several small pieces of ash and walnut this way. Anyway, I grabbed this piece of plywood thinking it would be good for something. It was a touch less than ¼ inch, 100 per-

cent clear on both sides, and had no voids in the edges. Still, I wasn't sure it was waterproof, so I subjected a small sample to the same testing that marine plywood undergoes: I boiled it in water for an hour or so. When the sample showed no delaminating whatsoever, I concluded that it was good enough to use on my boat.

The plywood was shaped into what resembled a short, thick, capital **I**. It was just a bit thicker than the cabin sides, so

(top) The plywood filler piece. It's been routed to lay flush with the outside surface.
(bottom) Next, I shaped the sides of the fillers, so that the inside edge of the ports would be rounded.

the top and bottom were dadoed off with the table saw until the piece laid perfectly flush with the outside of the cabin. The rest of the edges were shaved off with a jointer so that the fiberglass cloth could lay against it smoothly. Then it was sanded and the whole thing was coated with two coats of epoxy. This would become the core of the modification.

Next, I ground into the fiberglass of cabin sides, both inside and outside, for several inches beyond the filler piece. This was to give the surface a good, rough base for the epoxy to adhere to. The filler piece was glued in place with thickened epoxy, and once it cured, the clamps were removed and the cracks and joints were given a generous application of epoxy fairing compound. I then gave the whole thing a day to cure.

Next, I sanded and smoothed everything in. Just to be safe, another coat of epoxy was brushed onto the wood and allowed to cure, and then I began to laminate with fiberglass. I built up four layers on the inside of the hull, and three layers on the outside of 6.5-ounce high-strength glass cloth (an eBay special that

was a good buy, but hard to wet out—it didn't want to conform to curves, either; regular E-glass would have worked better). This was sanded, filled, and sanded again, until it was perfectly smooth on the exterior and the interior was blended in well. All the edges were well-sealed. When it was painted, it looked as if it had always been that way. I was pleased. The whole job took maybe four days to do, working about three to four hours each day, so it wasn't as time-consuming as it sounds.

Painting

Once I had made all the structural modifications, reinforcements, and repairs with the epoxy, I was ready to paint. The interior of a boat is a much less severe environment than the exterior. As long as standing water is kept out, you can use regular hardware store variety paint instead of marine paint. It's a good bit cheaper—and remember that saving money is an important goal in a small sailboat.

We can't use just anything, though. I found a gloss polyurethane for $8 a

(from left) The filler piece bonded in place with epoxy. Note that the plywood edges are well feathered. The edges of the filler piece will be compounded with epoxy. After the compound was sanded fair, it got three laminations of fiberglass that extended well onto the hull. Laminating the exterior. Note the fiberglass overlap.

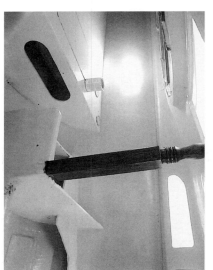

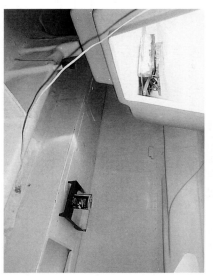

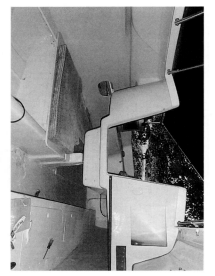

(clockwise from top left) Once the interior was sandblasted, I primed with Kilz . . . then rolled on a coat of polyurethane. A view of the interior paint. Needless to say, it was a fairly dramatic improvement.

quart that was a very strong, tough paint. (I even bought some dented close-out cans for $2 each!) It took about 3½ quarts to do all the surfaces, including the insides of the lockers and the underside of the cockpit. The glossy surface makes it much easier to wipe off mildew, and, unless you live in Nevada, it will mildew at some point—I promise.

You need to use some sort of primer, though. The polyurethane is so hard that its adhesive strength is sometimes less than ideal. I used 2 gallons of Kilz oil-based primer. Kilz has a reducer in it

that softens cured paint ever so slightly, allowing a very strong grip over old paint. So far, the Kilz-polyurethane combination is holding up very well.

One of the dangers with polyurethane is that it can't be sprayed without elaborate breathing protection. Spraying is fast, and it results in a super-smooth glossy finish, but it's not necessary for the rough interior surface. (If you're painting a liner, that's another story—but liners rarely need painting.) A roller works fine. I found several inexpensive short-nap rollers that worked fairly well, though some began to dissolve after a while and leave fibers in my surface. This paint contains some aggressive solvents, and it's also very sticky when it starts to dry. I tossed them when they started to go, and I put on a new cover. The expensive covers seemed to hold up better than the cheap ones. I also saved a bit by buying special solvent-resistant covers from BoatU.S., and cut them in half on the table saw. The smaller size made it easier to get into corners.

Painting the interior took about two weeks, not including the preparation time. The improvement is dramatic, and apart from new cushions, probably the most noticeable improvement to the boat's interior. Though it's certainly a major project, I wouldn't hesitate to paint the interior of a boat that doesn't have a liner.

Small Boat Wiring

Of course, the most reliable electrical system in a boat this size is none at all. That would have been far better than the rat's nest of lamp cord, corroded switches, and wire nuts that I found. I knew from the very first survey that every bit of the electrical system had to be replaced.

Remember: boat wiring is totally different than residential wiring. Techniques that work fine in the nice, dry, still environment of the average home interior will not fly onboard your boat. Using approved marine wiring techniques is no more difficult than residential work, but it requires a little learning, planning, and attention to detail.

In the learning department, you can make use of a few books. I found a copy of

Nigel Calder's *Boatowner's Mechanical and Electrical Manual* at the library. In it, he recommends THWN stranded wire, though others will say to only use fully tinned, marine-grade wire. The thinking is that tinned wire won't wick water in through the ends. I went with the stranded wire for reasons of cost. I was careful in sealing the ends, didn't have any terminals that would be exposed to standing water (hopefully), and wouldn't be running wires through the bilge. To completely replace all the wires, I used about 150 feet each of red and black 12 gauge, and about 15 feet each of red and black 10 gauge for the battery supply wires.

The bible of electrical marine installations is the *American Boat and Yacht Council's (ABYC) Standards and Recommended Practices*, section E-9, which covers DC installations in boats. I finally found excerpts from the ABYC spec on the Blue Sea Systems website, at www.bluesea.com/abyc.htm.

The U.S. Coast Guard (USCG) also has mandatory requirements for electrical systems in Title 33, CFR 183 subpart 1, section 183. You can look at these at www.access.gpo.gov/nara/cfr/waisidx_99/33cfr183_99.html.

In general, the USCG requirements are much less stringent and detailed than the ABYC standards. When I wired my boat, I followed the ABYC spec as closely as possible, though it's hard to say with complete authority. The ABYC electrical specification is directed primarily at manufacturers (their *Standards and Technical Information Reports for Small Craft* is $219 for members only) and there isn't a consumer version available. Much more affordable is Charlie

Wing's *Boatowner's Illustrated Handbook of Wiring*, available for $30 from the ABYC and regular bookstores.

The heart of your boat's wiring, and the logical place to start, is the electrical panel. You can buy one or make one yourself from scratch. They can get quite expensive, especially if you use marine breakers instead of fuses. It's an extremely simple thing, consisting of six fuse holders connected to six rocker switches. One side of the fuse holders are all connected together, which is where the positive connection of the battery goes. There's also a negative connection on this panel, but that's primarily for illuminating the rocker switches (they have neon indicator lamps in them).

When I planned my electrical layout, I added a bus bar and a terminal strip. The bus bar is just a strip of thick copper with several screws tapped into it. The bus bar serves as the main grounding point for everything electrical on the boat.

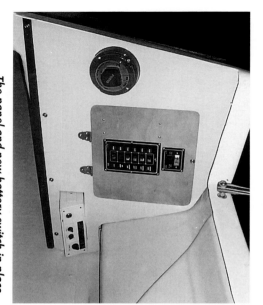

The panel and new battery switch in place. Since the battery isn't used to start an engine, the big battery switch is overkill, but it didn't cost much.

The terminal strip is to help distribute the positive end of the circuit, and avoids the common problem of several wires branching off of each switch in the electrical panel. A single wire goes from each switch to the terminal strip, where small jumpers further distribute the power. Each bulb or electrical circuit has its own spot on the terminal strip, where a single wire is anchored. This further helps to avoid the rat's nest syndrome, where snarls of wire branch off in all directions. The rat's nest makes troubleshooting difficult or, in extreme cases, impossible. Trust me, you'll have trouble at some point—electricity mixed with corrosion and the damp environment of a boat means problems are almost a given. You'll thank yourself later if you take the time to do it right now.

You should label everything neatly for the same reason. I printed out labels on the computer and taped them to the board on which the panel was mounted. I also used a fine-point Sharpie to identify the wires. I wrote the name of the circuit—bow bicolor lt, masthead anchor lt, steaming lt, and so on—on a small piece of an Avery label, cut it out with scissors, and wrapped it to the wire. Then I covered that with a small piece of clear packing tape. (If you can find it, clear heat-shrink tubing is a better choice—more about heat-shrink later in this chapter.)

There has been some debate about the best way to attach wire terminals. The ABYC says that you should use captive terminals (ring or bent-fork type) that can't slip off the screw on terminal strips. It goes on to say that solder connections can't be used alone to hold a terminal to a wire, but some type of me-

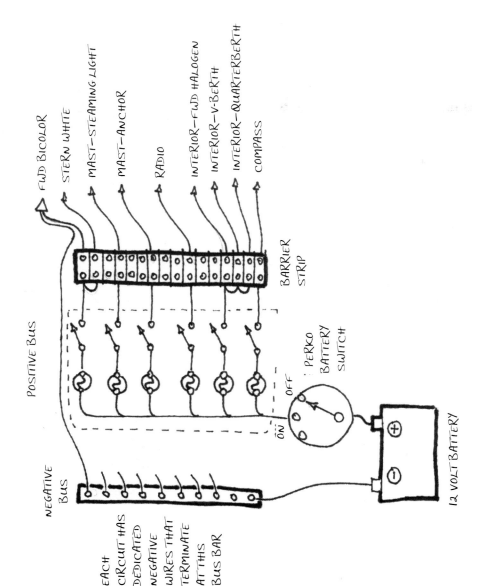

FWD BICOLOR
STERN WHITE
MAST—STEAMING LIGHT
MAST—ANCHOR
RADIO
INTERIOR—FWD HALOGEN
INTERIOR—V-BERTH
INTERIOR—QUARTERBERTH
COMPASS

POSITIVE BUS

BARRIER STRIP

PERKO BATTERY SWITCH

ON   OFF

NEGATIVE BUS

EACH CIRCUIT HAS DEDICATED NEGATIVE WIRES THAT TERMINATE AT THIS BUS BAR

12 VOLT BATTERY

My 12-volt distribution schematic.

chanical fastening must be used. They're talking about crimp-on connectors here, and they go on to say that crimp-on connectors must be installed with a crimper. I attached my terminals by crimping on the ring terminal and soldering the crimp, and then covering the joint with heat-shrink tubing.

Heat shrink tubing is great stuff. You slip the tubing over a connection, apply heat from a match or a heat gun, and it contracts to about half its diameter, forming a neat, permanent cover. Forget

that black, stretchy electrician's tape—it makes everything a sticky mess and doesn't hold up well in a marine environment. If you can find it, they even make a clear heat-shrink that's great for labeling the wires. I found heat-shrink tubing at a hardware store, but it was only available in black.

The ABYC spec also says that wires must be supported every 18 inches. I found a kit at an automotive store that contained a couple sizes of zip ties and several different sizes of nylon binding

Heat-shrink tubing at work. First, crimp and solder the ends, and then slide the heat-shrink over the terminal and apply heat. Neat, permanent, and not sticky!

straps for about $2. I bought three packs and used just about all of it. The wiring straps were mostly too small, since the 12-gauge wires made a fairly large package when bundled together. The zip ties help to keep things neat. I've also seen zip ties with lugs for screws molded into the ends. These would be ideal, but I've only found them at specialty electronics suppliers, and they're pricey if I remember correctly.

Once the panel was installed, the wiring went along smoothly. I used an old 12-volt plug-in "wall wart" transformer—one of those big, black, ugly transformers —to test each leg as it was installed, and each circuit worked the first time. The mast wiring was replaced as well, and I used a pair of two-conductor plugs for the disconnect. Since this connector is exposed to the weather, I'll certainly have problems in the future, but this is a common trouble spot.

If you've never done anything like this before, don't panic. Just read as much as you can, start on something small, and approach the problem one step at a time. It's really one of the easier projects on a small boat, as long as you keep the total system simple.

Painting the Exterior

After all the prep work, painting, and sanding of the hull and topsides, it was finally time to paint the exterior. There are several paint manufacturers to choose from, but I went with Petit because it was readily available from catalog suppliers and slightly cheaper than the competition. The exterior of a sailboat is a punishing environment for a coat of paint to endure, so I don't recommend scrimping on paint. Buy a good, marine-grade paint, and stick with one manufacturer for everything. Interlux thinner might do some strange things when used to thin Petit's paint. Maybe it'll work fine, but if I were you, I'd confine my experiments to the doghouse (the doghouse in your yard, not the doghouse on the boat). Don't experiment on something as large as your hull unless you really know what you're doing.

For painting the hull, polyurethane is the only way to go. Standard oil-based enamels, even the best marine grades, will have a life expectancy of about two years. It isn't unusual for polyurethane finishes to last five to ten years.

The very best finish is a two-part, sprayed-on finish. The only problem with this is that spraying polyurethane is so toxic that the fumes can kill you. Some two-part spray coatings are only available to professional refinishers, who use full-body protective suits and positive-pressure ventilation systems. Since we're talking about relatively small boats here, the cost to have a hull sprayed might be worth considering, es-

PAINT CHOICES

As I was completing the section on polyurethane paints, I read an article comparing different paint types for above-the-waterline use ("Topside Paint Kick-Off," *Practical Sailor*, Vol 28, #4, February 15, 2002). They applied different one-part and two-part polys, as well as other industrial and standard enamel coatings, to the side of an old Boston Whaler.

The initial results were that most two-part polys had excellent to good gloss, while most one-part polys had fair or poor gloss. The exception among the one-part polyurethanes was Interlux Brightside, rated excellent for gloss in red and white, fair in blue. My choice, Petit's Easypoxy, was rated as poor for all three colors.

Even though *Practical Sailor* didn't rate the paint very highly, I'm extremely satisfied with Easypoxy's performance and gloss. Maybe I'll try Interlux next time, but if the difference is as dramatic as they indicate, I'll need sunglasses to look at my hull. ∎

pecially if you can work out a deal where you do all the stripping, scraping, and sanding. A sprayed poly finish is beautiful—really. It can look as if the hull popped from the mold hours, rather than decades, ago.

If you decide that $200 per foot (a common rate to refinish just the deck; hulls are often less—around $100 per foot) is a bit too dear, there is an alternative. The major paint manufacturers have developed polyurethanes that are designed to be applied by roller and smoothed out with a dry brush. This technique is called drybrushing, and if you're careful, it can produce a finish that's nearly as glossy as a sprayed-on paint job (see the sidebar, Paint Choices, above). This technique is especially suited to amateur boat restorers who may not have access to all the necessary safety equipment.

One of the more recent developments in boat paints is one-part polyurethane paints. They're much easier to use than two-part paints because they don't need to be catalyzed before application, but they do need to be thinned a bit. They're less expensive as well. I used Petit's Easypoxy one-part polyurethane, Jade Green.

Painting works best if you have a helper or two, but it can be done by one person. Here's how:

Using the paint manufacturer's special brushing thinner, a batch of paint is thinned to a consistency of heavy cream. This is rolled onto the hull with a foam roller cover (not a household roller cover that you can get from a paint store—the household roller covers fall apart and ruin the job). At this point, the paint will slightly resemble the surface of an orange peel. While the paint is still wet, the finish is tipped off by gently stroking it with a good brush. This smoothes the finish considerably. I started by sanding the entire hull with a ¼ sheet electric pad sander. I had a few areas where the scraping had taken small chips from the

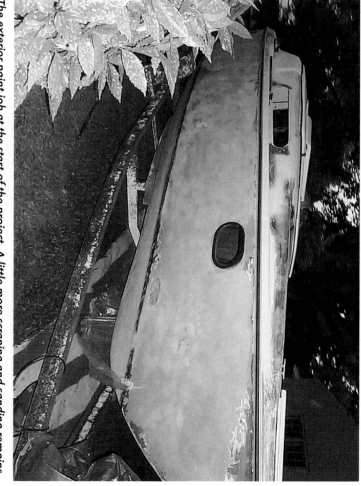

The exterior paint job at the start of the project. A little more scraping and sanding remains to be done around the bow.

hull, so I spot-primed these and sanded them in. (As I later discovered, this was a mistake. I should have primed the entire hull.) I removed the dust by wiping the hull down with a damp cloth.

If you have access to some help, it's great if you can get one person to mix paint and fetch rags, another person to roll, and a third person to tip it out. When I painted my hull, I did all three jobs myself. It isn't too bad if you do small sections of the hull at a time—roll out about 5 feet of hull, then brush, then mix more paint and start again.

As the paint dries, the brush marks seem to flow together. It also brings out even the slightest imperfection of the surface beneath, as I found out. My paint job still looks super, and I'm quite

pleased with the way it turned out. But if you examine the hull closely, you can tell it's been painted. Next time, I'll prime and sand the entire hull.

Bottom Paint

There are some considerations regarding bottom paint that I had to think about. Since my boat will be primarily sailed in an inland lake, I had several options. I could go without bottom paint at all, and haul out on the trailer to scrub off the slime every once in a while. Or I could use a hard paint finish with no antifouling properties, like the racers use. In the end, I chose a low-cost house-brand bottom paint from BoatU.S. My reasoning was that the cheaper paint would be somewhat less toxic, yet still protect the hull. The fresh coat of paint looks good on the trailer, too.

The bootstripe, which is the stripe of (usually) contrasting color at the waterline, deserves special mention. Part of the time it's dry; part of the time it's under water. And it needs a bit of antifouling chemicals to prevent grass and slime growth. There is a special bootstripe paint available that I used—though it's expensive, I felt it was worth the cost.

Painting the Deck

To prepare the deck, nearly all the hardware was removed, and nearly all the holes were filled. A few things—like the winches, for instance—remained in their original location, although they bothered me. The line from the jibsheet blocks to the winches should ideally be an unobstructed, straight line, and mine wasn't. As it was originally installed, the jibsheet would have rubbed against the cabin as it went to the winches. That would easily rub straight through my nice new paint job, as well as increase friction and wear on the sheet. My options were to install a small wooden or brass chafe strip on the cabin side, or move the winches outboard. In the end, I removed the winches, fabricated a pair of custom stainless steel brackets to mount the winches on, and reinstalled the whole thing. The new location works fine on the starboard side, but since winches turn clockwise, the port jibsheet still just touches the edge of the cabin. It's much better than the original arrangement, though.

The topsides were painted with Petit's Off-White polyurethane, and I used Sandstone for the nonskid areas.

The molded-in nonskid pattern, like most older boats, needed special attention. On most production boats, the nonskid is an area of tiny diamond-shaped patterns molded into the deck. Even when it was brand-new, it didn't grip terribly well. Now most of the recesses were filled with old paint, so it's even

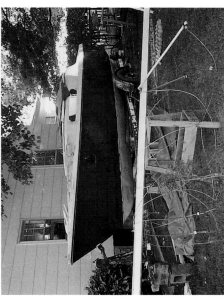

(top) Drybrushing the hull. The paint has been rolled on, leaving a very bubbly and rough surface. Lightly stroking with the brush pops the bubbles and smoothes the surface greatly. I was very pleased with the performance of the Petit one-part poly, though I've heard that two-part poly gives even greater gloss. (bottom) The hull after the first coat of green polyurethane.

less effective. And since this boat has no lifelines on it, the nonskid areas are especially important.

To renew my nonskid, I used a modern adaptation of an old method for treating wood decks. They were commonly painted, and then a coating of fine sand was sprinkled into the paint. When the paint dried, the excess was brushed away, leaving a surface that gripped well. Sometimes another coat of paint was added to increase the surface's durability. Although sand can work well, I've heard it can be hard on bare feet. (I've also heard that model railroad ballast, available in hobby stores, makes a great nonskid.) Instead, I used a polymer product from Interlux that is made of micro-

scopic spheres. The rounded surface of the grit is said to grip well, yet not hold dirt as much as sand. First, I sprinkled the polymer, which is a very fine, light-weight powder, onto the wet paint. I discovered that I could get equally good results by mixing the compound directly into a batch of paint. I tried adding a second coat of paint over the nonskid, thinking that this would make the coating more durable, but that didn't work. The Interlux polymer is so fine that the paint made the surface too smooth. I used a brush to apply the paint, but a roller would probably work well, too. This nonskid is comfortable on bare feet and grips well, but it always looks dirty and is impossible to clean.

The same technique applied to the deck. The color match for the deck and non-skid areas was particularly nice, and probably a side effect of sticking with the same manufacturer for the entire project.

Hardware Mounting

Locating the hardware is always a difficult choice while you're restoring, especially if, like me, you couldn't sail the boat before you bought it. Now you're forced to use your imagination to find the ideal locations for halyard cleats, fairleads, and so on. No matter how good your imagination is, there is nothing like a day on the water to point out the obvious. I was quite certain that once I got my boat launched, I'd be saying to myself, "What was I thinking when I put that there?"

This is why you should avoid bedding hardware in 5200, which is made by 3M and is legendary among the boatyard set. It's an adhesive polyurethane bedding compound that people swear by—and at. It forms a permanent bond, nearly impossible to remove once used. (I've heard, though, that a heat gun can work wonders to help remove the stuff.)

Sealants

In addition to 5200, 3M also makes 4200—a polyurethane caulk that reportedly doesn't stick like grim death. This is what I used to re-bed all the hardware that was mounted on the deck.

The old standby is polysulphide. This is good stuff and could be used to bed everything above or below the waterline except plastics. A commonly available brand is Life Caulk from Boatlife. It's available everywhere (except Tennessee, that is, which is why I used the 4200).

If you're wondering why I haven't talked about silicone, it's because it isn't nearly as useful as the other two compounds. You'll probably discover why, as you work on the leaky fitting that was bedded in silicone on your old boat. It

seems that people who are less than knowledgeable about boatwork commonly reach for silicone, attempting to stop leaks by surrounding the offending fitting with a big bead of the rubbery goo. To quote Rocky the Flying Squirrel, "That trick never works!" You have to remove and clean the underside of a fitting before setting it in compound, and if you use silicone improperly, you'll get plenty of practice removing, scraping, and re-bedding fittings. The problem with silicone is that it doesn't have much adhesive strength. It's strong and very chemical-resistant, though, and works well on plastic parts, like my portlights. These require a soft, rubbery seal to prevent stress cracks, and I used silicone to bed my new portlights when I installed them. Silicone should never be used below the waterline, though.

If you've ever had the extreme displeasure of having to sleep in a berth that's directly under a leaky fitting, you'll understand why I'm a little anal about properly bedding deck hardware. Leaks can travel a long way in the overhead from their original source, and they can be maddening to track down. It makes sense to stop them before they start.

To properly bed a fitting, both mating surfaces must be perfectly clean and dry. Since I repainted my boat, this wasn't a problem, but make sure there isn't a trace of old compound anywhere. A little light sanding followed by an acetone wipe isn't a bad idea. Next, apply sealant to the fitting. Make sure there's a little sealant donut around each bolt hole. Set the fitting in place, and put a ring of sealant just under the head of each bolt before you insert them into the fitting.

SAVING ON SEALANTS

Most hardware-store-variety sealants aren't up to marine use, which is a shame because things can be so much less expensive when bought outside the typical boat chandlery. I bought my silicone from the hardware store, and so far it's holding up as well as any marine variety would. I also found polyurethane roof caulk (not polyurethane construction adhesive) that was almost identical to 5200, both while wet and when cured. Still, I'd never use this in a critical or below-the-waterline application. But it worked well under the rubrail at the hull-deck joint, where it seemed that some kind of thin wood was used to fill gaps. I dug out the rotten wood, and filled the resulting gaps with poly roof caulk. For this application, it worked great. The entire job took three tubes, costing $7.50 instead of $45. ∎

Snug the bolts enough for the sealant to make good contact with the fitting surfaces, but wait until the sealant cures before tightening. Otherwise, most of the sealant will squeeze out onto the deck where it won't help stop leaks. Don't try to wipe away the excess sealant while it's wet; trim it with a razor blade after it cures. (How well the razor blade trim works varies with the type of compound you use, though. It didn't work too well with silicone; the soft compound seemed to roll under the blade. You may have different results than I did.)

Considerations

When a fiberglass boat is built at the factory, its hull and deck are often made differently to handle the different stresses placed upon it. Solid fiberglass is somewhat flexible unless it's really thick and heavy. Since the hull is supported, in a sense, by an even force (the water), it can be a little flexible. The deck, on the other hand, is subjected to "point-loading stress," meaning when a 250-pound deck ape jumps up and down because

he's dropped a winch handle on his foot, it places a high load in a relatively small area. Fiberglass boatbuilders discovered early on that people prefer a boat that feels "solid" underfoot, and a boat with a deck that flexed greatly was perceived as cheap. (This is a particular problem with the MacGregors, and it explains why the previous owner went to so much trouble to rebuild the foredeck.) As a result, decks are commonly built with some kind of stiffening core in them, usually plywood panels surrounded by fiberglass. Sometimes a special balsa core or polyurethane foam was used on expensive boats, but mostly you'll find boats with plywood. As long as the plywood remains sealed, this is fine.

The trouble starts when the builder drills into the deck to mount a cleat. The bedding fails after ten years or so, and your boat's previous owner didn't notice. Water started to slowly creep into the core, and once it gets in, it's hard to get out. Rot follows, and a big repair job is required because of a lack of attention to a small detail. I imagine the builders builder did, but don't bolt down the cleat yet. Next get a larger drill bit, and carefully enlarge the smaller holes, but don't drill all the way through. Only drill through the top layer of fiberglass and the plywood, but stop before you go through the plywood core. (If you do make a mistake and go all the way through, don't despair. It's just going to be a little harder to find the correct location of the hole, because we're going to use the small hole on the inside of the boat as a drilling guide later.)

Now go down below and tape over the little hole with masking tape. Mix up a small batch of epoxy. I used one of those dual syringe-type packages of epoxy glue that you can get at the hardware store for this job. Fill up the little well that you've drilled with the epoxy, and let it cure. If some soaks into the core, that's even better. The next day, peel off the tape, and run your drill with the correct sized bit through the hardened epoxy from the underside of the deck, and install your fitting. Not only have you sealed the core from water migration, you've created a fine little compression sleeve through the deck, and it won't crush the core when you tighten down the bolts.

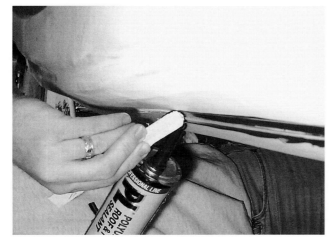

Caulking the rubrail. For this job, I found a black polyurethane roof and flashing sealant at a builders' supply store. It looks, handles, and smells exactly like 5200, except this product was $2 per tube, as opposed to about $12 per tube for the genuine article. I tested it first by squeezing a bead and letting it cure; it hardened into a very strong, flexible blob. By smoothing the bead with a paint stirrer that I'd sanded round, I got a good-looking, watertight seal.

thought that this would get boat owners back to the dealer to buy a new boat, which is one way to deal with the problem. Another way is to bed the fittings right in the first place and make the boat last.

The proper way to mount hardware is to seal the hole with epoxy. It isn't hard, but you should take the time to do it right. You start by locating the hardware—a cleat, let's say—and drilling the holes to mount it. Same as the original

Backing Pads

But wait, before you tighten up that cleat, let's further suppose it's a mooring cleat—a mooring cleat that happens to be holding your one remaining anchor—and it's howling 50 knots in a summer squall outside, and there's a lee shore 50 feet away. The last thing you would want to hear is the crunching sound that fiberglass makes when a bolt head is being pulled through it.

The proper way to mount high-load hardware—like mooring cleats or lifeline stanchions—is to make a backing pad. Backing pads can be made of stainless steel or plastic, but the best is probably epoxy-soaked plywood. Get a piece of marine-grade plywood, and cut a piece that's a few inches larger than the mounting holes all around. Drill it to match the cleat. If the cleat is mounted on a curved surface, shape the underside of the backing pad to match the curva-

ture of the fiberglass. Chamfer or taper the edges a little, and then coat all sides with a layer of epoxy. When it's cured, bed this well in a layer of compound, and then attach the fitting, using only stainless steel bolts and oversized washers (sometimes called "fender washers"). With any luck, you'll never need this kind of strength, but little details like this make a strong, safe boat, no matter what size she is.

CHAPTER 5

Boat Joinery and Woodworking

Materials, Techniques, and Procedures

Woodworking aboard boats is a subject that could easily take up an entire book. (Some good ones are listed under Woodworking Resources in Appendix 7.) Several things make boat joinery different from standard carpentry: higher strength is required, quality materials must be used for long life, safety needs dictate rounded corners and plenty of handholds (though this is more important in larger seagoing boats, there's no reason why you shouldn't make your boat as safe as possible—just remember that you'll never turn a trailer sailer into a Hinckley), and the small space of boat interiors requires planning. There's plenty to think about.

Wood Choices

Several woods are suitable for use aboard a boat, each with its own benefits and drawbacks. Your choices should depend on the application.

Teak

This is my favorite. When freshly milled, it's a beautiful tan color and finishes to a golden brown. Teak naturally has a high amount of oils in it, which makes it highly rot-resistant in the damp marine environment. Teak can be treated with oil, varnish, or both. A good example is the commercially available Deks Olje system, which uses a penetrating oil (probably a linseed-oil-based or tung-oil-based solution), followed by a high-gloss finish, similar to a varnish.

The downside of teak is its cost and difficulty in milling. I called around and finally found a lumberyard that was willing to sell me some for $16 per board foot. A company called Teakflex Products (www.teakflex.com) has both Burma and Asian plantation teak available for $6.50 to $13.50 including delivery, but there's a minimum three-month wait on all orders. I haven't ordered from these folks, but the prices are right. If you've never worked with teak, prepare yourself for some adjustments. It's very hard and brittle, and the resinous sawdust quickly dulls tools. Carbide bits and saw blades are a must, and hand-sanding takes forever (but produces a nice finish). I found myself using a sanding disc in an angle grinder to mill the teak and ipe parts that I used on my boat. The oils in the wood can make it difficult to glue, and some glues, like epoxy, require pretreating with an acetone wipe or a special primer to make the glue stick.

Teak's great looks make it a good choice for finish trim, while its strength and rot-resistance make it a good choice for structural work.

Ipe

This is a fairly recent entry into the hardwood market. Sometimes called Brazilian walnut, it's used to build high-end decks and outdoor furniture, and it's a fairly good teak substitute. It's a very hard, heavy wood, and it contains natural oils that make it rot-resistant, just like teak. In fact, it's so dense that it sinks in water. It's a similar golden color, though teak has more light and dark banding, making it a touch prettier. The really attractive aspect of ipe is the cost.

I've seen ipe advertised for as low as $1.53 per linear foot for a 1×6 board. Occasionally, you can find ipe in some very strange places. One of my best "scores" was when I noticed Lowe's was selling tomato stakes for about $4 a bundle.

Upon closer inspection, I noticed they were small (about ¾-inch square), heavy, and made of a tight-grained, dark wood. As near as I could tell, they were ipe. I bought all they had, and they've never carried them since.

I used ipe right alongside teak for my finish trim, both on deck and below. I'd choose all teak if cost were no option, but this is a very good second choice. So far, it's held up every bit as well as the teak, though I've noticed a little checking in the end grain that needs to be watched.

Mahogany

Compared to teak and ipe, mahogany is a poor choice for wood projects on deck. It was traditionally used belowdecks with good results, but it's gotten very expensive. I've never used it, but I've ripped out plenty of rotten mahogany from old boats. There are many varieties of mahogany, each of which has very different characteristics. African and the dark red Philippine mahoganies are harder and more decay-resistant than the light red Luan mahogany or Honduras mahogany.

Ash

White ash is commonly being used now for boat interiors, and its light color produces a much brighter atmosphere than a boat with an all-teak interior. It is not very rot-resistant, though.

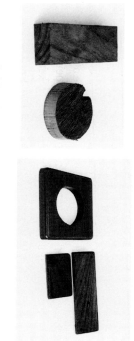

(left) Unfinished samples of teak and ipe. The block on the left is real teak; the circular cutout is ipe. (right) The same woods varnished. Teak is on the right–it shows a little more banding than ipe.

White Oak

This can be used successfully where high-strength framing is required. It's more resistant to rot than red oak, but it will still disintegrate if not kept treated and oiled.

Other Hardwoods

There are plenty of other hardwoods suitable for boatwork, but they can be hard to find. Okume, iroko, apitong, and greenheart are imports—iroko is a lot like teak, but not as strong. Greenheart is decay-resistant, and popular with European boatbuilders. Domestic hardwoods like elm (now largely unavailable, thanks to Dutch elm disease) can be used and are good for steam bending.

Softwoods

The better grades of pine and fir can be used as framing on a boat, especially when oiled and treated with preservative. Yellow pine is much harder and more resinous than white pine, and it lasts longer in a marine environment. It was commonly used in workboats built in the south. Cedar, spruce, larch, and redwood can all be used aboard.

Marine Plywood and Alternatives

Standard construction-grade (BCX) plywood is a coarse, poor-quality material that doesn't belong on boats—regardless of the fact that it was used quite a lot at the MacGregor factory. Don't use it in your repairs. True marine-grade plywood is ideal but very expensive, especially in areas far from the coast. It's beautiful material—thin plys, no knots or voids anywhere, and very strong. But you can expect to pay up to $90 per sheet plus shipping. Good thing there's an alternative.

When I was in college, I worked in sign shops. The sign painters there used a product called DuraPly to make signs that would hold up to the weather. It's a type of plywood that has a phenolic-type paper layer glued to the finish face or, in thicker pieces, to both faces. DuraPly is very rot- and water-resistant—we used to see billboards that had been up for ten years or more that could be renewed with just a fresh coat of paint. Since the hand-painted sign is becoming a thing of the past, DuraPly is getting harder to find—I had to do a bit of calling and driving before I found an old-time family lumberyard that had a few pieces. It was only minimally more expensive than construction-grade ACX plywood, and much less than true marine ply. The DuraPly I was able to find seemed to contain softer laminates of lower quality than I remember from my sign-shop days, but it still worked well and has a nice, smooth, painted finish. It's a significant cost-saver for the budget boat restorer. (Note: There is another plywood product being marketed under the trade name DuraPly that is intended to be used as container flooring. This isn't the same material as signmakers' DuraPly. Your best bet for finding DuraPly is to call a sign shop and ask where they get theirs, or if they'd be willing to sell a few sheets next time they order.)

There are more-complete discussions about boatbuilding woods and their characteristics in books about wooden boatbuilding. You can read an online chapter from *Boatbuilding with Plywood* by Glen-L Marine at www.glen-l.com/wood-plywood/bb-chap5.html. The authority is *WoodenBoat* Magazine, where current info about available boatbuilding woods can be found.

Adhesives and Fastenings

Just as there are several types of wood that will work aboard a boat, there are several methods for joining wood parts together. But in general, remember that conditions aboard a boat are much harsher than those in a house, and woodwork needs to be much stronger than you may be used to. It's best to use two methods whenever you can—in other words, screws and glue, rather than just glue alone or screws alone.

Mechanical fasteners that can work aboard ship include nails, screws, and bolts. I avoid most commonly available nails, though. Standard lumberyard nails will rust quickly and will work themselves out of their holes as the boat flexes in a seaway. If you want to use nails, buy bronze ring nails. These nails are almost impossible to remove once they've been driven into place. They're also almost impossible to find, but they can be ordered from marine hardware specialists like Jamestown Distributors. (For contact information on these and other suppliers, see Appendix 7.)

Stainless steel screws and bolts are more readily available. I was able to buy nearly all the fasteners I used from a local Ace Hardware store. The giant mega-retailers in my area didn't carry nearly as much stainless as the real hardware stores—another reason I prefer to buy from small, locally owned businesses.

For wood-to-wood joints, you have a wide range of choices that will work. The keyword is "waterproof," not "water-resistant." The newer polyurethanes, like Gorilla Glue, work well. Urea-formaldehydes, such as Weldwood, have a long boatbuilding history. Epoxies will work well and are tolerant of poor fits.

For joining wood to cured fiberglass, about the only thing that will work is epoxy or a polyurethane adhesive caulk like 3M 5200. Good surface preparation is essential, and it's important to follow the directions provided by the manufacturer. I primarily used epoxy for woodfiberglass joints and, if well supported with fillets and fiberglass, these joints are good and strong. The one time I tried to do a rush job, things didn't go so well. I attempted to glue a small block of wood to the inside of the hull with just a little thickened epoxy on the underside and no fillets, but the wood popped off when it was put under stress. So take the time to do it right, or you might be doing it over.

There is one special situation that you'll encounter, and that's bonding oily tropical hardwoods like teak. The natural oils that protect this wood so well also prevent good glue bonds, so the bonding surfaces need to be "degreased," in a sense. I attempted to bond my teak by prepping the surfaces with acetone, and then using thickened epoxy. The bonds failed after two years of exposure on deck. What I should have used is resorcinol glue. This is a two-part formaldehyde-based glue that needs to be carefully mixed. The bonding surfaces must be matched for a thin glue line, sanded and wiped with acetone or denatured alcohol, and clamped well for 24 hours. I understand that teak can also be bonded with the new reactive polyurethanes like Gorilla Glue, since they are less sensitive to oils in the wood, but I can't speak from experience.

Techniques

There's no way that I can discuss every type of potential woodworking problem that can be found on your boat. Instead, let's go over the basic philosophy that I used to guide the decisions I made when restoring my boat—it worked well for me. I divide the woodworking requirements on my boat into either structural or finish woodworking. Structural jobs aren't normally visible, while finish jobs are.

Structural Woodworking

Naturally, the underlying structure of your boat is important. The plywood panels that make up the berth tops and sides are a good example of what I consider structural woodworking. Usually, most of the structural woodwork will already be in place, requiring replacement rather than fabricating the structure from scratch. As you analyze these jobs, try to determine what caused the piece to fail in the first place, and address that

deficiency in your repair.

For example, one area of my boat that was badly rotted was the support structure for the keel winch. It had failed for a couple of reasons: the location of the winch near the companionway exposed it to drips; it was covered up behind a panel so that its deterioration couldn't be seen; and materials that weren't rot-resistant (blocks of fir and pine) were used. In this case, I decided that stainless would be a better choice here than wood, and it removed the entire problem. It was replaced with a custom fabricated bracket that's very strong in this application.

Another example was the plywood panels in my boat. Most of them were OK, but one berth top had some rot that was caused by an icebox. Instead of attempting to patch the rot with epoxy, I

SIZING LUMBER

Just in case you hadn't noticed, a 2x4 isn't 2 inches thick by 4 inches wide—it's closer to $1^{3}/_{4}$ inches thick by $3^{1}/_{2}$ inches wide. This discrepancy is a result of several factors. Wood shrinks as it dries, which reduces the size a little. More material is lost in the planer, which smoothes the surface. "Dressed" or "surfaced" lumber is much smoother than wood that comes directly from the sawmill. It can be purchased with one planed surface (S1S), or planed on both surfaces, top and bottom (S2S). It can be surfaced on one or both edges as well (S1E, S2E), though that designation is fairly uncommon. You're much more likely to find lumber that is dressed on both sides and edges (S4S).

If you live near a sawmill, you might be able to get "rough-sawn" boards, which are larger, but still contain a higher amount of moisture. Wood is generally called "green" if it contains more than 19 percent water.

Cabinet lumber is sized differently. It's listed in "quarters," as in $^4/_4$, which means 1 inch (four quarters) when green. $^4/_4$ lumber usually dresses to a slightly larger size, about $^7/_8$ inch finished. A "board foot" of lumber is the amount of lumber that's contained in a piece of wood 12" long, 12" wide, and 1" thick (in its rough, green state) or its equivalent. For example, 1 by 3 by 48 inches is a board foot, as is a 2-by-6-by-12-inch board. ∎

decided to cut away the rot by making a nearby locker opening larger.

At the MacGregor factory, access to the areas under the seats was made the cheap way—four plunge cuts with a circular saw, which left a perfectly rectangular opening. Ideally, any opening in a boat should have rounded corners. This reduces the chance of stress concentrating at the corners and developing cracks, and it eliminates sharp points on the lids. Since there were no cracks at the corners of any of the openings on my boat after 30 years, it seems that the factory method was OK strength-wise. But

it looked, well, cheap. The sharp lids were a potential cause of injury, and the small size of the openings made access to the lockers difficult. Enlarging the openings would allow me replace the lids with new plywood, and give me a chance to round the corners as well. Plus, I could extend the opening of one of the lockers to remove the rotten section.

So here was a good chance to do some structural woodworking—enlarge the locker openings, make new lids, and install cleats on the underside of the locker tops so that the lids wouldn't fall through. The main goal was to do work that was as good as, or better than, the work done at the factory.

I started with the layout. Using a square, I drew a large rectangle where the new opening would be, making sure the lines were parallel and square. The usual approach would be to draw in radiused corners and cut the opening with a saber saw, but this often gives less than satisfactory results. Instead, I drilled the corners with a 1½-inch hole saw and then connected the outside edges of the holes with the saber saw. The corners are much more accurately cut this way.

Once the opening was enlarged, I needed to add cleats to the underside of the berth top. These are just strips of wood that prevent the lid from falling through the opening. They also stiffen the top a little. Teak or ipe come first to mind in terms of rot resistance, but these would be expensive and difficult to mill and glue. And with the state of the world's rainforests, it's not a very logical choice, especially when we remember that this is a trailer sailer, not the *Sequoia* (Herbert Hoover's presidential yacht).

Structural woodworking. The panel below was taken from the locker near the centerboard winch, where splashing water caused it to rot. The top panel is its replacement and incorporates an additional cutout for increased stowage.

LUMBER GRADES

The different grades of lumber can sometimes be confusing. Here's a basic rundown—although, because different yards have different customs, it's rare to see all these grades meaning exactly the same thing. Lumber grades generally refer to the surface appearance, although the poorer grades will have a lower structural value because of defects. These are hardwood grades, like ash, maple, and oak. Softwoods like pine use a different grading, which refers to its strength rather than its appearance on the surface.

FAS (which stands for, "Firsts and Seconds,") is the best. It must be 83 percent clear on its poorest side, meaning no knots, cracks, or checks in the surface. Next is #1 Common, which must be 67 percent clear on its poorest side. # 2 Common is at least 50 percent clear on the worst side. # 3A Common is 33 percent clear, and # 3B is 25 percent clear. There is also a grade called "Select." Selects are FAS on the good side and #1 Common on the poor side. This is sometimes called "FAS 1 Face." ■

I used plain old pine. Yellow pine would have been a little better, but I didn't have any. I cut it to size, and then glued and screwed it into place. Waterproof glue and stainless steel screws are mandatory. Tempting though it may be, don't use drywall screws. Over time, they'll corrode into little rusty barbs. If you're going to completely seal the screws in epoxy, drywall screws could be used, but there are better choices.

If you're addicted to drywall screws as I am, you can use a new type of screw that's designed for building outdoor decks. They're called "single auger-point deck screws." They have square drive flat heads, and they're made of stainless steel. Sometimes they can be found at higher-end building supply centers, or they can be ordered from Jamestown Distributors. (Contact information is listed in Appendix 7.)

Before the cleats were screwed into place, I treated the pine with linseed oil to prevent rot. The oil will prevent the glue from bonding, so I left one side dry until after it was bonded in place. I paid special attention to the end grain, though, and gave this area several coats of linseed oil. After the oil soaked in for a couple of days, the oiled surfaces were given a coat of oil-based paint for extra protection.

I guess that now is a good time to address a question that may be lingering in your head: "Why is he going through all this when he could just use pressure-treated lumber?" True, pressure-treated wouldn't rot for 50 or 100 years, but I generally avoid pressure-treated wood like the plague. Here's why.

Pressure-treated lumber isn't treated with just pressure. It's soaked in a chemical soup containing copper, chromium, and arsenic (hence, the name "CCA-treated wood").

These are cumulative toxins in humans and are carcinogens. Arsenic is especially bad and is connected with lung and bladder cancer. Unless completely sealed, CCA-treated wood continues to leach chemicals out, and detectable traces of arsenic can be found on cloth wiped on the wood, even wood that has aged. A recent story in the *Washington Times* said, "The National Academy of Sciences' National Research Council, in its September study for the EPA on arsenic in drinking water, found that long-term arsenic exposures of 10 micrograms a day translate into a 1 in 300 risk of lung or bladder cancer. On average, the swipes used in a study of weathered, aged playground equipment made with CCA-treated wood measured 25 times that, or 247 micrograms." Landfills won't accept pressure-treated wood, and if it's burned, the smoke is toxic. In short, I don't want this stuff anywhere near my boat or my family.

There is a safer, though somewhat less effective, alternative to pressure-treated wood or commercial chemical rot treatments (which may contain copper). One is plain boiled linseed oil, which prevents rot by displacing moisture in the wood. Another is ethylene glycol. It is toxic—if you drink it, it'll kill you. But it doesn't migrate into your body through your skin like arsenic can; you have to ingest it. Ethylene glycol is the main ingredient in automobile antifreeze, a very inexpensive and readily available source of this chemical. A third treatment for wood is borates, which are borax-boric acid mixtures. Borax is an old-time laundry detergent additive and can be found in the grocery store. Boric acid is commonly sold at feed stores as roach killer. Both are inexpensive.

You can mix up a batch of borate rot treatment by heating up a blend of 60 percent borax, 40 percent boric acid, and water. It needs to be heated to dissolve. Just to be safe, don't do this indoors, and don't get it so hot that it boils. A similar solution can be made using ethylene glycol—50 percent glycol antifreeze, 28 percent borax, 22 percent boric acid. A really good article called "Chemotherapy for Rot" by Dave Carnell can be found on the Boatbuilding Community

SCARY BEDTIME READING

Shogren, Elizabeth. "Pressure Treated Lumber and Risk of Arsenic Exposure." *Washington Times*, Nov. 13, 2001. (www.lassc.org/_disc1/1000000c.htm)

Project on Playground Equipment. "Estimate of Risk of Skin Cancer from Dislodgeable Arsenic on CCA Pressure-Treated Wood Playground Equipment." U.S. Consumer Product Safety Commission, 1990.

Galarneau, D., et al. "Residues of Arsenic, Chromium, and Copper on and near Outdoor Structures Built of Wood Treated with CCA Type Preservatives." *Health and Welfare Canada*, August 1990.

Hennington, Byron, and Birgit Carlsson. "Report to the Legislature: Evaluation of Hazards as Posed by Leaching of Arsenic, Copper, and Chrome from Pressure-Treated Timber in Playground Equipment." The International Research Group on Wood Preservation. Document Number IRG/WP/3149, 1984.

website at http://boatbuilding.com/content/rot.html.

So back to structural woodworking and my berth tops. I had new cutouts and nice, new, rot-resistant cleats along the edges. New lids would complete the project. Out came the DuraPly.

I first cut an accurate outline of the opening. The DuraPly was thicker than the original berth tops, and I needed it to lie flush with the original surface. I thinned the edges by cutting rabbets around the perimeter that were about 2 inches wide using the table saw. I cut a finger hole using the hole saw, and then beveled all edges using sandpaper. The lids got the same linseed oil first coat, but these were primed with Kilz and sanded before they were painted since they would be seen. When the job was finished, the new lids looked better than new.

That's a basic look at structural woodworking. To summarize, you want high strength and rot resistance—good looks aren't as necessary, but keeping things neat usually helps in the strength and rot departments. Painting not only prevents rot but makes surfaces easier to clean as well, and clean surfaces are less likely to deteriorate.

Finish Woodworking

My next category of woodworking I'll call "finish woodworking," for lack of a better term. These are the parts of your boat that everyone will see. Not only do we need strength and rot resistance, but we need good looks as well. This leads us to a few guiding principles for finish woodworking:

1. Use high-quality materials. This usually means teak or ipe trim, good

plywood or DuraPly (not the construction-grade stuff you get at Home Depot), epoxy glues, and stainless fasteners. If you have unlimited funds, buy teak and Brunzeel marine plywood. If you're keeping a close eye on the bottom line, ipe and painted DuraPly is a long-lasting, cost-effective combination.

2. No unfinished plywood edges. This is something that no one at the MacGregor factory seemed to understand, but on a boat, you should never leave a plywood edge unfinished. The exposed end grain and glue lines are weak and will easily delaminate, splinter, or rot. Always cover it in solid wood, like an L-shaped piece of teak. On the very finest boats, like a Hinckley or Herreshoff, the "no exposed ply edges" rule would apply to structural woodworking as well, but for most boats, this is a "finish woodworking" item.

3. Corners need to be rounded. Having sharp corners and edges on the boat's furnishings increases the chance of injury if someone is thrown against it in a seaway. In a trailer sailer, with its tiny cabin and lack of standing headroom, this won't be nearly the kind of problem that it would be on a larger boat. But it helps to give an impression of quality if you take the time to finish your woodwork to the same standard as a more expensive vessel. Just because our boats are small doesn't mean they should have cheap, slapped-together interiors. A bullnose router bit with a pilot bearing does an excellent job of softening

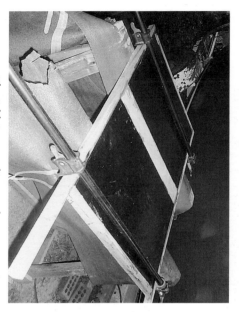

The tabletop was long and narrow, so I used a strip of ash in the center.

edges, but you'll need a carbide bit. Teak will dull a high-speed steel bit in a very short amount of time.

There are two examples that I can give of finish woodworking that I did on my boat: the galley cabinet and the dinette table. Let's start with the less successful of the two, my table.

The original table on my MacGregor was hideous, even when brand-new. It's just a piece of plywood that was edged with some sort of plastic RV-type edging, and surfaced with some sort of paper that had a woodgrain print. The pink-with-gold-flecked Formica that was ripped out of my old house might have been uglier, but only slightly. Fortunately, it was rotten, making replacement a no-brainer.

Since the table is a focal point on a boat, it was worth spending some time rebuilding it. I wanted to use real wood, though plywood with a solid off-white Formica laminate with real teak edges is a good-looking, easy-to-clean surface. Since the table on this boat will likely never be used while underway, I didn't

install fiddles. "Fiddles" are raised lips around the edges of the table that prevent plates from sliding into your lap when the boat heels. I have an uncle who owns a higher-end furniture business, so I paid him a visit. In the back of the warehouse was a cherry bureau top that had long ago lost its base, so he gave it to me. A trip to their scrap pile around the back turned up several pieces of ash that I could use for the edges.

When I began to build the table, I discovered that the cherry bureau top was too long and narrow to make a properly-sized table, but if it were cut in half and joined by a strip of ash in the center, it would just fit. Out came the circular saw, and I began to resize what I thought was a solid piece of cherry.

Then I made a startling discovery. The edges were solid wood, but the center was particle board! Damn. Damn, damn, damn! I thought long and hard about what to do, but in the end I decided to go against my own sermons and use it anyway. Particle board, which is a cheap home-construction material made of sawdust and glue, has no place in a boat, and this table is going to be the first thing I'll replace. It weighs a ton, but, heck, the cherry is pretty, even if it's only veneer. I glued solid maple on the edges with epoxy, and then sanded the entire thing smooth with an angle grinder fitted with a sanding disc. I finish-sanded it with a quarter-sheet vibrating sander, and then hand-sanded the scratches out. I rounded the edges with a bullnose router, and then the whole thing got a coat of epoxy to seal it. The epoxy left a somewhat rough finish, so I sanded this and gave it two coats of varnish. The finished table looks really

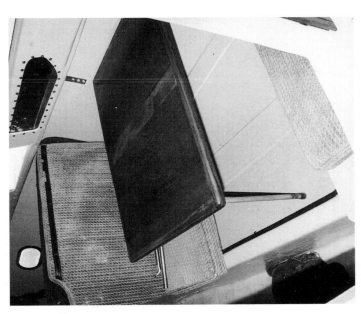

The finished table. The ash finished a little darker than I thought it would, but it looks much nicer than the original.

nice, especially compared to the original.

So I have sinned: I have used particle board on my boat. (You can't see it—it's encased on all sides with hardwood and encapsulated with epoxy, but trust me, it's there.) I think this illustrates an important point about restoring these boats: you should do the best that you can, and work to the highest standards possible, but there are times when it might be better to go ahead with a less-than-ideal solution and get the thing finished, rather than doing it to A-1 certification standards but taking longer to do it. At the time I made my decision, I was broke and had already invested many hours into what I'd started. To start over from scratch would have added a great deal of time and cost to the process. Maybe I'll build a "proper" table later, but for now there are plenty of more pressing jobs to attend to. So if you have to do a temporary repair, or one that's less than ideal to get on the water sooner, go ahead—don't lose any sleep over it, but know the difference.

There is just one little thing, though: you have this flexibility on cosmetic repairs, but not when it comes to safety. Never put a "temporary patch" on a leaking through-hull, for example, or use less-than-standard marine fittings in the rig. It just isn't worth the risk, especially when it's just to save a few bucks or a couple of hours.

My second example of finish woodworking turned out a little better. The original Venture 222 had no galley area, just a long berth space. Later models had "sliding" galleys, which seems to me to be a dubious arrangement, though in fairness I've never used a boat that had one. The previous owner of my boat had

built a huge plywood counter, complete with sink, battery-operated pressure water, built-in icebox, and drawers full of junk. This was rotten, heavy, and poorly-designed anyway, giving the tiny cabin even more of a claustrophobic air. And it no doubt threw the little boat off her designed lines (meaning that the extra weight probably either lowered the boat past the waterline, or gave it a list to port—the designer didn't anticipate all this extra weight) and it affected the boat's sailing performance. After it was removed, the additional space was welcome, but I decided that a small cabinet would be useful. Something to hold a single burner camp-type stove, a small food-preparation surface, perhaps a few drawers for coffee cups and silverware would be a welcome addition to this boat. (I'm a big fan of good coffee, and I consider a cappuccino at a cool fall anchorage to be the height of decadence.)

Naturally, I started with the design. I wanted a cabinet that was small, simple to build, and removable. In its most basic form, my galley cabinet is just a box with dividers in it, and that's how I started the design. I made a very rough sketch and decided what I needed the cabinet to contain, which was a few plates, a pot, the camp stove, and miscellaneous odds and ends like forks and knives. No sink—it would be easier and simpler to wash dishes in a Rubbermaid storage tub or a bucket on deck.

Once I had a rough design, I hacked up a cardboard box to make some panels, and then began a full-size model by taping them together in the boat. I trimmed the back to match the curve of the hull, and set the height of the top so that the cooking surface would be comfortable to use either standing or sitting. I measured the distance from the stove to the overhead so that surfaces wouldn't get too hot or catch fire. Once the basic outer dimensions were finalized, I made notes and removed the model from the boat. I brought it into the shop and made additional adjustments using the actual stove, pot, and plates that it would hold.

Now that I had a working drawing, I began construction. I decided to assemble the top and sides of the box first, and then fit the shelves and dividers. One of the biggest difficulties was having to use plywood that was curved. I had purchased two sheets of DuraPly some months earlier, and had no place to store

it except downstairs. The humidity in my basement set the plywood into a curve, and it was impossible to remove. This made measuring, layout, and cutting much more difficult than it should have been. Had I been able to use brand-new plywood, or had I been more careful with storing it, life would have been easier.

I used dadoed construction on the box. The dadoes were difficult to cut, especially since the panels were curved, but I came up with an interesting solution. By screwing the panels, outside faces together, I was able to pull the curves out and flatten the panels enough to cut the dadoes on the table saw. A radial-arm saw would definitely be the tool of choice for this job, or possibly a dado plane—but I had neither. After the dadoes were cut, I removed the screws. This left little holes that were easily filled and painted over.

A cardboard mock-up of my galley cabinet, used to check clearances and measurements.

the heads with epoxy putty.

So now, the box was assembled, and the screw heads filled. To really make this thing durable, I rolled on a coat of epoxy, which soaked into the surfaces and the end grain of the plywood nicely. The next step is painting, so remember to wipe down all surfaces with a damp rag once the epoxy has cured to remove any amine acid blushing that may have occurred. A coat of Kilz primer was rolled on, sanded, and then given a coat of polyurethane. Whew!

And we're still not finished. Remember what I said about no raw plywood edges? My cabinet still needed trim strips on the top and front. I used some

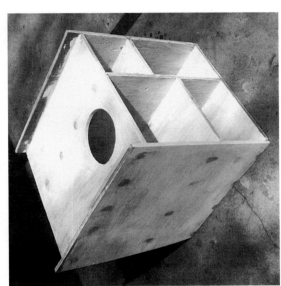

The cabinet assembled and primed, with the screws countersunk and filled.

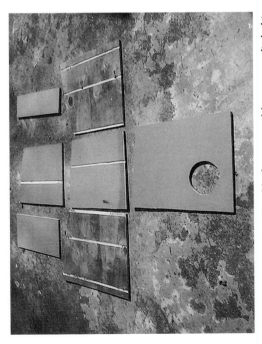

The panels cut and dadoed before assembly. It was a little bit like a jigsaw puzzle.

Once the dadoes were cut into the outside panels, I did a trial assembly by clamping the box together with pipe and bar clamps. The dadoes made the box nearly self-aligning, and the sides and bottom were parallel with minimal adjustment required. Now I could measure and mark the locations for the dividers. More dadoes and panels were cut, and the entire collection was assembled with clamps. Nearly everything fit, though I did miscut one dado that needed correction. After this was fixed, I could begin the final assembly.

The cabinet was put together with epoxy glue and screws. Nearly any woodworking joint made in a boat shouldn't rely on a single type of fastener, like glue alone. The exception, of course, is when something needs to be removable, but even then, bolts are usually stronger than screws. On my cabinet, I countersunk the screws and filled of my coveted stash of ipe tomato stakes; they turned out to be the perfect size for this job. I milled several feet of trim into an L shape, where the inside edge was the same width as the plywood. If you have a router table, it's best to round over the sharp outside edge of the trim now. If, like me, you don't have a router table, you can carefully round over the edges of the trim after it's installed, but your chances of making mistakes are greater.

Most of the plywood edges got an L-shaped piece of trim, with the exception of the vertical divider in the center. For this, I cut a thin strip of wood that was the same width of the plywood, and only as thick as one leg of the L.

The orientation of the trim strips is important, too, especially if you intend to fit drawers into the cabinet. The edges of the openings should be flush on the top

The cabinet was sanded and painted with a coat of polyurethane. Trim strips were epoxied in place, rounded over, sanded, and oiled. The cabinet will be bolted to the berth top.

and sides, but the bottom should have a little lip—about ⅛ inch or so. This lip is there to catch the edge of the drawer, so that when the boat heels, the drawers don't slide open and dump their contents on the floor. Some of these spaces will get drawers at a later date, and some won't. I wish I had measured these spaces just a little differently; if they were a hair larger, I could have bought some Rubbermaid storage tubs to fit them, though these aren't very "shippy."

The trim pieces were bedded in thickened epoxy, and then all the edges were sanded flush with the plywood. The paint needed touching up in a few spots, but this didn't take long. The dark wood contrasts nicely with the light-colored panels. It's important to avoid too much teak in the cabin, because it can make a boat interior look dark and small. But given the stock, low-cost interior of my boat, you'd have to use lots of teak before this would become a problem.

To finish the teak trim, I simply used linseed oil. There are plenty of proprietary teak care products that could be used, but I believe that the major ingredient in most is linseed oil. This treatment wouldn't last long exposed to sun and weather, but in the protected confines of the interior, it's a pretty good choice. It gives a nice satiny finish, and it can be renewed every few years with a rag and more oil, or it could be top-coated with varnish if desired. Tung oil might be a good choice, too.

Flotation

Now let's discuss the possibility of adding foam flotation to your boat, making it unsinkable. All trailerable MacGregors that I know of had foam flotation installed at the factory, though some owners choose to remove it in order to gain more stowage.

This subject always elicits a raging debate in sailing discussion groups, with some advocating its removal and others advocating replacement. On my boat, the previous owner had left the forward flotation but removed the blocks aft. I chose to replace it. Here's why:

The first thing that you need to realize is that these boats aren't the same as larger boats that regularly go to sea without foam flotation. While this may be obvious to some, most larger, heavier boats are going to be much stronger than most trailer sailers, and much, much more capable of handling an extended storm at sea without damage. These bigger boats are far too heavy to be towed behind a car—that's one of the trade-offs that we must accept with trailer sailers. So we can't expect to subject our little cruisers to the same sea conditions; they're just not designed or built for it. The foam is there for added insurance, just in case. Also, larger seagoing boats can't use foam flotation—the quantity of foam required to float the heavy vessel, in case she were holed, is far too great.

Just how much foam does it take to keep a holed boat off the bottom? Good question. Let's find out.

The total amount of flotation required to keep a boat up is equal to the volume of the hull below the waterline. In other words, if you filled the inside of your boat with foam up to the waterline level, it wouldn't sink, even if holed. The problem is that this takes up too much living space. But you can take this same amount of foam and chop it up into bits, and then stuff the bits into unused cor-ners and dead spaces in the boat, including spaces above the waterline, to achieve the same effect.

You don't have to fill up your boat with foam packing peanuts to figure out the flotation that you need, though. You can estimate the amount needed using a calculation. I found this information in Paul and Myra Butler's excellent book, *Upgrading the Small Sailboat for Cruising.* Find the loaded displacement (the weight of the boat plus the people inside it, and all their fishing rods, canned food, books, bug spray, everything). Take that number, in pounds, and divide it by 64, the weight in pounds of a cubic foot of salt water. If you want to be accurate and you sail in fresh water, divide by 62⅖, which is what a cubic foot of freshwater weighs in pounds. Using my boat as an example:

$$1{,}800 \text{ lbs boat weight (according to the manufacturer)}$$
$$+\ 600 \text{ lbs (2 adults at 150 lbs each, plus 150 lbs each for stores)}$$
$$\overline{}$$
$$2{,}400 \text{ lbs} / 64 = 37.5 \text{ cubic feet of foam}$$

That's how much foam is required to float the boat at the designed waterline. If we can live with the boat a little lower in the water, then that amount can be reduced, and in practice, this is always done. It can be reduced up to 70 percent, but if you try to calculate the very minimum amount of flotation, you risk the difference between the deck being awash, and the boat going to the bottom. Slowly. (Shouldn't have brought along that last six-pack.)

On my boat, I guessed that 50 percent would be a safe number, giving me a

2.6 cubic feet of scrap Styrofoam was sealed under each quarterberth. Another 5 cubic feet was secured to the underside of the cockpit.

total amount of foam required at 18.75 cubic feet. I estimated that roughly half that was in the form of foam blocks jammed under the V-berth, so I needed another 9.375 cubic feet somewhere aft.

Where you put the foam is important. In needs to be evenly distributed fore and aft as well as port and starboard in order to keep the flooded hull stable. If the foam is all low and along the centerline, the boat could turn turtle (capsize) and stay that way, stabilized by the foam. If all the foam is installed under the V-berths, a flooded boat will float, but with its bow pointing to the sky—not a very comfortable attitude in which to await rescue or attempt recovery. I placed about 5 feet of

foam under the port and starboard quarter berths, and the remainder in blocks secured to the underside of the cockpit floor. Remember, the foam will be pushing up with great force. One of the details that I needed to attend to was to screw down the inspection hatch in the V-berth. It would be extremely disconcerting to watch as blocks of foam float out of the cabin as the boat sinks ever lower.

And if you install foam in your boat, where are you going to put all your stuff? Simple: leave it at home. There is still more than enough room to store food, clothes, and toys on my boat with the flotation installed. Trailer sailers are lightweight boats, and if overloaded with stuff, they don't sail well. A heavy-displacement cruiser would hardly notice the difference if overloaded a few inches down at the waterline, but a trailer sailer would perform like a true pig if similarly overburdened.

I hope I never need the flotation that's in my boat, but it's nice to know it's there. It should not be considered a watertight life insurance policy, though. I heard a tragic story of a water-ballasted MacGregor 26, which has positive flotation, sailed by a drunken captain who apparently forgot to fill his ballast tanks. The boat capsized in rough weather, and two children (who were below, wearing life jackets) drowned.

CHAPTER 6

Marine Metalwork

Cost-Effective Solutions for the Small Sailboat

At some point during your restoration, you're going to come across metal stuff. Many times the metal stuff will be rusty, stuck, bent, cracked, broken, corroded—in other words, needing replacement. By doing some detective work, you can learn what your options are and discover the best course of action to take.

After you've donned your Columbo raincoat and cigar, the first thing to do is try to figure out why your metal part is failing. Metals on boats can deteriorate for several reasons—corrosion, electrolysis, and fatigue from stress come immediately to mind.

Simple Corrosion

Steel is a great material. It's very strong, very cheap, and relatively easy to work. But there's one drawback: it rusts. Or, to put it more scientifically, it oxidizes. It's a chemical reaction where free oxygen, either in the water or in the air, combines with iron atoms in the steel to form iron oxide. Steel rusts faster if it gets wet or is in a humid environment, like a boat. Worse still are the effects of salt water on steel. Despite this, steel and iron have been used aboard boats and ships for centuries, with various strategies developed for dealing with the inevitable corrosion. It nearly always involves sealing the surface of the metal from the elements. Remember, I'm talking about plain carbon steel here, not stainless—that's a different animal. I'll discuss stainless in a minute.

It isn't my intention to give a complete treatise on metal corrosion in boats—this subject could fill an entire book. In fact, the book is called *Metal Corrosion in Boats* by Nigel Warren (out of print). Warren's book tells you everything you ever wanted to know about rust, and probably then some. I'm more interested in the practical applications—what to do about the cruddy bits you're likely to find in your old trailer sailer.

Painting

Metal can be sealed from oxygen by enamel paints, epoxy paints, or paints containing tar. As long as the finish is occasionally renewed, this method looks good and can last a long time. The problems start when you try to paint a corner or sharp edge. The paint film is very thin and weak there, and if the piece is rubbed or abraded, corrosion will shortly follow. Sunlight also breaks down paint films, resulting in earlier corrosion if the paint isn't replaced every year or two.

Coal tar paints are often used on steel boats, and they're very strong when applied to steel. I didn't use any on my boat, but this might be worth a try if you have some mild steel fittings that you need to renew. Coal tar paint is available by mail-order from BoatU.S., West Marine, Defender, and other mail-order marine suppliers.

Powder coating is similar to painting, but stronger. A special powder is blown onto the surface of the metal, and then the whole thing is baked in an oven. You have to go to a specialist for this kind of treatment, though, and it's somewhat costly. Powder coating services are often found in most larger cities; they're mostly used by industrial customers and auto restorers.

Galvanizing

Galvanizing is a very common method of protecting steel. The entire piece to be protected is immersed in a bath of molten zinc. Steel rusts because its electrons move around, and zinc always gives its electrons up to steel, thus protecting the steel. (That's why you see "sacrificial zinc anodes" on underwater metal parts: the zinc sacrifices its elec-

trons to protect the steel. As long as there is sufficient zinc present, the steel is protected. I'll talk more about zinc and different metals later, under Galvanic Corrosion, so bear with me if you don't understand this stuff yet.) For an example of how well the system works, take a look at the old anchor that came with your old boat. If it's a good-quality anchor, like a genuine Danforth, then it will have been galvanized years ago, and if it's been used where the bottom is soft, there's probably no rust on it at all. Even when the galvanizing wears off, anchors, chains, and other pieces can be re-dipped, extending their usable life greatly.

Galvanizing is somewhat of an art, though, and some shops are better at it than others. If the bath is too hot, the coating will be too thin and too cold, and you get a thicker coat, but it's more likely to flake off. There is also a process known as "cold galvanizing," which isn't really galvanizing at all, but painting with a zinc-rich primer. It isn't nearly as effective as the real thing (but it's better than plain primer). Also, it's very possible that by the time you read this, your corner galvanizing shop will be closed down. Galvanizing is a rather toxic process, and the EPA has taken a dim view of small shops without strict pollution controls in place.

Surface Preparation

Whether a piece is to be painted, powder-coated, or galvanized, surface preparation of steel parts is critical. The steel must be perfectly clean, with every bit of corrosion, grease or oil, or old paint removed before the coating goes on. Otherwise, the corrosion will continue to work underneath the coating, rendering your surface treatment useless.

In most cases, the method of choice is sandblasting. This gets rid of just about anything that isn't sound metal, and leaves a slightly roughened surface, which helps paint or zinc grip tightly to the metal. An ideal way to sandblast small parts is to take the piece to a sandblasting company and pay them $20 or so to do the job for you. Be sure to bring along a can of primer, and don't do this on a rainy or humid day—a single drop of water can ruin the job. If you want to do it yourself, an industrial sandblasting cabinet is the way to go. These things cost $1,200 and up, though you can find bargains at machine shop auctions if you're very lucky. They also require sizeable compressors to run. If you're galvanizing, the shop will usually sandblast the piece before they dip it and the cost is included in the price.

There are a couple of options to sandblasting that don't require investing in heavy industrial equipment. One is chemical treatment. First, old paint is removed with a chemical paint stripper, and then rust is treated with a phosphoric acid compound. This is another trick that auto restorers sometimes use. Phosphoric acid (H_3O_4P) is somewhat hard to find. I had a tough time locating it when I was working on my boat. Auto parts stores didn't carry it, and the only source I could find was an industrial chemical supplier—and I didn't want to buy 55 gallons of the stuff. I did eventually locate a quart at a hardware store under the trade name Ospho in the paint department. Like all acids, it can be dangerous, so read the MSDS (Material Safety Data Sheet) on phosphoric acid if

you actually find some, and learn how to handle it safely. You'll read about skin burns, poisonous fumes, the fact that it'll probably kill you if you swallow it and blind you if it splashes in your eyes, that sort of thing—so be careful. It reacts with the rust itself, turning it into a black inert compound that can be painted over. Proprietary products, like Corroseal, can be used, but they're expensive (around $49 per gallon), though small bottles can be bought in auto-parts stores.

Electrolytic Rust Removal

My favorite trick, though, is electrolytic rust removal. It's a completely nontoxic process, converting the rust electrically. It lacks the mechanical surface preparation that sandblasting offers, but it's not nearly as messy, noisy, or expensive. All you need is a DC power source, like an auto battery charger, some baking soda, a bucket big enough to submerge the part you're cleaning, and a chunk of sheet metal to use as a sacrificial anode. (It will get eaten away in the process.) Here's how you do it.

First, get a DC power source. For tiny jobs, a small 12-volt DC power supply that plugs into the wall will work, but it'll take a long time to be effective. You need amperage—the more the better. If you can find a large transformer from some scrapped electrical equipment and you're handy with a soldering iron, it's simple to wire in a full-wave bridge rectifier to the transformer's output for your power supply. If you don't know what a full-wave bridge rectifier is, perhaps you shouldn't be fooling around with bare wires and power circuits, as they can be dangerous. (Really, you could learn how

(left) My keel winch. While this really should have been replaced, I thought I'd try to rebuild it. (right) The rust-removal setup. Be careful that the anode and cathode don't touch.

to design a power supply in about two evenings of study with a book from the library, but do take the time to learn all the safety precautions involving power circuits. This is a relatively benign power supply, but you should still be careful.)

Using an automotive DC battery charger for your power supply is much easier. I bought a brand-new one from an auto store just for this purpose, but this is a good thing to look for at a garage sale or flea market. Bigger works better, but the small ones are OK. Using a permanent marker, write ANODE in big block letters on the positive (+) connection, and WORK on the negative (−) connection. If you get this backwards, your sacrificial anode will come out nice and shiny, while your boat part gets eaten away.

Now for your container. A large Rubbermaid tub works great, but a 5-gallon bucket from a construction site will do. Anything that will hold water and is nonconductive works. Fill this about three-fourths full of water, and toss in a few handfuls of washing soda. (If you can't find washing soda, baking soda will do. I was unable to locate washing soda, but I've heard that it works better. According to one to chemistry professor, the difference is that " . . . washing soda will consume two equivalents of acid, while baking soda will only consume one equivalent.")

Now prepare your work to be cleaned. It's important that you get a good electrical connection on the piece, which might

be difficult if the piece is deeply rusted. Scrape away the rust in a small spot and attach a piece of wire. "Alligator clips" from an electronics supply or hardware store can be useful for this purpose, or you could get creative and fabricate some sort of custom attachment. If you use a battery charger, try not to submerge the spring clips that came with the charger, or they will eventually be eaten away, especially the positive clip. You're better off attaching short pieces of wire to the part and the anode, and then attaching the clips to the wires.

Anything can work for the sacrificial anode, but remember two points: (1) a large surface area is beneficial, and (2), don't let the anode touch the part being cleaned, or the circuit will short and overheat your power supply. A piece of scrap stainless makes a good, long-lasting anode, but I used a flattened tin can. It worked fine, and I've got a million of them.

Once everything is wired up, plug it in and let it bubble. I used this method to clean my keel winch, and it took a few days. A larger or more finely-tuned system might work faster. Every now and then, I had to brush away some black crud that formed where the rust was converted, but this was easy to do. After three days, I removed the winch, dried it, and painted it. You need to work quickly, because new rust will begin to form almost the minute that the current is removed. There is a small amount of free hydrogen created by this process, so don't seal a lid on your container or work in a poorly ventilated area. Remember the Hindenburg!

I had so much fun with my electrolytic rust-removal setup that I would run around my shop looking for rusty things to clean. It works amazingly well on tools and antiques.

Galvanic Corrosion

I was hoping to avoid this subject because there's a great deal about it that I don't fully understand, but it's a subject that needs mentioning whenever you talk about metals and boats. The problem involves using different metals together. Whenever two dissimilar metals are in contact, corrosion will occur. Exactly why this happens is a long story, but I'll try to be brief. It involves atomic chemistry, electron bonding, and the readiness of one molecule to give up electrons to another. This readiness is called "electrical potential." (When the electrons actually travel from atom to atom, that's "electrical current.") Every metal has a particular electrical potential. It's been studied for a long time, and as a result, scientists years ago came up with—drum roll, please—the galvanic series (see table). This is a fancy name for a list of metals in order of their increasing tendency to lose electrons.

When two metals on the list are used together, they corrode. If the metals are far apart on the list, they corrode more quickly. For example, a copper screw can live pretty happily in a silicon-bronze casting. It will corrode, but this will happen very, very slowly. That same copper screw, though, will quickly corrode in an aluminum casting. In fact, I've heard that a copper penny lost in the bilge of an aluminum-hulled boat can corrode the aluminum so quickly that it can hole and sink her.

Also, the lower metal—more anodic or base—is the one that gets eaten away. If there are three metals, the lowest gets eaten first. In other words, the lower metal will lose electrons, while the upper gains electrons. Both metals change, but the one losing the electrons is the one that deteriorates. That's why we use sacrificial zincs. But note that zinc wouldn't protect a magnesium alloy fitting. In fact, if magnesium were cheaper than zinc, we'd probably be using "sacrificial magnesiums."

(left) The winch after treating and wire brushing. (right) Primed and painted, I should be able to get a few more seasons out of this before I have to replace it.

THE GALVANIC SERIES OF METALS IN SEAWATER

Metals located closer to each other on the scale are more inert in the presence of seawater, and those further apart are most likely to corrode. For example, if you have a type 316 active stainless steel prop shaft protected by a zinc anode, you won't see much corrosion on the zinc. The same zinc, however, would get eaten away more rapidly if you had a silicon bronze shaft. A worse situation would be an aluminum outboard motor near a bronze rudder blade, with no zinc anodes protecting the metals.

CATHODIC OR MOST NOBLE

Platinum
Gold
Graphite
Silver
Titanium
Hastelloy C
Stainless steel (types 304 and 316, passive)
Iconel (passive)
Nickel (passive)
Monel (400, K-500)
Silicon bronze
Copper
Red brass
Aluminum bronze
Admiralty brass
Yellow brass
Inconel (active)
Nickel (active)
Naval brass
Manganese bronze
Muntz metal
Tin
Lead
Stainless steel (types 304 and 316, active)
50-50 lead-tin solder
Cast iron
Wrought iron
Mild steel
Cadmium
Aluminum alloys
Galvanized steel
Zinc
Magnesium

ANODIC OR MOST BASE

The practical application to this list is knowing where a potential problem exists, and what to do to protect against corrosion where it's likely. For example, one of the most common problems are stainless steel screws in an aluminum mast. Though it appears that galvanized steel screws would be a better choice, it doesn't work that way in practice. The normal environmental corrosion of galvanized screws appears long before electrolysis becomes a problem. Self-tapping stainless screws are a standard practice, though it helps greatly to isolate the fitting as much as possible. Plastic washers under screw heads are sometimes used on better boats, and lubricating the threads with grease helps minimize corrosion. I've recently been experimenting with Desitin (yes, the diaper-rash stuff) for this purpose. It contains zinc oxide in a very water-resistant petroleum jelly base. It's too early to tell if the zinc oxide adds much galvanic protection to a particular screw (since it's an oxide of zinc—essentially, zinc that's already corroded), but I'm fairly certain that it doesn't hurt. It'll take years before we know the practical results of my experiments. (I've learned not to use this on mast fittings, though—I treated the bolts on my mast cap with Desitin, and it worked so well as a lubricant that three tightly secured screws apparently backed themselves out of my masthead, and the mast fell while the boat was at anchor. My forestay turnbuckle unscrewed itself as well. All this was the result of ski boat wakes, which can be quite a problem on some lakes—see the sidebar on page 125.)

Another very real problem exists when you mix metals below the water-line. A stainless prop shaft supported by a bronze strut is just asking for trouble. If you see a boat with two or three zincs attached to the prop shaft, it could be indicative of an overly cautious owner, or it could indicate a larger problem with dissimilar metals below the water-line. Or it could indicate the presence of yet another type of problem: electrolytic corrosion.

Electrolytic Corrosion

Our electrolytic rust remover is a good demonstration of the power of electricity to corrode metal, and our sacrificial anode proves this assertion. Now imagine our little battery charger on a much larger scale. Suppose the power mains at your favorite mom-and-pop marina are a little old and sag into the water a bit. Nobody notices ten missing amps, which could drift through the old insulation, energizing the water around the marina. Then along we come and plug into their shore power, completing the circuit. Then the metal parts of the boat that are below the waterline, if bonded to the electrical system, can essentially become the anode, causing deterioration to occur at an alarming rate. This is electrolytic corrosion, and it can be caused by shore power, or stray currents and different electrical potentials within the various metal parts of your own boat. Don't panic, though—this kind of problem is relatively rare, and it's more often seen on metal boats, but it can occur. It's best prevented by properly bonding all metal parts that are below the waterline to a single bonding strap. This prevents differentials if stray currents occur. If you have an inboard motor, make sure your shaft zincs are in good condition, and

(from top to bottom) Refinishing stainless by buffing. These are the chainplates before . . . and here's the result. A wire brush removed the paint, and then the whole thing was polished with a buffer.

renew them every year or two. If you have an outboard, most problems can be prevented by simply lifting the foot clear of the water.

So to generalize corrosion prevention:

- Try to avoid screwing different metals together.

- If you have to combine metals, insulate and lubricate as best you can (except the mast).

- Avoid different metals below the waterline whenever possible.

- If you have to use different metals, make sure they're bonded and protected with sacrificial zincs.

About Stainless

Stainless steel is a very different material from mild carbon steel. It's a steel alloy, containing as much as 14 percent chromium. The chromium adds a high degree of corrosion resistance, and other alloys (like titanium, silicon, nickel, molybdenum, or tungsten) can be added to increase the effect of the chromium, resulting in a wide variety of different types of steel. The most commonly used on boats is the 300 series of stainless, like 302, 304, 308, or 316. This series is an alloy containing chromium, nickel, and carbon. The 300 series is nonmagnetic, whereas some of the cheaper varieties of stainless don't have this handy identifying characteristic. By bringing along a small magnet, you can easily see if the less expensive stainless fittings at your local hardware store are suitable for use on a boat. Generally, if a magnet sticks, leave it— it's a low-grade stainless.

Stainless works in a manner quite different than plain steel. The chromium in the steel forms a very thin oxide layer on the surface, protecting the steel. Oxygen is required to maintain the film, and if the stainless is starved for oxygen a type of corrosion called "pitting," or "crevice corrosion," occurs. This is why stainless isn't generally used below the waterline—there isn't enough oxygen in the water to maintain the oxide film. The exception is type 316, which can maintain much of its corrosion resistance when submerged.

In order to preserve its protective film, stainless shouldn't be painted or left with a rough finish. If stainless is ground, the resulting scratches should be sanded out and polished with a buffing wheel. Deep scratches, cracks, or gaps can hold enough water to starve the steel of its oxygen, and rust will form as a result. That's why most decent stainless fittings are polished. Stainless steel fabrication is a somewhat technical process, but some limited work can be done in the home shop. Just what can you do for your old boat in terms of metalwork? Let's find out.

Marine Metal Fabrication

If you take the time to learn how, and if you spend the money for the right equipment, there is no limit to the amount of metalwork that you can do in your home shop. In fact, you could build an entire steel boat in your backyard if you wanted to. However, for the purposes of trailerable sailboat restoration, I like to get the most bang for the least buck, in terms of both money and time. You can do quite a bit with a fairly small investment in tools, and once the tools are bought, you'll find other uses for them.

First and foremost, though, is safety. Safety glasses are a must when doing any sort of metalwork, as a hot metal chip in the eye is often a serious matter. I'm also a firm believer in leather work gloves and hearing protection.

One of the most basic things to have is an arc welder—not a MIG or wire welder, but a stick unit. An arc welder allows you to join two pieces of metal together, and the joint is very strong and instantaneous. Kind of like super glue on steroids. I bought an inexpensive import for $140 years ago—long before I had a boat—and I've found many uses for it. An AC/DC welder is better than an AC-only unit, though more expensive. Learning to weld isn't too terribly difficult, but it can be pretty scary the first time if you're not in a class. A shock from an arc welder is serious business, so if you decide to try to teach yourself to weld, be very certain that you know all the precautions and hazards associated with this activity before you attempt it.

I learned the basics in a high school shop class decades ago. Check out an adult-education class at your local community college if you'd like to learn how to do it right, but you can probably learn how with a basic welding textbook from the library and diligent, careful practice.

Welding Stainless

Joining mild steel is fairly simple. Position the steel, use a 6013 or 7014 electrode, and fuse the pieces together. Clean the weld and protect from corrosion, either by painting or galvanizing. Joining stainless, however, is more tricky. When heated to the melting point, the chromium tends to precipitate out of the steel. The result is rusting at the weld joint. It also conducts heat poorly, which results in a greater tendency to warp when welding. The pros weld stainless steel by using a TIG torch (which stands for "tungsten inert gas"), but it is possible to weld it using an arc welder.

The trick is to use special electrodes. Sometimes called "maintenance rods," these are high-performance rods developed for particular applications, like high strength, corrosion resistance, wear resistance, or other uses. (They even make special tubular electrodes that are filled with carbides, so you could, in theory, make your own carbide-tipped tools.) The downside is that these rods are usually very expensive. The special stainless rods that I was looking for cost nearly $26 per pound (about 12 rods). Once again, eBay to the rescue! Maintenance rods are commonly overbought by industry, and then sold as surplus. New, unopened boxes of electrodes are often available, often at a fraction of their over-the-counter price. After some patient searching and a few tries, I bought 15 pounds of maintenance rods by Chronatron—5 pounds of high-wear rod, 5 pounds of corrosion-resistant for stainless, and 5 pounds of high-nickel rod for welding cast iron. I paid about $28 for the lot, including shipping. The stainless rods were too thick for welding tubing or thin stainless, so I bid on another lot of 10 pounds of ½-inch stainless rods by X-Ergon, and I paid about $40 for that lot. I plan on using those to fabricate a bow pulpit and boarding handles for the stern. You do need to be wary about buying electrodes that aren't sealed. Once they're opened, they need to be properly stored or they will absorb moisture from the air, and become very difficult to use. A dead dorm-type refrigerator with a 100-watt light bulb as a heat source makes a perfect welding rod storage cabinet.

I used these electrodes with great success to fabricate a new stainless winch mounting bracket. I mentioned this briefly on page 83. At the factory, the keel winch was supported with wood, and a proper stainless bracket should have been used in the first place. There was evidence of several repairs to this area that had been made over the years. A bracket could also be made of mild steel and galvanized, and it would be easier to make.

First, I bought 3 feet of ¼ by 4-inch stainless steel bar stock from my local steel supplier. It wasn't cheap; I think I paid about $25 for the piece. Moreover, they had no idea what kind of stainless it was, but it was marked "304."

I needed to cut the bar. A

metal cutting chop saw is the best thing to use here, and often the supplier will cut your steel to size by charging a fee for each cut. An alternative is to carefully use an abrasive disc mounted in an old circular saw. Carefully, because if you let the blade jam and kick back while cutting, it could break and send pieces flying about at high velocity. I know I've said this before, but wear safety glasses! Gloves, heavy clothes, and earplugs are good ideas as well. Don't do this in a wood shop—the sparks will easily ignite the sawdust, and you'll have a fire in short order.

Now imagine a T-shape, made of ¼-by-3-inch flat stainless bar. I welded this together using Cronaweld corrosion-resistant rod, then heated and bent the center bar almost 90 degrees, but not quite. I heated the stainless to a dull red using a coal forge, but an acetylene torch with a rosebud tip would probably work better. Hopefully, heating to a dull red kept the chromium loss to a minimum, and the steel will still be corrosion-resistant, but time will tell. I added a "foot" to the bottom, which rests on a thick plywood pad that is bonded with polyurethane adhesive to the top of the keel trunk, just behind the keel cable

(left) A stainless bracket welded with maintenance rod.
(right) The rebuilt winch mounted on its new bracket, a much stronger arrangement.

A stainless bracket for the bow light. Start with a paper pattern, mark the bends and mounting holes. Center-punch the holes for drilling.

(above) Round sharp edges with a file and/or sandpaper. (right) Drill the holes using a drill press and cobalt bits.

hole. The entire arrangement is neat and very strong.

Drilling metals can be done with a ⅜ hand drill, but it is a very slow and laborious process. It's often necessary to "step-drill," starting with a small (say, ⅛-inch) drill bit and using progressively larger bits. Stainless is even harder to drill. It's much, much easier to use a drill press. I have a small benchtop import press that handles the small (¼-inch) thicknesses of metal quite easily. The only downside to my small drill press is that it was lightweight and eas-

ily stolen. That's why I'm on my second press. Buy new bits before you try to drill stainless. A TiN (titanium nitride)-coated drill bit, well lubricated, will go through stainless if it isn't rushed. A cobalt bit does a much better job.

Fabricating without Welding

Some useful things can be made out of stainless without welding. I used stainless steel sheet to make mounting brackets for my sheet winches and new Aqua-Signal Series 25 navigation lights. All that was required was cutting out the shape of the bracket, drilling it, and bending. I made a paper template to start with, marking the location of all the holes and bends.

Next, I cut out the shape using a hacksaw with the finest blade that I could find. When you use a hacksaw, at least two teeth should make contact with the metal being cut at all times; otherwise the teeth could be broken off. Since the stainless sheet was very thin, I had to cut it at an angle, which was a general pain in the—well, let's just say it was a pain, but I managed. I drilled the holes using a TiN-coated bit and plenty of cutting oil. Still, it protested quite a lot, and I had to stop several times to cool the bit.

Lastly, I bent the steel to shape using a bench vise and a wooden mallet. Stainless can be readily bent to shape if you don't bend it too tightly, and cold-bending stainless tends to work-harden

(top left) Buff the surface of the stainless using a buffing wheel.
(bottom left) Bend the bracket at the marks using a bench vise. Using wood blocks prevents scratches. (top right) The finished bracket.
(bottom right) I built these winch bases using methods identical to the bow light bracket.

the steel a bit. You only get one chance, though—any attempt to straighten an incorrectly-bent piece of stainless will usually result in cracked steel. Even if it doesn't crack, the strength of the steel will be seriously compromised, and it shouldn't be used.

Finishing the stainless was done with my stationary 6-inch wire wheel and buffer, which I've talked about previously. Buffing the stainless results in a good-looking, bright shine that should be followed by a stainless polish.

CHAPTER 7

Canvaswork and Upholstery

Sewing Basics for Small Boats

Now we can finally move on to an area where we can work without getting too grimy: the boat's canvas. I'm grouping the upholstery in the same chapter, though this may not be traditionally known as "canvaswork." Since it's accomplished with essentially the same tools and materials, it seems logical to talk about it here. (Note: If you've never touched a sewing machine before, don't start by recovering your cushions. Begin with the smaller projects described in the Canvaswork section below. Get comfortable with those first, and then tackle the covers.)

Sewing Machines

One important tool for doing this sort of work is a sewing machine. If you don't have one, don't panic. I did all the canvaswork on my boat using a $10 garage-sale special that a friend gave me. (He had three sewing machines.) It's an old machine from the 1940s, straight-stitch

only, and it weighs a ton because there are no plastic parts in it. It isn't the most powerful machine in the world, but it can slug its way through four layers of cloth for brief periods. These older machines can be modified for heavier use. SailRite has a super article on modifying a home machine for boat work at www.sailrite.com/Tips/homemachine.htm. One of their tips is to increase the inertia of the balance wheel by adding strips of adhesive-backed lead. You can get this stuff at any auto-parts store; it's used for balancing magnesium wheels. SailRite is a good company; they carry high-quality supplies at good prices; though I was able to buy a finished mainsail for less than their kit price, it isn't nearly as nice as their sail. Others who have built sails from their kits are very pleased with the results and the company.

Once you've begged, borrowed, or bought a sewing machine, you need to learn how to operate it. The manual that comes with the machine is usually best, but manuals are often missing with secondhand machines. The manual for my machine had probably been scrapped and repurposed as a grocery list for the Last Supper, so I went to the library and checked out a basic sewing manual—I think the one I found was by Reader's Digest, but any basic manual should show you how to oil, thread, and operate most sewing machines. They're pretty similar in design, especially the older machines.

Canvaswork

Cloth items have held a place of importance on sailing vessels for hundreds of years. Their natural flexibility has obvious advantages in the constantly moving, pitching, and rolling environment of a boat in a seaway. Add the advantage of compact stowage, and it's no wonder so many things were made of cloth. The boats have changed, but the environment hasn't—cloth is still a logical choice for lots of things that are extremely useful aboard. The high cost associated with marine canvaswork is usually a result of time required to make things more than the material, so if you can teach yourself a few simple skills you can outfit your boat with tons of custom-made accessories at comparatively little cost.

I have to admit that I particularly enjoy marine canvaswork, especially when projects aren't too overwhelming. I've always liked making small canvas bags, bug screens, spray shields, sun covers, tool holders, and so on. As usual, you could write an entire book on the subject, and several are listed in Appendix 7. I have Karen Lipe's book, *The Big Book of Boat Canvas*, and I'd say it's pretty

good overall—plenty of good information, and lots of projects for you to make.

As far as specific projects go, this section will have to be a bit brief, simply because I haven't yet had the chance to sew all the things that I want to make for this boat. One of the things that I have made, and so can speak about from experience, are handrail covers.

Handrail Covers

This little project was lots of fun. I had installed a brand-new pair of teak handrails on the cabin top, with three coats of new varnish. In order to preserve the life of the handrails, I made a pair of handrail covers from natural canvas. Sunbrella would have been a better choice, but I found a dark green canvas in a fabric store for about one-third the cost of a Sunbrella. Unfortunately, using natural canvas instead of Sunbrella was a false economy. After three years, these covers faded completely to a grayish white, so I had to remake my handrail covers with Sunbrella. Natural canvas is fine for practice, or belowdecks projects, but for anything on deck, using acrylic canvas is worthwhile. If you do use natural canvas, note that it shrinks a little, so you need to allow for that in your design. Otherwise it sews just like acrylic canvas.

If you've never done any sewing before, this is the place to start. I got really good results on my first try, and I saved a bunch of money over a pair of covers from a catalog. They look a lot better than catalog covers, which are wrinkly one-size-fits-all covers. Using a contrasting-color thread looks nice, but it shows off your mistakes. If you're a complete novice, then I'd use a matching color thread. I used a heavy carpet thread and a denim/canvas needle in the machine.

First, I made a paper pattern from newspaper. I took a strip of paper and wrapped it over the handrails, not too tightly, and marked it where it contacted the deck. I cut this out, and then marked and cut the length, again not too tightly, as the fabric will shrink a bit. Remember that the pattern made this way will give an outline of the finished cover, not the cloth required to make it—you need to add a bit for the hem.

Back inside, I laid the pattern on a piece of fabric, added ¾ inch to all sides, and marked the cut line. One of the advantages to using natural canvas is that it had some sort of sizing in the cloth added during manufacturing. It made the cloth stiff enough so that it would stay folded, almost like a sheet of paper, and I didn't need to pin it. I folded the top and bottom edges and sewed them into place.

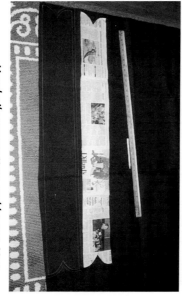

Handrail cover pattern and layout. Note the cut line and stitch line marked on the cloth.

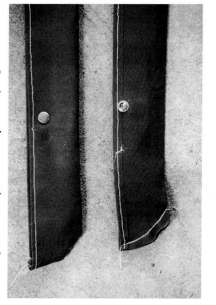

Sewing up the covers. The one on the top hasn't been turned yet, the one on the bottom has.

Next, I folded the covers in half lengthwise, with the hems facing out. I did the same to the pattern, marked where the end seams should go, and then stitched the curved ends. Then I trimmed off the excess and pulled them inside-out.

After a quick trip to the boat to double-check the fit, I was ready to add the snaps. Real marine-grade snaps by Taylor-Made are best, but I've had good results using Dritz snaps, available at sewing outlets for a good bit less money. There have been some inferior snaps showing up of late, and I'd stay away from the very cheapest snaps, which might be made of plated steel. Plated steel snaps will rust quickly, staining your canvas. You can check them before you buy them by holding a magnet up to the unopened package . . . if the magnet sticks, they'll rust. Snaps are easy to install, and instructions and an installation tool come in the package. I put in two snaps to secure the covers between the handrail loops, and voilà, the job's finished! I took me about half an hour to

The completed handrail covers installed on the cabintop.

make one of these; you may be able to do it a bit faster.

A Bimini, Dodger, or Shade Awning

Where I sail, it can get extremely hot in the summertime. Some sort of cockpit shade is a welcome addition when the sun makes an outing on our lake seem like a trip across the river of the damned. (OK, so I'm exaggerating—it doesn't get that hot, but it can make your crew mutiny.) A bimini or a dodger can help.

A bimini top is a cloth panel that is stretched over an aluminum or stainless frame, while a dodger is a fabric "windshield" that's also supported by a frame. While either project is considered canvaswork, and could be made by

a dedicated amateur, I decided to buy mine rather than try to make it. I got a brand-new surplus powerboat bimini on eBay for $76 including shipping. It's really a dodger, and while a custom-built one would fit the boat better, it would cost $400 or more. In practice, I think a true bimini would be more useful. The shade offered by my dodger is too far forward to be much use to the helmsman, and the frame is a bit too tall, so it interferes with the boom. Folded, the frame lies just across the sheet winches, so that needs to be corrected as well. So there's quite a bit of bother associated with my dodger—and negligible benefits—that I hadn't considered.

A bimini, though, would do a better job of shading the entire cockpit, though the low boom height makes installation and use troublesome. The very best way to figure out if either of these options would be a good addition to your boat is to launch it first, and then see how much room you have available. I installed my dodger before I checked the height of the sail, and so I had to remove, adjust, and reinstall it.

A different approach to the problem of summertime heat is a simple awning for use at anchor. These can range from a simple square of light fabric stretched between two poles to elaborate cockpit tents that surround the entire cockpit. The tent approach has some merit, since this increases your available space at anchor. The challenge is to come up with something that's strong, lightweight, easy to rig, and preferably not too expensive. Nearly all shade awnings are custom-designed for the individual boat, since there are such a wide variety of cockpit shapes; there isn't a "one-size-fits-all" or single "best" design. A few ideas are shown below.

Another idea that might be workable would be to scavenge an inexpensive tent for shade awning parts. A small, simple tent with dimensions that are close to that of your cockpit might be modified to use as a shade cover by removing the floor and re-sewing one end to be narrower. At the very least, you could use the fiberglass poles and nylon as raw materials for your shade awning.

Whatever choice you make—bimini, dodger, or shade awning—is bound to be an improvement in comfort on your boat. The further south you sail, the more important this becomes. While cruising in the tropics, people often debate, not just the cockpit. If you find yourself spending a lot of time at anchor, you might consider this as well.

Upholstery
New Cushions and Covers

The cushions and covers on my old boat weren't too bad, especially considering their age and the abuse that they'd suf-

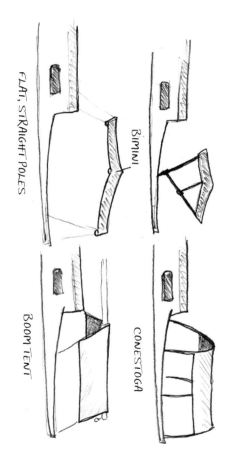

BIMINI

CONESTOGA

FLAT, STRAIGHT POLES

BOOM TENT

Shade on your boat can take a number of different configurations. Consider strength, simplicity, and stowage requirements when you design one for your boat.

fered of late. I tried cleaning them by taking them to a car wash and pressure-washing them in the bed of my little pickup. The original covers aren't re-movable, so you have to clean them in place. While this isn't so bad, the trick is getting enough water out of the newly cleaned cushions so they'll dry quickly. Otherwise they tend to acquire a lovely mildew smell, which is why I needed to clean them in the first place. The original foam still had a fair bit of spring left, but it smelled rather gross. My cleaning experiment was only partly successful, and even after they were cleaned, they still looked old, worn, and tired, so I bit the bullet and threw them all out.

I ordered all new foam from a foam rubber supplier here in Chattanooga. It cost about $123 to do the entire boat in 3-inch foam, rather than the stock 2-inch foam. I also ordered a blend of 1-inch medium laminated to 2 inches of firm foam. I had originally specified 1 inch of soft, but the foam supplier talked me out of it. In retrospect, I shouldn't have trusted their profes-sional judgment. The medium-firm blend is fine for sitting, but not for sleeping. When laid on, you can tell ab-solutely no difference between my new cushions and the old ones, and it feels too hard. Since the foam was cut and laminated to order, there was no return-ing it. Moral of the story: go to the ware-house and sit/lay on some samples before you have it cut.

I saved a little by buying the foam in sheets and cutting it myself. An electric carving knife works, though it doesn't cut quite as cleanly as the hot wire cut-ter that the foam suppliers use. If you

give them full-size patterns of your cush-ions, they'll cut out the foam for you, usually charging an amount per cushion. Ask. If they can do this, and the charge doesn't seem too bad, I'd recommend let-ting them cut it. Cutting the foam myself was more difficult than I anticipated. But I did get acceptable results with the carving knife, and besides, no one will ever see my ragged spots.

Once the cushions were cut out, work could begin on the covers. I found a pretty fair deal on some dark green upholstery cloth on eBay. It isn't "boat fabric," but a synthetic blend that was purchased surplus from an upholstery shop. I bought all they had—12 yards—and it was just barely enough. I proba-bly could have ordered a little more by taking a sample down to our local up-holstery shop, but by careful layout and piecing together long strips for the edg-ing, I stretched the 12 yards to cover all the cushions, including some that were missing. (When I removed the original "galley" construction, this left a long space that was originally berth/seating space. The replacement galley cabinet is a fraction of the original size, and this allowed for two small seats on the port side.)

Making the covers wasn't really all that difficult, but I'll be honest: I found it pretty tedious. The last two covers seemed to take forever to finish, just be-cause I was so tired of sewing them. Each cushion cover took an average of six to seven hours to complete. The de-sign of these was a little different. I wanted removable covers so that they could be washed, but I couldn't find any decent-quality YKK Delrin zippers any-where. (Since then, I've discovered

SailRite has them at about $1 per foot, without the sliders—those are $1.50 each. This would have added about $6 or $7 per cushion. If I had to do it again, I'd use the zippers, even though they're more difficult to sew.) I designed the covers to close with laces, much like you'd lace up a pair of tennis shoes. This way the lacing could be slightly tightened or loosened in case my sewing was a bit off. Also this low-tech solution was less likely to jam or break, though the likelihood of this actually happening is slim if you use the proper zipper. (A brass or metal zipper is sure to fail after a few years, but a Delrin zipper would probably outlast you if kept out of the sun.)

It might be easiest to understand the theory of sewing covers (for the complete tyro) if we design a cover for a hypothetical cushion that's a 12-inch cube. I know, this is a little strange, but bear with me—the construction details will be the same for our cube as for real cushions, even though the dimensions will change a little. OK, so to cover this thing, we need a top and bottom, and four sides, each a little larger than 12 inches. Let's call it 14 inches square, which gives us an inch on all sides for a hem. Next, we cut the sides. You can piece the sides together using squares of material, which leaves a seam at the corners. Looks nice. Or you can cut one long strip that wraps three sides.

Why not four sides? Because we want to leave an opening in one side to get the foam in and out. The easy way to do this would be to sew a zipper right down the middle. The cheap way would be to install eyes and lace them up, as I did. Either way, you need to cut the cloth oversize to allow for the hems, and you need to fold the cloth at the opening and sew it down so that the edges don't unravel.

Now here's the neat part: you sew the panels of the cloth with the good side facing in. The actual stitches are a 12-by-12-inch cube drawn on the cloth. Use a ruler or use the foam cube itself to trace where the stitches are supposed to go. Some books recommend reducing this dimension by about a half inch. This allows the cloth to stretch a little, and the foam to compress slightly, resulting in a tighter cover. But if overdone, your covers will be difficult to fit over the foam, and possibly will warp the finished cushion.

Sew up the lines that you've drawn on the cloth on a sewing machine, then the very last step is to reach inside the cover you've sewn and pull, turning it in-side-out—or outside . . . no, inside in—well, anyway, you pull on the fabric until the good side is facing out. All the seams that you've sewn should now be on the inside, giving you a cloth cube shape with nice corners. You can't even see your stitches. Most people with sewing experience will shake their heads and

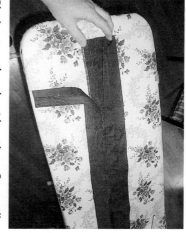

Piecing together the sides. These flaps will get eyelets and lacing when the cushion is finished.

mutter how easily amused I am, but for folks like me with little exposure to the fabric arts, this is high science!

All the cushions on my boat were made using a variation of this basic box. I just adjusted the sizes a little. Oh, sure, the V-berth cushions were a little trickier, as were the settee backs with cutouts in the corners and curved sides. But I got through it by always referring back to my simple box, and remembering that any cushion is just a variation of it.

Making a Cushion Cover

I started by drawing on the backside of the upholstery fabric. (Tip: Save those thin slivers of a worn-out bar of soap that you find in any bathroom. They make great markers for cloth.) First, I rolled a length out on the floor, face-down, and positioned the cushion to be covered on it. Each panel of cloth required two lines. One was the "seam line," which was a tracing of the edge of the cushion, actual size. The other line was the "cut line," which was the same shape, but ¾ inch wider. A narrow yardstick or ⅞-inch-wide strip of wood was handy for marking the cut lines. I flipped the cushion over and drew the other side, and cut both of these panels out.

The smaller edges were slightly more difficult, as they needed to be laid out with a yardstick. I cut strips that were 4½ inches wide—3 inches wide for the foam, plus ¾ inch top and bottom seam allowance. Measuring the edge gave me the length, and I added 1½ inches for the seams. Three of these were cut out.

Now comes the assembly. I pinned one of the edges to the top, bad side out—the good sides of the fabric were facing each other. I put pins straight through

the seam lines to make sure the two pieces of fabric were correctly aligned, removing the pins as the seam was sewn. This was where I messed up most often, as getting the panels of cloth correctly aligned was difficult. They would sometimes slip out while I was sewing. Some people swear by two-sided tape, and others have suggested using a stapler. I got the best results using plain old pins, but your results may vary. It does help in aligning the panels if all your seam allowance is the same—in other words, if all the seams are exactly ¾ inch wide.

The fourth edge, where the cushions would be inserted into the covers, was a good bit more complex. What I envisioned was a pair of cloth strips, 1 inch wide, on the top and bottom, through which brass eyelets would be installed. Behind these would be a 2-inch strip of fabric to hide the foam and give the lacing a more finished appearance. I built a length of this strip and pinned the whole assembly together, and then sewed this strip into the cover just like the other three.

When turned inside out, all your stitching and construction will be on the inside.

After I sewed the corner seams, I went around all the seams with another row of stitching, just for insurance. I believe that these stitches get a considerable amount of stress, and the extra rows may add enough security to keep things together a bit longer.

Marine upholstery is an area in which I don't consider myself much of an expert—even after seven cushions. I'm quite satisfied with the way they turned out, though my biggest mistakes were:

1. Not being careful enough with the

location of the lacing—some are facing the outside edge, and some face the backs of the cushions. I put lacing on the longest edges to make inserting the foam easier, but I should have gone for more consistent looks.

2. Not allowing for the difference in foam thickness when designing the backs. My settee back sits up too high, because I used the original cushion as a layout. I should have shortened it an inch so that the top would be even with the bulkhead. It doesn't bother me enough to re-sew the darned thing.

All told, I saved a bundle by doing the work myself, but it was a big job that I don't think I fully appreciated before I started. I'd do it again, but only if I had to.

Odds and Ends

Screen Bags

Without a doubt, though, this next trick is my very favorite, most-useful, lowest-cost modification I've done on my boat. These bags cost very little, allow you to see the contents without opening, and allow full air circulation so things stored inside are unlikely to mildew. They can be used above- and belowdecks, made as large or as small as needed, and are just as handy as anything. Make yourself at least one or two, and you'll see what I mean. You can use them for food, for clothes, for dishes (even dirty dishes can be placed in them and towed over the side for a few minutes, feeding the fishies and prescrubbing the plates!), for winch handle holders, hatch boards, sails, life jackets—there's literally no end to this one.

The new interior with all the cushions installed. It's a vast improvement over the original cushions, and it makes this essentially a brand-new boat down below.

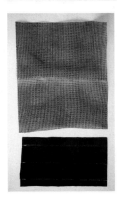

(clockwise from top left) Layout for a small winch handle bag. Fold the cloth for the hems, and then fold this piece in half again. Insert the screen and sew the bottom edge. Fold in half again, and sew along the bottom and sides with a double row of stitching. Turn it right-side out, and it's finished.

I only wish that I could take credit for the original idea, but I can't. The suggestion for these was posted on the MacGregor/Venture e-mail list. It was one of those things that I read, stuck away in the back of my mind, and then forgot about for a while. It was only after I made some that I discovered what a neat idea this is. I've attempted to find out who made the post without success; of course, it may have been in a book somewhere—who knows?

The key to these bags is fiberglass screening that you can buy by the roll at a hardware store. It's light, strong, and inexpensive. I think I paid about $7 for a 2-by-10-foot piece. I'm still making bags from my original roll. Easily sewn together on a sewing machine, fiberglass screening is a touch slippery and needs to be carefully positioned and guided through the machine. My contribution to this idea is using strips of canvas (or other heavy cloth—using upholstery scraps to make matching bags for the interior would be

neat!) to edge the tops of these bags.

Make the edging the same way as you made the handrail covers (that is, fold the top and bottom edges inward, and then fold in half and stitch with the screen in between). Drawstring bags can be made by adding grommets and a line before you fold and trap the screen. Self-closing bags could be made by replacing the line with a length of small-diameter bungee cord with stopper knots on the ends. Or the bags could be left open and snaps added to secure the bags to the boat. I did this in several places in the cockpit, and it makes a great place to put the tails of sheets and halyards instead of the usual method of letting them lay all over the seats and floor, where they are constantly getting in the way. Try it, and you'll like it—I promise!

Insect Screens

Another simple project is an insect screen for your companionway or forward hatch. Many people who make their own are content to glue bits of Velcro along the edge of a piece of window screen. Functional, yes, but not very durable or seaworthy. If you've tackled the screen bags project, you've practically made a high-quality insect screen for your hatch.

As we've seen before, it's a simple matter to add a canvas edge onto a piece of fiberglass screen. Where the screen bags have one or possibly two canvas edges, an insect screen will have four. You'll need to measure carefully so that your finished screen has a few inches of overlap. Also, it's quite possible to get away with a single thickness of canvas on the edge rather than a double thickness. The screen can be directly sewn to the back side of the canvas. An optional roll-up spray flap makes this screen much more functional for the companionway.

The companionway screen is secured with snaps rather than Velcro. It's important to locate the top snaps on the underside of the companionway hatch. This way, drips are channeled onto the canvas, rather than inside the boat. If you treat the finished screen with Scotchgard or a similar water repellent (having, of course, sewn in the optional rain flap), the finished cover will do a

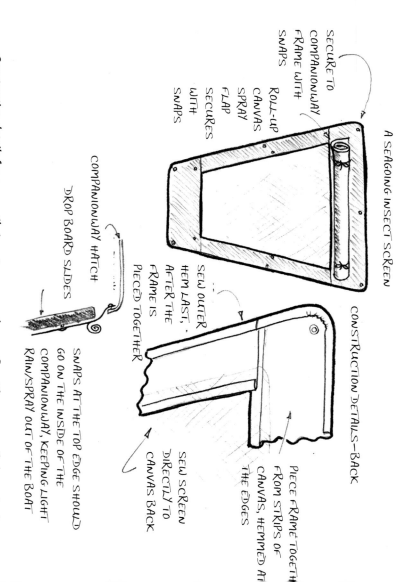

A SEAGOING INSECT SCREEN

SECURE TO COMPANIONWAY FRAME WITH SNAPS

ROLL-UP CANVAS SPRAY FLAP SECURES WITH SNAPS

CONSTRUCTION DETAILS—BACK

SEW OUTER HEM LAST, AFTER THE FRAME IS PIECED TOGETHER

PIECE FRAME TOGETHER FROM STRIPS OF CANVAS, HEMMED AT THE EDGES

SEW SCREEN DIRECTLY TO CANVAS BACK

COMPANIONWAY HATCH

DROP BOARD SLIDES

SNAPS AT THE TOP EDGE SHOULD GO ON THE INSIDE OF THE COMPANIONWAY, KEEPING LIGHT RAIN/SPRAY OUT OF THE BOAT

Construction details for a versatile insect screen and spray flap. They can easily be resized to fit any opening on your boat.

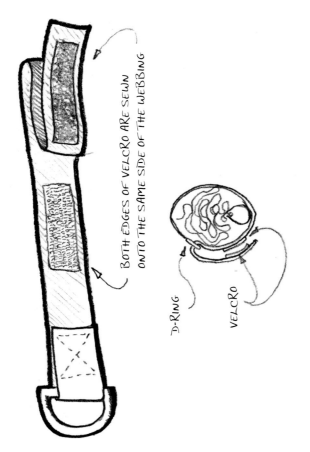

BOTH EDGES OF VELCRO ARE SEWN
ONTO THE SAME SIDE OF THE WEBBING

D-RING

VELCRO

Velcro sail gaskets. They're strong, easily made, and won't tear your sail or whack you in the teeth.

good job of keeping out light rain and spray. It's no match for really rough weather, though.

Velcro Sail Gaskets

As you may have already guessed, I'm not a big fan of Velcro aboard my boat. It's not that I have some strange psychological affliction concerning the stuff; it's just that I think Velcro tends to be a bit overused on some boats. That was certainly the case on mine, as I peeled up little bits of the stuff from every corner. It shouldn't be used for everything, but there are some applications where it excels.

Consider its strengths: it's flexible, adjustable, and although its peel strength isn't that great, its shear strength is pretty good. The perfect place to use it is in making custom sail gaskets. Gaskets are short bits of line that are

used to secure the sail to the boom. People often use bungee cords for gaskets, though this isn't a good choice, because the hooks can tear the sail, especially if the sail is older and degraded from UV exposure. Bungee cords with balls and loops are better, because they can't tear the sail—although the balls can spring back and knock you in the teeth when you release them.

A better idea is to make a custom gasket out of webbing, a brass or bronze D-ring, and some Velcro. First, sew the D-ring to one end of a length of webbing, and then take it to your furled sail for measuring. The webbing goes around the sail, through the D-ring, and back onto itself, where it is secured by the Velcro. The 2:1 purchase of the D-ring lets you snug up the sail really tight, and cuts the load on the Velcro by half. Using a longer strip of Velcro makes these straps more adjustable, and they can be used at different places on the boom. But they're limited in terms of their useful diameter, and they usually need to be custom-made for one specific position—for example, one long strap to gather the sail close to the mast, another short one for mid-boom, and another for the out-

board end. These can also be made into handy-dandy line binders, for securing coils of line for storage.

There are lots of other useful canvas projects that you can make for your boat. All the books listed under Canvaswork Resources in Appendix 7 have enough projects to keep you busy for years.

CHAPTER 8

The Rig

Inspection, Repair, and Replacement

"Standing rigging" on a sailboat refers to all the cables that hold up the mast, usually consisting of the forestay, backstay, and shrouds. The running rigging is the system of lines that raise and control your sails. Both will probably require attention during your boat's restoration.

Standing Rigging Inspection and Repair

The standing rigging will need to be given a very close inspection, from the chainplates (the large metal pieces that anchor the standing rigging to the hull) to the masthead. Since these cables will most likely be the same ones that were put on the boat at the factory, they will certainly be nearing the end of their expected service life and should be checked carefully.

There are two basic signs of failure that indicate a stay needs replacement. These are rust stains and "fishhooks," which are single, broken strands of wire,

usually found quite painfully by running your hand along the cable. Rust stains aren't very common, but fishhooks are. A less masochistic way of looking for fishhooks is to run a rag or paper towel along the wire, as the hooks catch the cotton fibers as easily as flesh. Either way, you need to replace the wire immediately, as the remaining 18 strands in the wire take on a heavier load than the broken one, and those remaining are probably fatigued as well.

If you find a fishhook, you should go ahead and replace the stay and its opposite counterpart. For example, I found several broken strands on my port lower shroud, so I ordered enough cable and fittings to replace the port and the starboard shroud. If your backstay is bad, replace the forestay, too—it doesn't cost that much in materials.

End Fittings

Now we come to decision time. What end fittings should you use? There are several

121

choices, with arguments for each. These are—in ascending order of cost—spliced eyes, Nicopress swages, roller-swaged fittings, and mechanical terminals (Norseman, Sta-Lok, and similar).

Spliced Eyes

Normally, standing rigging is made from 1×19 wire—that is, a single bundle of 19 large strands of wire. It's used because it has the least amount of stretch. Another type of wire is 7×19, which is made up of 7 bundles of wire, 19 strands each. It isn't as strong and stretches more, but it's more flexible and can be spliced by hand. This is how Lin and Larry Pardey set up the shrouds on *Seraffyn*, and the extra flexibility would be a benefit to a boat that is trailered. Splicing 7×19 requires a rigging vise, which is expensive, but a workable substitute could probably be built by modifying an inexpensive drill-press vise. Splicing wire is not too easy the first time, especially in the smaller diameters, but you can learn it with practice. If you want to try splicing wire, you should probably get *The Complete Rigger's Apprentice* by Brion Toss. This is another excellent book, though some of the rigs and information covered would not normally be found on trailer sailers. There are instructions for making the Liverpool eye splice, and you'll get a look at a rigging vise in this book.

Nicropress Swages

To use a Nicropress swaged eye, you loop the wire back on itself and insert the end into a special copper sleeve. A special tool is used to compress the sleeve, gripping the wire. It's quick, reasonably strong, very inexpensive, and quite con-

spicuous. This is the first thing that people will point to and say, "See . . . I told you MacGregors are cheap! Everyone knows you shouldn't use Nicopress swages on standing rigging." And they would be correct, if we were talking about an oceangoing heavy cruiser.

Trailer sailers aren't meant for ocean passagemaking. True, Nicopress swages aren't as strong as other swaging methods. In fact, according to *Practical Sailor*, only bulldog clips are weaker. (Bulldog clips are special U-bolts for cable that you can buy at hardware stores. They're useful for temporary and emergency repairs, but that's about it.) Nicopress swages are hard on the wire, too, and you'll often see failures occurring at the swages. But remember, the loads on a trailerable sailboat are smaller than larger boats, and we can get away with a few liberties. Most of the original swages on my boat were fine, after nearly 30 years of use. (Most, but not all, of the wire failure on my lower shrouds was right at the swage. I replaced both. The following season, I replaced the rest of the rig when I installed a new masthead.) When I replaced my lowers, I used Nicopress swages, but I put a dab of epoxy glue on the inside of the sleeve just for fun.

There are a couple of ways that you can install Nicopress swages. One is illustrated in the photo. I modified an old bolt cutter by first building up the cutting surfaces with an arc weld bead, grinding them smooth, and drilling a hole for the swages. I used this for replacing my lower shrouds. While the swages have held up so far, they're kind of ugly and uneven-looking because of my homemade swaging tool. (One of my

hundreds of small business ideas would be to make a pattern for just the jaws, and have a hundred cut out of alloy steel by a laser-cutting operation. These you could sell as direct replacements to be bolted on to a standard bolt cutter when needed, instead of having to buy a second large tool. Remember, you heard it here first.)

When I replaced the remainder of my standing rigging the second season, I used a different approach. A special swaging tool that uses bolts can be bought for not too much money, and I had one from my previous boat that would swage up to ⅛-inch cable. And as luck would have it, the stock cable size on the V222 was ⅛ inch. (I went up a size on the lowers—another reason why I built a swager rather than using the bolt type.)

The bolt-cutter type of swager is much, much faster than the inexpensive screw-in type, but the slower method

Nicropress swages being installed. I made a Nicropress swage tool from an old bolt cutter. I took it apart, built up the cutting edges with weld metal, and then drilled a hole through the jaws. It works almost as well as the more expensive tool, but the resulting swages don't look as evenly made.

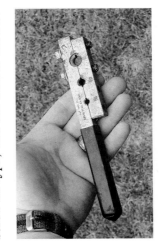

A commonly available Nicropress swager. These are generally effective but slow. The resulting swage has a better appearance than those made with my homemade swage.

looks neater and is probably slightly stronger.

When replacing the rigging, you have to measure the existing shrouds very carefully. If your boat is at a marina and you have wooden docks, you can lay down the shroud and stretch it between two small finishing nails that you drive into the dock. Then use these nails to measure the new shroud. (Don't forget to pull these nails when you're through, or someone might find them with bare feet!) Unless your existing shrouds are very short, it's not a bad idea to make the new ones about an inch shorter than the old ones, as new cable will stretch a tiny bit as it works. I didn't have a dock to work on, so I cut the old eyes carefully, leaving a hook shape. I swaged one end of the new shroud in place on the mast, and then hooked the old shroud in the same tang beside it. I then carefully pulled the two lengths of wire taught, marked where the new lower eye should go with my thumb, and bent on the new eye. Handling the stiff cable is difficult, but you'll get the idea after a few tries. Be sure to buy a few extra eyes and swages to practice with first, and then cut and swage your shrouds.

Roller Swages

These are the kind of fitting that you'll find on 90 percent of the production sailboats afloat. The cable fits into a fitting that consists of a tube and eye (or fork, or turnbuckle bolt) that's a one-piece forging. The tube is squeezed onto the cable using a special roller swage that squeezes the tube while revolving around it. In the best of cases, it results in a smooth, even grip over a large length of the wire. Swaging errors show up later in the form of curved fittings, when one side of the wire starts to slip under load. Curved fittings should be immediately replaced, as these will abruptly fail without any more warning. I've also seen a particularly gruesome case where these fittings were installed with a Nicropress swager, resulting in a mangled look reminiscent of large mechanical dogs chewing on a stainless stick. If you encounter this, plan on replacing the entire shroud. (The one time I saw this was a repair job. It's unlikely that you'll find an entire boat mistreated this way.)

Where Nicropress fittings cost pennies per end, roller swages cost dollars—but it isn't as expensive as I once thought. Defender's 2001 catalog lists roller-swaged eyes at about $7 each, including layout and installation. So my 12-foot lowers would have cost about $20 each—$14 for the ends and $6 for the wire. Not too bad. Had I realized this, I probably would have gone this route rather than swaging these myself. By the time you add the cost of the swaging tool (\$40), Nicropress swages aren't that much of a bargain. And you won't have self-righteous book-sailors pointing at your shrouds all the time, which is worth something.

Mechanical Fittings

These are the cream of the crop, the best end fittings that money can buy. It's what fashionable long-distance cruisers are wearing these days. Sta-Lok and Norseman are two popular brands. These fittings use conical wire formers to secure the individual strands. They're installed using ordinary wrenches, so one of their great advantages is they can be repaired at sea. Their disadvantage is the cost—they start at about $25 each, and they don't come in sizes small enough for trailer sailers, unless you want to increase your shroud size. They're nice, but for the kind of sailing we're talking about, they're serious overkill.

Restoring Tangs and Chainplates

Mast tangs are small straps of stainless steel that are used to connect the stays to the mast. The mast tangs are, naturally, much smaller and lighter than chainplates since they're located high above the boat's center of gravity. The chainplates are on the other end, and connect the stays to the hull. Between the chainplates and stays is some form of tensioning/adjusting device, either vernier adjusters or turnbuckles. Vernier adjusters are straps of metal with sev-

"YOUR MAST IS DOWN . . ."

Sometime after I got my boat, I received a distressing phone call from my wife's aunt—beside whose lakeside home I kept my boat moored. I raced to the boat, and sure enough, the mast had fallen.

A quick survey revealed minimal damage. The step was badly bent, and some bolts were deformed here and there, but the mast and boom were still straight. Repairs would be fairly easy.

Trying to figure out why the mast had come down was harder. Three bolts at the masthead were missing, and the turnbuckle at the forestay was gone completely. Apparently, numerous ski-boat wakes had caused at least the masthead bolts to back themselves out (which I still have a hard time believing; they were torqued in very tight, and the threads had been lubed against seizing—a bad idea in retrospect). The forestay turnbuckle had also unscrewed itself completely. It is unclear if the loss of the masthead bolts caused the mast to fall, or if was the combination of the loss of the masthead bolts plus the turnbuckle. Either way, I found it amazing that four tightly-secured, threaded fittings could unscrew themselves.

Correcting the problem is simple: secure all mast bolts with LocTite and lock washers, and secure all turnbuckles with wire. The potential for damage caused by simple boat wakes is amazing, and if your boat will be moored where this is a possibility, be sure to take this sort of intense cyclical loading into account. As a result of what happened to my boat, I now secure all rigging bolts with Loctite and seizing wire. ∎

eral holes through them, and they're adjusted by pulling the stay as tight as possible and inserting a clevis pin through the correct hole. (See page 103 for an example of vernier adjusters.) They aren't as strong as turnbuckles, but they are quite adequate for a trailer sailer and much quicker to set up. My boat has a single turnbuckle on the forestay, which tensions the mast fore and aft.

Restoring these parts is often a simple job. First remove them by unbolting from the mast or hull. Carefully inspect the parts for small cracks, bends, or corrosion. Since the chainplates are heavier, you're much more likely to see problems on the tangs. Replacement

tangs can often be purchased directly from marine catalogs. Also look at the bolts, and if they look rough or stressed, go ahead and replace them—they're cheap. On my boat, most of the clevis pins in the adjusters had been lost and replaced with bolts. This is poor practice, since clevis pins are stronger than bolts for a given diameter. Clevis pins are surprisingly expensive for what they are, but this isn't the place to pinch pennies. A mast failure under load is at best terrifying and expensive, and at worst, could result in a serious injury if someone happens to be standing downwind when, say, the bolts in the adjusters break.

Some boats' chainplates are secured in different, less convenient ways. Some, for example, take the form of a giant square washer—a "backing plate"—secured with a special eye bolt to the underside of the deck. The most difficult to deal with are the ones that are laminated into the hull itself. Often water finds its way in between the chainplate and hull, an ideal situation for crevice corrosion. Replacing these is an expensive and complicated proposition. Even testing them is expensive, since the only way to see if cracks exist is by x-ray testing, which requires a specialist. If your boat has integral chainplates, the only suggestion I can offer is to keep them well-sealed to prevent water migration. If you suspect the chainplates are bad, (if you see rust stains at the joint, for example) consult with a professional. Stained chainplates can give way suddenly, with little warning and often dire results.

If everything looks OK, all you need to do is polish the parts with a buffing wheel and a fine compound. Since the compound is suspended in a wax stick, this process tends to warm the piece and give it a fine wax coating, which you can improve by following up the buffing with a coat of regular paste wax. Reinstall the hardware, and you might want to put a drop of LocTite on the threads (see sidebar on previous page). A dab of bedding compound on the threads also works. If you see any corrosion on the mast, it's a good idea to isolate the stainless from the aluminum with a plastic or rubber washer before assembly. When I replaced the masthead, though, I found very little corrosion after 30 years—an indicator that stainless and aluminum, while dissimilar metals, are reasonably close on the galvanic scale (see table on page 101). It will eventually corrode, but depending on the alloy it can be a fairly slow process.

Mast work in general can be tricky, since you're working on a long tube. Securing anything with bolts—the mast tangs, for example—can be incredibly difficult, because you can't access the inside of the mast. In less expensive boats, the standard practice was often to pass a bolt directly through the mast, and place a nut on the outside of the mast opposite the bolt. Tightening the bolt then crushes the hollow mast, weakening it significantly. The correct way to bolt tangs is to pass the bolt through a hollow aluminum tube inside the mast. Locating this tube, as you may have guessed, is a nightmare. You could tape the tube to the end of a long piece of wood, and then slide the whole thing into place. When it's through-bolted, a sharp tug breaks the tape to remove the wood.

For this reason, you'll find most hardware secured to the mast with one-sided fasteners, such as sheet-metal screws or stainless pop rivets. If loads are spread over a large area through multiple fasteners, this method can be quite satisfactory. Again, Brion Toss's *The Complete Rigger's Apprentice* goes into this in detail.

Running Rigging

Unless you've bought a boat that has been recently upgraded, it's very likely that all your running rigging will need to be replaced. All of the lines on my boat had seen better days, and while they can still hold most of their load, several spots were chafed badly, and all were stiff and faded. I replaced everything. The halyards (remember, halyards lift, sheets control sails) were replaced with a special low-stretch line (Samson Sta-Set X), and for the sheets I selected a nice fuzzy braid that's easy on the hands. It helps inexperienced crew members if you have different colors for your lines—it's less intimidating to say, "Pull the green line" than to say, "Pull the jib halyard."

As you get your rope from the supplier, be sure to neatly whip the ends after it's cut to length. Here's a little nautical trivia: the raw material is generally called "rope," but after it's cut to length for a specific job, it becomes a "line." There are exceptions to this rule, like the bolt rope on your sail and the bell rope that rings the bell. But if you say, "Pull up the anchor rope," you'll immediately be branded as a lubber by all the old salts. If there aren't any old salts around, and everyone else is shouting, "Yank that rope on the left!" you can smile and think to yourself, "Bunch of lubbers!"

Believe it or not, whipping line ends is one of my favorite ways to relax at anchor. There are several ways to whip a line. Most common these days is simply a wrap of electrical tape with the end melted with a match or hot knife. While this is serviceable, you won't impress anyone with your marlinspike seamanship abilities. The traditional sewn whip, made with thread, is how I like to do it. My favorite book on traditional marlinspike seamanship is a little paperback called *The Arts of the Sailor* by Hervey Garrett Smith. Written in the 1950s, it's long out of print, but you can still find the paperback version in used-book stores. The book is very small and will fit on the tiniest sailboat.

Synthetic lines can be reconditioned rather than replaced. If they're just

filthy, you can put the line in a pillowcase and run it through the washing machine (without bleach). After the washer is through, let them soak for a day or so in a bucket of water with liquid fabric softener added. Rinse and air-dry. Sometimes this treatment can extend the life of a line considerably—dirt is abrasive as well as ugly.

The blocks and cleats will probably need attention, too. At the very least, they'll need cleaning and lubricating. A silicone spray does wonders with plastic blocks (please, don't call them pullies), replacing oils that naturally dry out and crack plastic parts. If you can disassemble the block, do so, cleaning and lubricating everything. Often, plastic blocks are riveted together, though, so it's impossible to do a thorough job. Ball bearing blocks, such as Harken, shouldn't be disassembled. Harken recommends flushing ball-bearing blocks with fresh-water and using a dry lubricant, such as McLube's Sailcoat.

If your blocks are really old or cracked, replacement is the only option. Some of the old mainsheet blocks on my boat were the original phenolic blocks. (Phenolic looks like a hard, reddish plastic with some kind of fabric embedded in the material.) These had to go, but if you've never sailed before, and if it's at all possible, I'd recommend taking the boat out once before you decide about replacing the blocks in the cockpit. You may find that the original arrangement works fine, despite its age or appearance. You can quickly run up a hefty bill at the chandlery if you have to replace everything.

Unfortunately, I was unable to follow my own advice. There was no way this boat could be sailed before working on the blocks, winches, and cleats, so I had to make educated guesses about where to locate things. Having some sailing experience helped in one way, but hurt in another. It helped because I knew what to expect—I knew, for example, that having the headsail cam cleats face directly aft would be a big pain to release, especially when the boat heeled. You'd have to get up, crawl to the downwind side of the cockpit, and lift the sheet to release the cleat. If the cam cleats face the opposite side of the cockpit, though, they can be quickly released by simply flipping the sheet upward to snap the sheet out of the cleat. If you're heeling way over, on your way to a knockdown because of a sudden squall, this feature becomes a safety issue rather than a matter of convenience.

But my sailing experience was a disadvantage, too, because it made me prejudiced against most of the sail handling hardware in the cockpit. I replaced just about everything because "I don't want any of that old junk on my boat!" Some of it may have worked fine, but because it looked bad, I wanted it off. As a result, I spent more money in this area than was probably necessary. Remember, we're only sailing from point A to point B, and old hardware can get you there the same as new. That said, I've sailed on boats before with old, worn-out, or badly-located hardware before, and for me, it isn't nearly as much fun as sailing a boat on which things are laid out in an intelligent and efficient manner. That's one of the aspects of sailing that appeals to me, and so I made it a priority on my boat, even if I spent a little more money than was absolutely necessary. My point is that this sort of thing

is a personal choice. You may see it as wasteful, or you may say that I didn't replace enough. So get as much advice as you can, but remember, it's your boat, and you should set it up in a way that appeals to your way of sailing.

With this in mind, here's what I did to improve the running rigging on my boat:

1. Replaced the original mainsheet system with a Harken traveler and new fiddle blocks.
2. Moved the winches outboard and relocated the jibsheet cam cleats.
3. Replaced halyard cam cleats with regular cleats.
4. Replaced the single jibsheet lead block with twin sheet blocks on tracks.

Mainsheet Traveler

A traveler system, if you've never used one, is a nice improvement on just about any boat. It allows you to fine-tune the shape of the mainsail by changing the angle of the mainsheet in relation to the sail. In strong winds, you want a flatter sail, so the traveler car is let out all the way to leeward. Now the mainsheet pulls more downward on the boom, flattening the sail. Just the opposite happens in light winds—the car is pulled to windward, and the boom is free to lift a bit, making the sail fuller. I enjoy tweaking my sails, so I knew that I wanted a traveler, but I didn't know how I was going to get one.

Then I found a brand-new Harken small-boat traveler car on eBay for about half-price, so I bought it. Harken generally makes really nice equipment, and their travelers are certainly no exception. The problem is the price. A com-

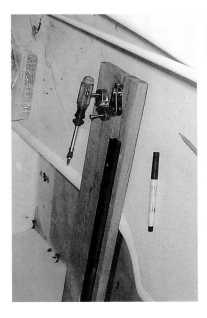

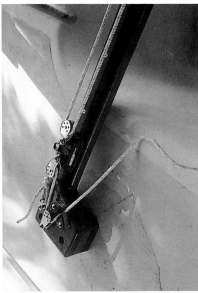

(top) Measuring the traveler base and laying out the hardware. (bottom) The new traveler installed. The base has riser blocks on the ends to mount the hardware at the correct height, and sharp edges are rounded over for safety and varnish strength. It's strong, looks good, works well, and costs less than stock.

plete traveler system for my boat, including the track, costs about $370. I had the car and was out about $30 so far.

Because Harken track almost never shows up on eBay, I went ahead and bought a 4-foot section from the catalogs, but I didn't buy any of their stops or ends. Instead, I found an inexpensive source for small stainless dinghy blocks from a local importer, so I bought four and modified two of them by bending the sheaves a little so that they could be screwed onto the traveler car. Then I designed and built a bed for the track out of ipe so that I could use standard blocks to control the ends. This will be a bit of a maintenance chore, because it needs to be varnished annually. The finished result looked great and works well as the standard Harken system, but it cost about $100 instead of $370. Sadly, I made a mistake when building my traveler base: I used epoxy to bond everything together. The epoxy wasn't strong enough to hold the wood as it expanded and contracted with the seasons, and it's now warped and cracked. It functions fine, though it looks bad. I'll probably end up replacing the wood and adding the Harken ends in a few years. To prevent this problem, I should have done two things: (1) I should have used resorcinol glue rather than epoxy, and (2) I should have used several screws to help the glue hold everything together.

Relocating the Winches

The winches on the original MacGregor 222 are poorly located. That's being kind, actually. In use, the lines rub against the house, and the cleats are located directly aft on the coaming. I built a stainless-steel bracket to move the winches out a few inches, so that the jibsheets just clear the house (see photo on page 107). This gives me room to add a pair of cam cleats where the winches were, facing inboard. Now all I have to do to free the sheet is give a quick tug upward from the helm—I don't even need to leave my seat. This is a nice feature when the wind picks up and the boat starts heeling past 20 degrees. The jib can be quickly eased, keeping the boat on her feet and easing the strain on the rigging.

Creating the base itself wasn't difficult; the procedure is outlined in Chapter 6. This area comes under considerable strain, though, so whatever you do, make it strong. In retrospect, a thicker support base might have been better. These actually flex a tiny bit when the wind is up. Also, my cam cleats don't have fairleads on them. As a result, I've had to recover the sheets from overboard on a few occasions.

If your budget is unlimited, you could consider upgrading your winches. Yacht surplus suppliers often have smaller single-speed winches at a reasonable cost, since a common upgrade on many boats is to replace stock single-speed winches with two-speed self-tailing winches. All-bronze winches are preferred over aluminum, as the aluminum is more likely to corrode.

Replacing Halyard Cam Cleats

My boat came with the turning blocks installed for leading the main and jib halyards aft. The halyards were secured using cam cleats. I removed the cam cleats and installed regular cleats. These can be tensioned easier than cam cleats. You just take a half-turn on the cleat, grab the halyard ahead of the cleat and pull up, and then quickly take up the slack on the cleat. (This is called "sweating the line.") Made fast, regular cleats are much more secure than cam cleats. Cam cleats are a better choice when a line needs frequent adjustment—like a sheet. In actual use, though, I prefer to go forward and secure the halyards at the mast base; the gear to lead the halyards

to the cockpit is unused, and a needless complication on my boat. You may feel differently about cockpit-led halyards.

Replacing Jibsheet Lead Blocks

The original Mac came with single stand-up jibsheet lead blocks bolted to the deck, one on each side. This is a low-cost arrangement that works, but it doesn't allow any adjustment of the sheet lead angle. I installed T-track with new twin sheet lead blocks, and they are a marked improvement in the rig. Now the headsail shape can be altered by moving the sheet blocks forward or aft to suit the wind strength and sail size—especially important if you're sailing with old headsails, as I am. While twin sheet blocks are great for racing, where you need to change headsails quickly, on a cruiser they're a bit of a mistake. A stopper knot on the tail of my headsail sheet will pass right through them, and I've had to fish the jib-sheet from the water several times. A single block wouldn't allow this to happen.

This arrangement doesn't work for large headsails, like a 170 percent genoa or a drifter. I had to install turning blocks at the aftermost corner of the cockpit to handle this job. The old stand-up blocks worked well for this.

There are hundreds of other little details to the running rigging that will vary from boat to boat. Again, it helps immensely if you can sail the boat before relocating hardware. In fact, it might be advisable to put together just enough hardware to take it for a short sail before making any extensive modifications to your sail-handling hardware. Even small decisions like how long to cut your new sheets are much easier with a little sail time.

The Sails

Your sails are one of the most important parts of your boat. Without sails, it's just a powerboat! So you should give them proper consideration.

There are two ways of thinking about sails. One way is to "fly 'em if you've got 'em"—as long as they're holding together, put them on the mast and point the boat as best you can. The other school of thought is that sails should be optimally shaped and tensioned at all times, and you should do (or spend) whatever is necessary to get the best sail shape possible. You'll most often, but not always, find cruisers in the first category, and racers in the second.

Either approach can work. Although sails are not items that usually lend themselves to owner rebuilding, you can do some things to improve them a little. Some aspects of sails have to be left to the pros, though.

One common problem with old MacGregor sails is boltrope shrinkage. Over time, some of the early sails had boltropes that would shrink, even though they were synthetic. The result was a mainsail that is wrinkly and baggy. The solution is to carefully cut the stitching free, pull the sail tight, and restitch the boltrope by hand. It's one of the few improvements that can be successfully done by a non-specialist, but I'd suggest reading a manual on sailmaking and repair before tackling this job.

The sails that come with your boat will probably be like mine were. The original mainsail was wrapped around the boom (not the proper way to store a sail), dirty, and soft from age. The headsail wasn't original but made by a different manufacturer, and while it was old,

it was a better-quality sail and included a set of reef points—a good option for cruising sails. But it, too, was quite soft and just stuffed into the bag.

Sailmakers are constantly trying to combat stretch in sails. When they stretch out of shape, they become less efficient. The exceptions to this rule are sails that are only used off the wind, like spinnakers. Spinnakers are made from stretchy nylon to absorb puffs of wind. Sails that are used upwind are best made from a stiff cloth that holds its foil shape in varying strengths of wind, and to make the cloth stiff, manufacturers add resin filler to the cloth, which adds strength and reduces stretch. The resin also makes them very hard to sew, either by hand or with a machine.

While both of my sails worked OK, their softness made them wrinkly and baggy, and they were pretty dirty as well. A sail that is "blown out," or stretched out of optimal shape, will result in more heeling, less forward drive upwind, and a reduced pointing ability. I decided to replace the mainsail, which was the worst offender, and wash and repair the headsail. I also added a newer used 150 to give me a range of choices for the foredeck.

A sail shouldn't be tossed into a washer, though people have done it. Spread it out on the lawn, and scrub with a mild solution of soap and a soft brush. Rinse, and hang it up to dry in the sun. While this usually helps, this won't get out mildew stains, which are often the result of storing a wet sail.

To get mildew stains out, you have to send it to SailCare. This company will not only wash your sail, but they'll go over it and make proper repairs, and then recoat the sail with resin. I've

MEASURING HEADSAILS

You'll often hear headsails referred to by number, like a 110, 135, 150, or 170. This number is a percentage of the distance between your mast and front/bottom end of the forestay. If this distance is 12 feet, then a headsail with a foot that is 12 feet long is a "100." A foot that's 10 percent longer is a 110, 50 percent longer = 150, and so on.

Headsails can have other names as well. Genoas, or genoa jibs, are generally larger than working jibs—anything from about 135 to 170 could be called a genoa. Headsails bigger than that are sometimes called "drifters." These are made with light, thin sailcloth to catch the lightest breeze. Still larger are the "cruising spinnakers," which are asymetrical like a genoa, but used for very light downwind work. ∎

heard that the results are truly amazing, and folks who have used SailCare are quite pleased. But it is expensive: a quote to do my mainsail was over $200.

I also got quotes to replace the sail. I found that there are wide variations in new sail prices. It's always good to have your sail made by a local sailmaker if one is available. They know the local conditions, will measure your boat, and can make adjustments if the fit isn't quite right. To get this kind of service, though, you should expect to pay a premium price. Sometimes local sailmakers can be very competitive depending on the season; get a quote around Christmastime, for example, and it will be different from the same quote at peak racing season. Your next option is to order your sail from a larger loft like North or Hood. These folks are famous for producing high-quality, fast sails. They're also generally pretty expensive.

There is another option, and that is to have your sails made overseas. This option is usually the least expensive, and it's what I chose for my boat. I got a very

low price from Sails East. They're based in Chicago, but the sails are made in Hong Kong. My new mainsail was just a touch too long. At some point, my mainmast may have been shortened a little. In any case, with the new sail bent on, the boom hung a little low in the cockpit. I made adjustments by adding a new masthead and a sliding gooseneck, which raised the boom a few inches. The new sail looks good and has a great shape. I'd probably go this route again, though I'd carefully double-check my measurements instead of depending on the sizes the loft had on file.

I like my new sail, but truthfully the old one would probably have been OK for the occasional trailer sailer use. If your sail is just dirty, use it for a season to get a good feel for what you like and don't like about it. If it fits perfectly but is blown out, you could send it in for the loft to measure. Do this in the off season, though, since it can take a while to have the sail made. (Mine took over three months.)

CHAPTER 9

Outboard Motors

A Cost-Effective Power Plant

I never really cared too much for outboard motors. They're noisy, fussy, and have a reputation of being unreliable. Given a choice, I'd much prefer a big, old Atomic Four or, better yet, a Yanmar Diesel rumbling away under the cockpit sole. But on smaller boats, inboard engines are generally impractical because of their weight, so I was faced with a choice: either sail without an engine altogether, or face my bias and learn as much as I could about outboards. Unfortunately, the no-motor option isn't too practical, so I chose the latter option. (Another alternative is a large oar, which isn't as crazy as it sounds; see Appendix 2.)

About Outboards

One of the fist things I discovered is that motors are pretty darned expensive, all things considered. Even a seized, non-operational "junker" outboard will sell on eBay for around $100. A used but functional outboard in the 4 to 7 hp range will commonly sell for around $400. Newer ones, or those in better con-

dition, sell for quite a bit more. I realized this early on with my boat—it came with an old Mercury, but apparently someone (the seller claimed it was the repair shop, but I have my doubts) had left the motor in an oil drum filled with water, which froze solid during an unusual winter cold snap. The resulting stress cracked the motor's foot assembly. Replacing this single part would cost over $400—more than the motor was worth. So I sold it on eBay, and got about $75 dollars for it. The buyer had another Mercury and purchased it for the parts.

So if you can buy a boat that has a working outboard included in the price, that's a big plus. But it didn't work out that way with my boat, and I needed an outboard.

At one end of the spectrum is a brand-new outboard motor. It is an option if you have the funds. New outboards are cleaner-running and more dependable, especially the newer four-stroke engines. Some inland lakes have banned two-strokes altogether, and the industry is in the process of phasing out the manufacturing of these motors in favor of more efficient, cleaner four-strokes. The problem is the price—nearly $1,200 for a new 5-hp Nissan long shaft (though the price of four-strokes has dropped slightly in recent years—the same motor was around $1,400 when I first bought my boat). Since I was spending a bunch of money on restoration supplies, a new motor was an expensive proposition for me.

At the other end of the spectrum is an old outboard that you'll rebuild yourself. In keeping with the general theme of this book, it would seem that buying a worn-out motor and rebuilding it would be the best thing to do, but I don't advocate this approach for most restorers. Outboard motors, being complex mechanical assemblies, do wear out past the point of no return, much like an old car. The repair parts can cost nearly as much as a new motor. Outboard repair is a good skill to have, but it takes a lot of learning, practice, and tools to be successful. I didn't want to devote the time, energy, and money into rebuilding an old outboard for my boat, as I don't particularly enjoy engine work. Now, if you have some skills as a mechanic—you enjoy working on cars, for example, and you already have a box full of specialized tools—go ahead and buy yourself an old motor and a shop manual and have at it. But I was fairly certain that this approach wouldn't work too well for me, and I believe the same is true for many potential sailboat restorers.

There is another, more moderate path you can take, and this is what I recommend for most of us mere mortals.

Learn as much as you can about outboards so you can evaluate a motor. Find a good one that has been well-maintained and has some life left in it. Spend the money to get a motor in above-average condition, and then carefully maintain it to keep it that way.

Research

Like so many of our sailboat endeavors, the first step is research. The best sources of information are people who own outboard-powered sailboats. If you have any acquaintances who meet this description, just ask them casually, "So, how do you like your outboard?" You're very likely to get a passionate diatribe about how great the motor is or, conversely, an expletive-laden speech about how "The #&!* left me stranded a hundred times!" As with all anecdotal information, take it with a grain of salt. Oftentimes there are other, unspoken reasons as to why a motor gets a good or bad rap. Maybe your source never bothered to carefully measure the amount of oil in the fuel—getting this wrong can greatly affect the operation and lifespan of a two-stroke engine. So in order to balance out factors like this, speak with as many different people as you can.

Can't find any opinionated outboard owners in your neighborhood? The Internet is full of them. Check the archives sections of any of the bigger sailboat owner e-mail lists. One of the biggest I've found is sponsored by SailJazz (http://www.sailjazz.com/list manager). While their search function is somewhat difficult to use, I did find some usable information by typing in "outboards." If you check the archives and can't find any specific recommendations, you can sign up as a member and post a question, such as, "I'm rebuilding my first sailboat, and I need a good, dependable outboard that isn't too hard for a beginner to keep running. Does anyone have any suggestions?" That should generate a few responses. And here's a little tip about e-mail lists: Always sign up for the digest version. That way, you get one condensed e-mail with all the day's posts, rather than a separate e-mail for each message. On the MacGregor list, the postings often exceed 75 messages per day!

There are a few other good websites devoted to outboard repair. One of the better ones I've found is by a company called MasterTech. Their website (www. maxrules.com/fixtuneitup.html) shows how to fully tune a small 4-hp Johnson. While they call it a tune-up, it's really more of a minor rebuild, because they install new coils, head gasket, impeller, and rebuild the carburetor as well. They also sell parts and service manuals, primarily for Johnson and Evinrude motors. There are other websites as well; a Google search for "outboard repair" comes up with a number of promising sources of information.

If you're lucky, you live in an area that has a number of good mechanics. These people can be an invaluable source of information. Some will naturally be too busy to answer a bunch of questions. But if he or she were willing, perhaps it would be worth it to pay a mechanic his shop rate for a half-hour. In certain areas and situations, adult beverages can work better than cash. However you do it, you'll learn more if you arm yourself with as much knowledge as you can beforehand so that you

can ask intelligent questions. But having a real person show you how to check out and maintain an outboard can help you more than a stack of books.

Evaluating a Used Motor

I purchased the motor for my boat on eBay. Because I couldn't physically inspect the outboard, I had to rely on the seller's description, photographs, and ultimately, a little luck. The seller said that the motor, a 2-stroke longshaft Tohatsu 5 hp, had just come back from the shop where it had gotten a rebuilt carburetor and routine annual maintenance. It was, for me, rather expensive (the final price was $450). But the seller had a good feedback rating (I checked before I bid) and a fair number of sales, so I sent him a check and hoped.

The motor arrived some two weeks later on a Greyhound bus, which is a cost-effective alternative shipping method for things that are too large or heavy for UPS. I was relieved to find that it was exactly as described. It was in great shape and clearly had recently been worked on. I had to spend a little more on a fuel line, tank, and special fuel connector, because anything that has been used to handle gasoline cannot be shipped. You'll save yourself some time and aggravation if you buy a motor that includes these items. Once I got everything together and connected, I mixed up some fuel and placed the lower unit in a trash can filled with water. It started up after two pulls and ran smoothly.

If you decide to buy a motor online, be sure to check the seller's feedback rating. Look at the photos closely, and avoid motors that appear heavily corroded or otherwise abused. Insist on a detailed description of the motor's condition. Ask how often and what was done for annual maintenance, and how long the seller has owned the motor. I'd prefer to buy from another sailboat owner rather than a dealer, since a dealer has to add his profit. But a dealer will be more concerned with keeping a good reputation intact, so there are advantages either way.

Buying Locally

If there's a motor for sale in your area that you can inspect in person, your job is both easier and more complex. It's easier because you'll take less of a chance with your decision, but determining condition is now your responsibility. Obvious signs of neglect are easy enough to spot. Large areas of corrosion, dents, or broken castings can have a big impact on the price of a motor, thus lowering your risk a little. The real trick comes when a motor looks good externally, when internally it could be anything from a Swiss watch to German potato salad. How can you tell if it's a good motor? Fortunately, there are a few tricks that can help. Some of these I learned from a great article by Bob Grubb called "Digging In: Some Tips on Evaluating and Fixing Up an Old Merc," at www.oldmercs.com/basics.html.

There are a few tools that are useful to have with you when evaluating a motor. A "muff," officially known as a "cooling system flushing adapter," can supply cooling water to the engine, allowing you to run an outboard motor on dry land. You'll also need a spark plug wrench and perhaps a compression tester. The spark plug wrench will be an essential maintenance tool. The compression tester might not be, but they aren't too expensive and can save you a world of grief by flagging an engine that needs major internal repairs. Sometimes, though, poor compression can be cured by using a good engine cleaner. Also bring along a set of Allen wrenches and a large flat-blade screwdriver.

Visual Checks

First, give the motor a careful external examination. There are several things that you can look for that could indicate trouble. Take off the motor cover, and look at the overall finish. Paint that is discolored by overheating the power head is a warning sign. Another red flag might be bolts, nuts, or screws that are chewed up, indicating a motor that needs constant work or adjustment. The exception to this would be the drain plug on the lower unit, which should be a little scarred, since the owner should have changed the oil in the lower unit every season.

There should be two plugs on the lower unit for the lower gear, one upper and one lower. On my motor, these look like giant flathead screws, but the plug might be an Allen head. The upper one is a vent; the lower one is the fill hole. What you want is a sample of the oil in the lower unit. With permission, remove the upper plug to check the oil. It should be full to overflowing. Replace and tighten the upper plug, and then slowly loosen the lower one until some oil dribbles out. If rusty water comes out, that's not good; the prop shaft seals are probably bad and the gears are possibly corroded. If there's no oil at all, that's also bad, as the gears are possibly burned up. While you're looking at the foot, turn the prop by hand. If the motor has hit a stump and bent the shaft, you'll feel a slight corkscrewing effect. Any of these problems can indicate moderate to very expensive repairs.

Ladies and Gentlemen, Start Your Engines . . .

Occasionally, you might come across an unscrupulous seller who is trying to unload a clunker engine. If you ask such a person if he can start the motor for you, you'll be met with a barrage of excuses. One of these will likely be, "I can't get cooling water to the engine." So just for fun, buy and bring along a pair of muffs. They're inexpensive, and you'll need one anyway once you purchase your motor. Bring them with you when you look at an engine. Since you can now easily get cooling water to the engine, a slightly-less-than-honest seller will now have to scramble around for another excuse.

Ninety-nine percent of the time, though, sellers are regular folks with genuine motives. They'll give you the straight story about the engine they're selling and let you start it up. If it runs, pay attention to a couple of things. Clouds of blue smoke can indicate improperly mixed fuel or, if it's an auto-mix engine, a bad oil-injection system. If it's a four-stroke, smoke can mean bad rings or a bad head gasket. An engine that idles roughly can indicate cracked or leaky fuel lines; a clogged fuel filter; old, stale fuel; or a problem with the spark plug or ignition system. There's a great two-stroke troubleshooting chart in Edwin Sherman's book, *Outboard Engines: Maintenance, Troubleshooting, and Repair*. Another important item to check is cooling water. Make sure a nice, steady stream is running from the power head while the motor is operating.

Checking Compression

If you've gotten this far with your motor exam, and everything looks okay, the motor is probably good. But there are a few more checks you can do if you want to be really thorough, or if the seller is asking a premium price. One of the most telling tests on an outboard is a compression check, but it isn't necessarily definitive. As I mentioned before, poor compression can sometimes be caused by simple carbon buildup, and a good engine cleaning can restore compression. But a worn-out engine will not have good compression, and it's easy to wear out a two-stroke by not adding enough oil to the fuel. The test is a little involved, but for any engine that's selling for more that a couple hundred dollars, learning how to do the test is probably worth your while.

A truly accurate compression test requires a warmed-up engine, so it's best do take this step after the motor has run for a few minutes. Remove the spark plug, and if you're checking a motor with more than a single cylinder, disconnect the remaining plugs. Warning: Leave the other plugs in their holes, because an explosive fuel/oil mix will come out of any open cylinders. All you need is an open spark, and pop goes the weasel. Either disable the ignition completely—some motors have a lanyard clip that will cut off the ignition if removed—or ground the plug wires to the engine case, just to be safe. Do not remove the plugs and leave them laying around, attached to the plug wires; that's a very dangerous condition.

Pull the starter rope to spin the flywheel at about the same speed as you would to start the engine and note the reading. Exact numbers vary widely from engine to engine, but a reading of about 80 pounds is considered good compression.

If the compression seems low, try the test again, only first add a few squirts of motor oil. If the compression rises appreciably, you can suspect bad rings, scored cylinder walls, or, if you're fortunate, simple carbon buildup. If there's no change, a bad head gasket or, in a four-stroke, bad valves, may be the culprit.

A professional outboard mechanic might suggest a variation of the compression test called a "leak test." It involves injecting the cylinder with compressed air and measuring the rate of leakage. While this kind of test is more definitive, it is generally beyond the scope of "user maintenance."

If, after you've performed all these tests, you're faced with a choice between two similar motors, use your personal intuition and buy from the seller you feel best about. It is rare that I have ignored my "gut feeling" in cases like this and not regretted it later.

Principles of Operation

So let's assume you're now the proud owner of a new (to you) old outboard motor. Great. Now let's further assume that you want to protect your investment and give the motor the care and attention it needs to do its job for as long as possible. Financial considerations aside, it's important to properly maintain your motor so that it won't let you down in a tight spot—like docking in a crowded marina, or running for shelter before a fast-approaching storm.

I touched on the difference between two-stroke and four-stroke engines earlier, but now might be a good time to examine the two systems in a little more detail.

Four-stroke engines are what we're most familiar with—they're in our cars and most lawn mowers. Two-stroke engines are commonly used for smaller engines, like gas-powered weed eaters. One big advantage of two-strokes is that they have fewer moving parts—no valves, for one thing—and are generally lighter in weight. Four-strokes, while heavier and more complex, have a key advantage: they're easier to lubricate. But I'm getting ahead of myself. Let's look at the more familiar four-stroke first.

Basics of a Four-Stroke Engine

Engines operate by using a piston that slides up and down in an enclosed space, the cylinder. The rings seal the piston to the cylinder to form a nearly airtight seal. Fuel (gasoline) is mixed with air by the carburetor and supplied to the cylinder. In a four-stroke, a valve opens in the top of the cylinder and lets in the gas/air mix. This happens while the piston is traveling downward, and at the bottom of the stroke, the valve closes. This is the intake stroke.

Now the cylinder is sealed off and the piston travels upward to the top of the cylinder, compressing the explosive fuel/air mix. This is the compression stroke.

Just after the piston passes the top of its stroke, the spark plug fires, igniting the fuel and driving the piston downward again. I like to think of this as the drive stroke, though some books like to call this the ignition stroke.

Once the piston starts to travel upward, the exhaust valve opens and the smoke is pushed out of the cylinder by the piston. This is the exhaust stroke.

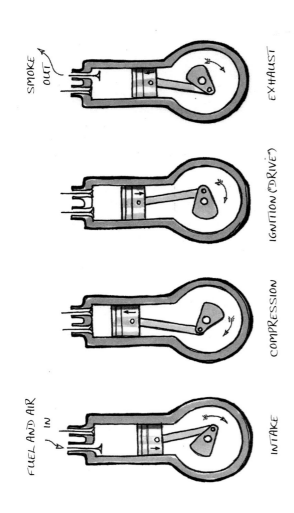

FUEL AND AIR IN   SMOKE OUT

INTAKE   COMPRESSION   IGNITION ("DRIVE")   EXHAUST

Four-stroke operation.

As the piston reaches the top of this stroke, the exhaust valve closes, the intake valve opens, and the cycle starts all over again. That's four strokes—down, up, down, up—for each explosion.

Basics of a Two-Stroke Engine

In a two-stroke engine, things are quite different. As you've probably guessed, there are only two strokes—one up, and one down—for each explosion. Further, there are no valves in the cylinder. Fuel gets in and smoke gets out through ports that are strategically located in the cylinder walls. The piston seals and opens the ports as it travels up and down the cylinder. It's quite ingenious, really.

The two-stroke still has to do the same operations as a four-stroke; that is, intake the fuel, compress it, ignite it (and harness the "drive"), and exhaust the smoke. But it does all this with half the piston movement—each stroke containing two opera-

tions instead of one. It works because it uses the backside of the piston to help move fuel through the system.

First, at the bottom of the stroke, both the exhaust and the intake ports are open. Fuel comes into the cylinder via the crankcase port as smoke is exhausted. As the piston begins traveling upward, both the intake and exhaust ports are sealed by the piston. The fuel is compressed as the piston passes the top of the stroke.

To start the downward stroke, the fuel is ignited and the piston is forced down. The exhaust port opens first, allowing most of the smoke to escape, then the intake port is opened. This lets in the fuel/air mix, displacing the remaining smoke and charging the cylinder for the next cycle.

Pros and Cons

So why is all this important? Well, with a basic understanding of how each motor

Two-stroke operation.

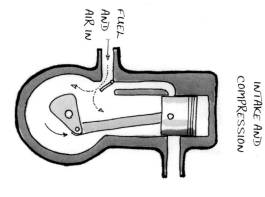

INTAKE AND COMPRESSION

FUEL AND AIR IN

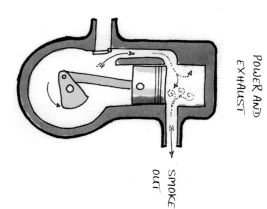

POWER AND EXHAUST

SMOKE OUT

works, we can talk about the pros and cons of each. It's easy to see that a two-stroke engine, with more explosions, can develop more horsepower with less weight. With no valves, two-strokes are simpler engines and are a little cheaper to manufacture. Sounds great, right?

One of the two-stroke engine's big disadvantages has to do with lubrication. On a four-stroke, the backside isn't used to deliver fuel to the engine, so the crankshaft, connecting rod, wrist pin bearings, and so on, can be continually washed in a nice, warm bath of oil. This is one of the things that gives it a long, happy life. In a two-stroke, the parts behind the piston are lubricated by mixing oil with the fuel. When mixed correctly, the cylinder's backside gets enough oil. But it has to be mixed by the operator (you) and it has to be mixed per the manufacturer's instructions. Too little oil and the engine is starved of critical lubrication. Too

much, and the engine doesn't work well. You'll get lots of smoke and fouled plugs, and deposits from burning oil will quickly gum up the engine. Even when the fuel is perfectly mixed, a t wo-stroke burns some oil, producing gummy deposits and polluting more than a four-stroke (in good working order).

A four-stroke, on the other hand, needs more internal parts, and is heavier as a result. Some of the weight is required to provide the inertia to carry the piston around four full strokes until the next explosion—but there are a lot of additional parts there, too. This extra weight is a disadvantage when you have to lift the engine and carry it around, but heavier engines have more torque or power at low revolutions. This advantage is somewhat offset by the greater complexity of the valves, camshaft, and so on. But in general, despite their higher complexity, four-strokes are rugged and dependable engines. Most early four-strokes were bulky and unreliable, but many people report a high degree of satisfaction with the modern engines.

Regular Maintenance

So just what should you do to "regularly maintain" your engine? First off, read your manual. Your seller should provide a copy when you buy the engine. If he or she doesn't have an owner's manual, that's a red flag. How do they know what the regular maintenance procedures are? Check the engine carefully before buying from a seller without a manual.

The maintenance procedures that I'm going to suggest are just that: suggestions. My comments shouldn't supersede that of your mechanic or your manual. Remember, I'm not a mechanic, just an owner. As of this writing, knock on wood, my little outboard has given me great service, so I must be doing something right. But like everything, take it with a grain of salt.

Every Time You Run the Engine

Use only clean, fresh fuel. And, if you have a two-stroke engine, be sure to mix the fuel with the right oil in the right proportions. That's a simple sentence with a lot of implications. In terms of fuel, there was quite a bit of hubbub over RFG fuels when they were first introduced. RFG stands for "re-formulated gasoline." According to Tim Base in an article called "Know Your Fuel" (www.boats.com), refining methods used for 87 octane regular gas were changed in the late 1990s. Among other things, oxygenates were added. There should be a little sticker on the pump that says so. The oxygenates are additional oxygen molecules in the form of added ether or ethanol. While this reduces carbon monoxide-, smog-, and acid-rain-producing compounds when burned, RFG fuels deteriorate much more readily than non-RFG fuels. Gummy, sticky compounds are formed as lighter molecules evaporate.

For this reason, I use only the highest grade of gas I can get, 93 octane. I always add a fuel stabilizer, and I always get rid of the old gas at the end of the season. I usually just dump the quart or so of the leftover fuel into the gas tank for my lawn mower. Some folks add it to their car and dilute it by topping up the tank—I don't think this hurts your car, but I can't say for sure. Whatever you do, don't just dump it on the ground or down a storm drain; doing so is illegal and pollutes a massive amount of groundwater.

The right oil, for nearly all two-strokes these days, means grade TC-WIII. For a time, grade TC-WI or TC-WII oils were available, but these cheaper grades were less refined and didn't burn as cleanly. You're not likely to find these oils for sale anymore. Opinions are split as to whether or not more-expensive oil equals better performance, but as long as the oil says, "Meets or exceeds grade TC-WIII specification," you should be okay. Whatever you do, mix your oil carefully and follow the manufacturer's instructions.

Seasonal Maintenance

Once a year, you should work on your engine a little more thoroughly. It is best to do these procedures in the fall, before the engine sits idle through the cold winter. I like to do the following:

- Change the oil in the foot.
- Change the fuel filter.
- Change the spark plug.
- Lubricate moving parts.
- Check the impeller and starting rope.
- Spray a coat of "fogging oil" or storage oil into the cylinder.
- Check the zincs and patch any corrosion or damaged paint.
- Flush the cooling system, especially with salt-water engines.

When changing the oil in the foot, technically known as the "lower unit," use the more expensive lower-unit oil sold at outboard shops. I understand these oils are formulated for reduced foaming and breakdown if a small amount of water gets in, which is common around shaft seals. Plain 90-weight gear oil sold at auto shops is not the same thing. Also, many outboard shops sell special oil pumps that will make this job easier and less messy. If you have a lifting outboard bracket on your boat, lifting the motor clear of the water after each use helps reduce the amount of water drawn into the foot around the shaft seal.

Changing the fuel filter is a no-brainer. They aren't usually too expensive. Same thing with the spark plug, though I've gotten by for three seasons of light use on the same plug. They don't cost too much, though, and you can save the old one in case you get a fouled plug. I like to lubricate the inside of the plug boot with a special silicone dielectric grease to help seal the plug against water and make the boot easier to remove next season.

Your manual should show you where to lubricate moving parts. Use a waterproof grease sold at outboard shops. Some mechanics recommend changing the impeller every season. If you run your engine a lot, or operate it in salt or heavily silted water, this is a good idea, since a bad impeller can quickly ruin a good engine. However, others say that if you run your engine lightly (just to clear away from a dock, for example) in clear, fresh water, there's no need to replace an impeller every year. An overheating engine (with a clear water intake) or reduced flow of cooling water out of the motor head are signs of a bad impeller. Inspecting or replacing the impeller involves removing the lower unit, which on some motors can be a tricky procedure requiring special tools; check your manual. If you do need to replace it, be sure to notice which way the little vanes are supposed to bend before you remove the old impeller. If you install them backward, the vanes will shear off the minute your engine is started and it will quickly overheat.

Replacing a starter rope is a common repair. Follow the advice in your manual, or try a general shop manual like *The Outboard Service Manual* (Intertec Publishing), which covers repairs and service for all major motors under 30-hp from 1969 onward.

Spraying the cylinder with some kind of rust inhibitor is a good idea. Although it's expensive, I'd use a specifically-made marine fogging oil for this purpose, though others have used Marvel Mystery Oil or similar stuff. They say it works fine, but until I hear differently from a mechanic, I'll spend the bucks.

Replacing the sacrificial zincs is extremely important in salt water. Freshwater engines need this too, though not as often unless your sailing waters are badly polluted or have stray electrical currents in them. (This is not as uncommon as you might think near marinas, especially older docks. If you can do it, lifting the motor clear of the water after each sail helps in this department, too.)

Flushing the engine with fresh water is extremely important for saltwater engines. You don't want your motor to sit all winter with salt water in it, or you'll surely have greatly restricted cooling water flow in the spring. I run my engine in fresh water only, but I still flush the motor once a season. If you sail in salt, I'd ask a mechanic what works best for flushing engines and cleaning out deposits. Usually, the best solution is plain tap water. There was a story in *Good Old Boat*, "Cleaning Out an Atomic Four" by Hugh Straub, (July/August 2003), about an owner who flushed an old saltwater-cooled Atomic Four engine with muriatic (hydrochloric) acid, but I'd be wary of home-brew solutions. Muriatic probably wouldn't work on an outboard because many motor blocks are aluminum.

Electric Outboards

One of my favorite new developments for sailboat propulsion is the electric outboard. A few folks have tried mounting the largest trolling motor they can find to their sailboats, and in a few cases they've had quite a bit of success. For example, on an American Mariner 24 (with 4,700 pounds displacement) an owner mounted a trolling motor with 107 pounds of thrust in place of his 6-hp Mercury (http://members.cox.net/sholley1/electric.htm). The

top speed with the Mercury was 6 mph, while the top speed with the trolling motor was 4.7 mph. With three batteries wired in series, he has about three hours of full-power running time. Since the batteries weigh 210 pounds, locating the batteries is an important consideration. Somewhere low down along the centerline is best. An application like this draws a lot of amps (around 40 at full power), so you need a heavy-gauge wire to run power to the motor.

Cost is a bit of an issue, since a saltwater-grade, high-thrust trolling motor can sell for as much as $700 if brand-new. A used unit would probably work fine if you could find one, since these motors can have a long service life. Add the cost of three good batteries, and you're approaching the cost of a new four-stroke. Also be aware that batteries need to be replaced every few years, so although it may cost you only $1 in electricity for a full charge, battery replacement can raise that figure quite a bit. But it is certainly an idea that can work well in some cases, and electric systems are very dependable.

There is another electric alternative that would be a good contender as a sailing auxiliary. Briggs and Stratton has (according to its website) a newly developed electric outboard that is about the same size and thrust as a 3-hp gas motor. Current pricing is around $1,800. It's a power guzzler, with the ability to drain four batteries in an hour at top speed, but it develops 150 pounds of peak thrust. Back off the throttle a bit, and battery life increases to 2.3 hours. Add more batteries, a wind generator, or even a small Honda generator, and you've got your own hybrid system!

CHAPTER 10

Sea Trials and Commissioning

Finishing It All Up

At some point in the restoration process, the jobs left to do cease to be "rebuilding projects" and start to become "ownership projects." I spent two years and five months of part-time work restoring my boat. It wasn't "finished" at that point, but it was ready for its sea trials (perhaps we should call them "lake trials") and commissioning.

Sea trials of your newly restored boat will be more important than with most boats. No matter how much planning and thinking you do, you'll find some glaring deficiencies in your boat the first time you sail it—I promise. Launch your boat, and bring a ruler and a clipboard. Take notes of all the things that need to be done, relocated, changed, and so on. Hopefully, you won't need to change or add that much.

I first launched the boat in late August. I left her in the water for most of the fall, taking several sails in varying conditions. Each time, I noticed something that would need changing—not immediately, but when I hauled the boat for the winter. For example:

The mainsail headboard chafed against the backstay, and the new main is a bit too long. The stock MacGregor masthead for the year my boat was built uses cheek blocks on the sides of the masthead a little extra room. Hopefully, the change in halyard lead will make them a little less likely to foul the steaming light, which has also been a problem.

Stowage below is inadequate, and I need to make an inventory list of things that will stay on the boat, along with locations for each item. Small eyelets for bungee cords need to be installed pretty much everywhere, as I've had a few sails where everything ended up on the floor.

Many other small things were deferred until later, like installing the VHF, final bolting of the head cabinet, screen bags and snaps, and so on. All these things are going on the "winter boatwork" list. You'll find that you have a list like this every winter. I find that some boatwork is enjoyable in the winter, as long as it isn't too ambitious.

Outfitting for Sailing

One of the shortcomings of restoring a boat will be felt acutely now, and that's the fact that you have to buy a ton of little doodads that would normally come with a better-kept vessel—fenders, docklines, life jackets, whistles for each, a horn, a fire extinguisher, some sailing gloves . . . the list can seem endless and can get pretty expensive. But these are the inescapable costs that you'll have to pay for just about any kind of watercraft, so just grit your teeth and get out the wallet. It only hurts for a few moments when you're handing over those bills anyway; you'll forget all about it once you get on the water.

At the very least, though, you should have aboard the complete list of equipment required by the Coast Guard. For the size boat we're discussing here, this means Coast Guard Class 1, 16 to 26 feet in length. The list includes (but may not be limited to):

Personal Flotation Devices (PFDs). One for each person onboard, plus one throwable. We have four aboard, properly sized for kids and adults.

Fire Extinguishers. Not specifically required, since my boat is under 26 feet and outboard-powered, but we have one anyway.

Ventilators. These are required on inboard boats, and on boats that keep their gas in lockers. I keep my tank on deck, in the outboard well.

Whistle/Bell. The Coast Guard requires Class 1 boats (of which your trailer sailer is an example) to carry a device capable of making an "efficient sound signal." We have a Freon horn in a dedicated cockpit holder. Plus, we have whistles tied to each of the life jackets. Whistles are not commonly considered "efficient sound signal devices" by the Coast Guard, but they are useful in man-overboard situations. If you sail in areas with fog, a ship's bell becomes an important signaling device, rather than a shippy nautical decoration.

Visual Distress Signals. Although sailboats under 26 feet are exempt from this, Coast Guard regulations require that you carry a bright orange flag with a black square and disc for daytime use. It's a good idea to have a distress flag aboard no matter what size boat you sail. Smoke signals can also be used, but they have to be currently dated. At night, the visual distress requirement can be satisfied with a flashlight capable of signaling SOS, but we carry flares as well. A new development in nighttime distress signaling is a small handheld laser. These look much like inexpensive laser pointers, but rather than a single dot of light (which is very difficult to aim) these new lasers produce a vertical band of laser light that can be pointed towards a tar-get at a very great distance.

Surprisingly, this is all that is required by the Coast Guard, but the list is far from complete. Good anchors are ex-tremely important. You should have at least one anchor, preferably two, with plenty of line. Don't scrimp on anchors . . . get good ones, properly sized for your boat. There have been whole books devoted to the subject of anchors and anchoring, and anchor manufac-turers have published tables of recom-mended sizes for different sailboats. For example, Simpson Lawrence rec-ommends an 11-lb Claw anchor for boats up to 23 feet, and Danforth says that their 5-lb Danforth Hi-Tensile anchors with 1,000 lbs of "holding power," are good for boats 24 to 31 feet in length. It's good to have several dif-ferent types of anchors aboard, because different bottom conditions have a great impact on holding power. Again, *do not buy cheap anchors* . . . those lit-tle PVC-coated "mushroom anchors" do little more than sink your line to the bottom, and will not hold a sailboat in position in anything but a dead calm. With most anchors, a length of chain is required to help them set properly. Correctly-sized rodes (the line connect-ing the anchor to the boat) are a neces-sity, as well as strong cleats to make the rodes fast to the boat. An oversized "storm anchor" is often carried on many boats, but I'm of the opinion that a correctly-sized, high-quality anchor (such as a genuine Danforth, CQR, Delta, Bruce, or Claw) is better than an oversize, inexpensive copy.

Oars. Some kind of alternate propul-sion, like an oar, is a real blessing to have if—or perhaps I should say when—your engine croaks in a flat calm. I'm still trying to come up with some way to row my boat: the oars need to be quite

A NOTE ON HORNS . . .

You should always know exactly where your horn is stowed and be able to retrieve it quickly. I learned this the hard way. Once, when I was a liveaboard, I was onboard my boat during a very large storm. I was anchored upriver, along with several other boats. When the windspeed increased to over 80 knots, most of the boats upwind of me began to drag anchor, including a large powerboat who was trying to use his engines to keep headed bow-to-wind. At one point during the night, the captain was getting tired, and began to drift straight for my still anchored boat. He was very close. I vividly remember tearing through the cockpit locker, tossing lines, winch handles, and other junk out of the way, frantically looking for my freon horn. I finally found it and blew a long blast . . . the power boat was within fifteen feet of me. The moral of the story is that you won't need your horn every day, but when you do need it, you'll likely need it immediately. In my case, it very nearly cost me my boat. So give it a dedicated spot to live and make sure it's ready when you need it. ∎

Various used boat electronics, all purchased on eBay. Some were brand-new, some needed repairs, but most were pretty good buys. If you're all thumbs when it comes to electronics, though, you're better off buying new or doing without.

long to work. Sculling is a possibility, though I haven't yet mastered the fine points of this art form. (See Appendix 2 for a discussion on how to build your own oars.)

Tie-Downs. One of the other things that you'll need to do when commissioning is figure out ways to secure all this stuff that you're bringing aboard. I had a couple of early sails where everything ended up on the floor, since my boat will heel past 40 degrees relatively easily (at about 18 knots of wind). Lightweight items are rather easy to secure with small or medium-size bungee cords and

stainless eyes. Larger items, such as the water tank and battery, required larger cords and eyes. Figuring out the best place to put things, and the best way to secure them, will definitely require some trial and error.

Electronic Equipment for Small Boats

As I neared the completion of my boat, I began to consider adding a few electronic extras. These things aren't essential—yachtsmen got along fine without them for years—but they were things I wanted to have, mostly just for fun. They added cost and complexity to my boat, to be sure. But

WHAT'S DSC?

It's short for "digital selective calling," and the hope is that it will revolutionize the way rescue operations are handled. DSC uses a digital signal to transmit specific information, such as:

- The caller's unique ID number (similar to a telephone number)
- The ID number of the unit being called, for example all Coast Guard stations
- The caller's location and the time of the call
- The requested working frequency
- The priority and type of the call (collision, crew overboard, fire, sinking, piracy, and so on)

Ideally, DSC will eliminate much of the human factor in monitoring radio frequencies for distress calls. There are still plenty of bugs in the system. For example, the Coast Guard is being plagued with large numbers of relayed DSC distress signals, 99 percent of which are accidental transmissions. It remains to be seen if DSC will mature into a vastly improved communications system as promised. ■

---

a few trade-offs can keep the downside of electronic equipment to a minimum.

VHF Radio

I installed a VHF radio and a depth sounder. New radios can get quite expensive, so I figured I'd save some money by buying a used one on eBay. I did save money—my VHF cost only $56. But it didn't come with any power connections or antenna. So I bought an antenna on eBay for $45, but then I had to figure out where to install it. It was too big for the masthead, so I bought an antenna mount and put it on the stern quarter. It will fold down, and it's in the way only part of the time. But I should have bought a handheld. They can be purchased brand-new for $130 or so, require no installation, and their range on the lake is more than adequate. As it is, I've had quite a bit of grief installing the radio. It's an old unit that could fail at any time, and I didn't

save that much. To add insult to injury, when I finally got everything powered up, no audio. Everything seems to be working, it appears to transmit, but you can't hear a thing. So here's a case where it's definitely better to buy new if you really want a VHF.

A VHF radio isn't a necessity, but it's nice to have for safety and convenience. Cell-phone coverage is kind of iffy in coastal waters (but this is improving all the time), and cell phones are useless for ship-to-ship communication. (You aren't likely to know the phone number for a tug that's rounding the river with a big tow, nor does he broadcast security information via cell phone.) VHF weather broadcast information is very handy to have aboard, especially with our smaller vessels, where being caught in a storm can make a bigger impression. You no longer need an FCC license to operate a VHF ship station, but you need to know the rules. A good website that outlines VHF operations is at www.boatsafe.com/nauticalknowhow/radio.htm#ch.

Depth Sounder

My depth sounder was another story. The cheapest brand-new unit I could find was $100 on sale, and they're more usually found at about $150. A depth sounder is nice to have, as it can really help with your navigation by following a contour. A grounding isn't nearly the inconvenience with a trailer sailer that it is with a keelboat, but it's good to avoid. I had one on my previous boat, and it was a great comfort to know how deep the water was where I was sailing.

There are two basic types of depth sounders. Older ones of the type most commonly used on sailboats have analog dial readouts. The other type is the old fish-finder-style, which uses a revolving neon bulb on a dial face. These are usually larger than the digital type, but they can give a little more information about the bottom density and obstructions, and they can locate schools of fish. They'd be an excellent choice to use in your dinghy to scout out anchorages.

I bought a used sounder on eBay, but I had a world of trouble with it, so I wouldn't recommend this route. I've learned the hard way that used electronics are often false economy. Newer sounders, and new electronics in general, are more compact, work better, have greater functionality, have more readable displays, and come complete with all the parts and factory support. When it comes to marine VHF radios, only a new unit will get you DSC, which is a very cool new feature (see sidebar).

There is, however, a good, low-tech alternative (or supplement) to an electronic depth sounder.

A Lead Line. While you're out buying stuff, pick up a big fishing sinker and some lightweight cord to make a lead line. Even if you have a depth sounder, there will be a time when you'll need to heave the line—the battery will die, or your sender will get dirty, or you'll just want to verify that there really is only 3 feet of water under you.

Ferenc Maté gives instructions for making a traditional lead line in his book, *The Finely Fitted Yacht.* A traditional lead line has a large, heavy weight, about ½ inch in diameter, and weighing about 5 or 6 pounds. The line is marked with different materials at varying depths, as follows:

2 fathoms	Leather with two ends
3 fathoms	Leather with three ends
5 fathoms	White calico
7 fathoms	Coarse red fabric
10 fathoms	Flat leather with a hole
13 fathoms	Thick blue serge
15 fathoms	White calico
17 fathoms	Coarse red fabric
20 fathoms	Cord with two knots

Normally, I like traditional ways and gear aboard boats, as time-proven designs are often the best, but not this time. The traditional lead line was designed for use aboard sailing ships, and the boats we sail are closer in size to the ship's dinghy. Everything can be much smaller—the line, the weight, and the spaces between the marks. Boat chandleries sell little plastic tags with numbers on them. I'd skip these—they don't last, and they're impossible to read by feel.

Launch day. The boat is rolled out of the drydock it's called home for the last two years and headed for the lake near our house. Don't forget to buy insurance before taking this step!

My lead line is made of ⅛-inch-diameter braided cord. I have knots in the cord every 3 feet. Measured from the bottom of the weight, one knot for 3 feet, two knots for 6 feet, three knots for 9 feet, and a piece of leather at 12 feet (two fathoms). You can even stamp a 12 on the piece of leather to help remind you of the system. From then on, the line follows the traditional system, with the addition of single knots at 4 fathoms and 6 fathoms. My line stops at 40 feet, though I'd use a longer line on a blue-water passage. If you really want to get traditional, bore a shallow hole in the bottom of the sinker. Put a little Crisco in the hole, and you can bring up a small sample of the bottom to help determine what type of

anchor you should use—try that with an electric depth sounder! Yet another method, which may be a little easier, is to use nylon zip ties to mark the depth, though this may be a little harsh on your hands when you're heaving the line.

The Payoff

A few weeks after the initial launch of my boat, a few other MacGregor owners brought their boats to Chattanooga for an inaugural day sail. Six people I hardly knew drove half a day just to help me celebrate. The wind was blowing nicely, and as we heeled to the freshening breeze, I looked up at the sails. That's when I realized that, finally, I was sailing again with my own boat under me. It

(above) Four hours later, and we're in the water. The first time out will definitely be taxing as you try to figure out where everything goes. (right) The first day out, we had very little wind. My 7-year-old son prepares to abandon ship after loudly proclaiming, "This is boring," and, "I can walk faster than this!" Sailing with children requires quite a bit of advance preparation and ready diversions, but that's another book.

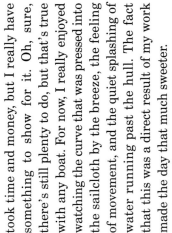

took time and money, but I really have something to show for it. Oh, sure, there's still plenty to do, but that's true with any boat. For now, I really enjoyed watching the curve that was pressed into the sailcloth by the breeze, the feeling of movement, and the quiet splashing of water running past the hull. The fact that this was a direct result of my work made the day that much sweeter.

If you choose to rebuild an old sailboat, and I hope you do, I wish you all the success in the world. May all your bolt holes line up, and may all your epoxy cure without a hitch. Make no mistake: it's a serious commitment of time and money. Don't give up—keep at it. When you get to the point of actually sailing, be sure to savor that moment. Everyone deserves that feeling once in his lifetime.

Fair winds,
Brian Gilbert

A Replacement Rudder

After the first season of sailing the boat, I did a very stupid thing. While hauling the boat for its winter repairs, I removed the rudder at the dock so I wouldn't drag it across the parking lot as I pulled the boat up the ramp. It was late and quite dark, and my little Nissan Frontier could barely pull the boat up the ramp—I thought I may have ruined my transmission—and I busied myself with lowering and stowing the mast. When I launched again in the spring, it dawned on me where I last saw my rudder: lying on the public dock five months ago.

So one of my first jobs that season was to build a new rudder. Fortunately, I had an excellent resource for replacing a rudder blade: my friend Tom Stockwell has written an article about making a MacGregor rudder using a stitch-and-glue boat-building technique. This article can be found at www.geocities.com/thomas_m_stock well/rudder.html.

Tom's article was the starting point for fabricating an entirely new rudder assembly. I built the blade of the rudder mostly as he described, except that the leading edge was reduced from 3 inches forward of the rudder post to 2 inches. In other words, the whole rudder was shifted aft 1 inch. This meant a slight alteration in the plywood core pattern. Tom calls this part a "key." My blade is 40 inches long by 12 inches wide. This may be a touch oversized for a Venture 222, since Tom's design is for a MacGregor 25, but in use, this rudder gave me excellent performance—better than the stock rudder, I think. Rudder area can be an important design parameter on a sailboat. If it's not correct, the boat will not balance well, either constantly trying to point into the wind or run off downwind. Sometimes balance issues can be addressed by shaving an inch or two off the bottom of the blade, or raking the mast, but neither was required on my boat.

But before we go any further, a caveat. Tom has had this design fail on him twice, where the rudder blade twisted and broke at the core. Others have experienced similar failures, but my rudder has worked like a charm. This could be because I sail in relatively protected waters, in usually calm conditions. The point to remember is that this is a relatively experimental design, and if you sail in rough waters it may not be suitable. In fact, as a condition of publishing his design, Tom has asked that I include the following disclaimer:

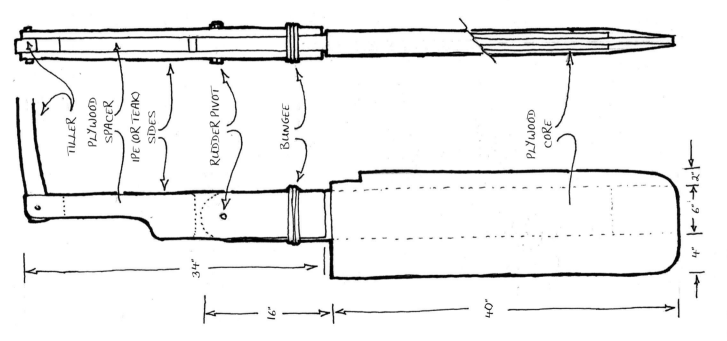

Dimensions for the new rudder.

Notice: By using this design, you are acknowledging that you bear full responsibility for any liability that may be incurred in the use of the resulting rudder. This includes accidental injury, death, or hardship that may result from the use of this rudder. By using these plans, you and your passengers relinquish all legal and financial claims against Thomas M. Stockwell. You acknowledge that should harm or injury result from the construction or use of this design, you will be liable for all damages, including (but not limited to) legal fees, medical fees, hospitalization costs, and so on. Authorized or unauthorized modifications to this design will not alter this agreement. This design is copyrighted by Thomas M. Stockwell, all rights reserved.

Building the rudder blade was a fairly straightforward process, thanks to the help that Tom's article provides. The core, or "key," is cut from a half sheet of ½-inch exterior plywood. Three layers are laminated together to create a 1½-inch-thick core. The keel is glued with a special woodworking glue called Gorilla Glue, which foams and expands as it cures. It's a strong, waterproof, gap-filling adhesive that is very well suited to this application. The core was completed by coating all surfaces with epoxy resin.

The blade was formed by wrapping the core with a piece of ¼-inch plywood. Exterior fir is recommended, though I had to use luan, as it was all that I could find locally. The two halves are secured by nylon zip ties until the glue cures, then the entire thing is coated with epoxy. I took the additional step of laminating the entire surface of the rudder with a layer of fiberglass. The rudder shell is open at the top and bottom of the blade, allowing water to fill the cavity. It results in a lightweight yet neutrally buoyant rudder.

Where I had to be inventive was the upper part of the blade, where the rudder attaches to the transom. The piece I ended up making was designed primarily to accommodate my very last piece of ipe hardwood, which was 5½ inches wide and 54 inches long. The assembly can be thought of as a kind of sandwich—1½ inches of plywood is captured by two ipe sides, which support both the rudder and the tiller, allowing them to pivot. The illustration explains it best.

The kick-up system is simply several wraps of bungee a few inches below the pivot point of the blade. If the pressure against the blade causes it to kick up too easily, it's a simple matter to increase the tension or number of wraps on the bungee cord.

This rudder design has several advantages over the stock MacGregor rudder. The foil shape causes less turbulence through the water as well as decreases the likelihood of stalling in sharp turns. The original rudder was just a slab-sided board with rounded leading and trailing edges, which is a hydrodynamically poor performer. It's lighter than the stock rudder as well. The hollow construction might make it more fragile, but I don't really think so. The entire thing is coated with epoxy resin inside and out, and the outside is laminated with fiberglass. It's as likely to pull the pintles and gudgeons from the transom before the blade itself breaks.

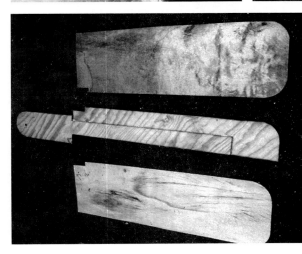

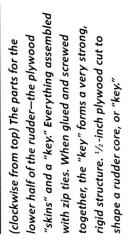

(clockwise from top) The parts for the lower half of the rudder—the plywood "skins" and a "key." Everything assembled with zip ties. When glued and screwed together, the "key" forms a very strong, rigid structure. ½-inch plywood cut to shape a rudder core, or "key."

One mistake that I made on my first blade was trusting a salesperson who said this was exterior plywood—it wasn't, and the trailing edge of my rudder began to separate after about a month in the water. It was fairly easy to correct with a little more Gorilla Glue and some epoxy and glass over the trailing edge. When I built my second rudder, I used ¼-inch BCX plywood. This one is heavier and should hold up better than luan plywood.

Making Oars

Since your sails are your primary method of propulsion, the outboard motor must be considered alternative propulsion. So let's talk about an alternative to the alternative. Even when motors aboard sailboats were uncommon, the prudent mariner usually carried some form of backup in the form of a pair of sweeps (fairly large oars) or a single sculling oar. The lower freeboard and narrower beam found on older boats made rowing more practical, but this still works on most trailer sailers to a degree. Larry and Lin Pardey routinely sculled their engineless *Seraffyn* (at over 24 feet long and 10,600 pounds displacement), so I imagine that I could do the same on my 22-footer.

The easiest way to get a pair of oars is to trot down to the chandlery and buy some, but where's the pleasure in that? You can go to the Internet, search for "making oars," and come up with a few pages of instruction that would produce some nice oars with a few afternoons of work, though in general these oars are lighter than their commercial counterparts. I think the design that I like best came from an early issue of *Yachting* magazine, via Bill Wallace at www.boat-links.com/CheapOars/. For the shaft, he uses closet poles available from any building-supply yard, and then he adds plywood blades. A few coats of epoxy and glass makes a nice, strong blade. Here are the materials you'll need:

- Two 8-foot closet poles, 1½ inches in diameter (larger if you can find it)
- Two panels of ¾-inch exterior plywood, 24 by 8 inches
- Your favorite waterproof glue
- A few flathead wood screws
- Fiberglass and epoxy resin (Optional)

I started with the handles by cutting a small groove, about 1/8" deep, by rotating the pole.

Oar materials from a builders' supply.

And cut at an angle. This was done freehand on a table saw, but a band saw would be better.

At the blade end, cut a 1/4" notch.

The handles are sanded at the groove but left round at the outboard end. First, sand opposite sides, and then make it square. Then sand the corners to make the handle octagonal.

The handles are shaped with an angle grinder fitted with a coarse sanding disk, affectionately known as a "boat eater."

The handle is finished by hand-sanding with 180-grit sandpaper. When the sharp corners are softened, this makes a very comfortable handle. Be careful with the boat eater; over-sanding will weaken the loom at the handle. It requires a light touch.

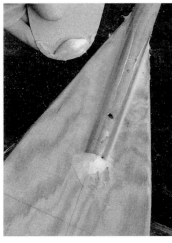

... out comes the epoxy. I made fillets at all the joints.

The blades were shaped with a table saw and angle grinder, then drilled with a 1" hole.

Then I laminated both sides of the blade with epoxy and fiberglass cloth.

After rounding the edges and sanding, the blades were glued and screwed to the poles. Actually, you could paint them and use them at this point for light-duty oars, but I never can leave well enough alone, so ...

The blades are cut from two pieces of ¼" plywood stacked together. Actual size and shape is up to you. My blades were about 8" x 24". The concave shape allows you to use the oar to fend off pilings, while the notch allows you to pick up lines in the water. This is not as strong as, or a substitute for, a proper boat hook, but the unique blade shape is useful nonetheless.

When properly laminated, the glass cloth should have a transparent quality. Avoid bubbles.

The fiberglass is easy to wet out with a chip brush.

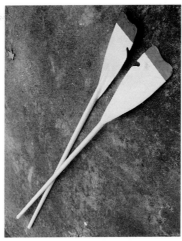

Here are the new oars with a coat of paint. Epoxy is very sensitive to UV rays, so paint any epoxy that will see a lot of sunlight.

The laminated edges were cleaved up with a sanding disk.

Trailer Restoration

Trailers are often neglected and in need of restoration, just like your boat. Your trailer is very important; a failure of the trailer can often bring about disastrous results. For this reason, I recommend seeking professional help if you're at all uncomfortable with working on things mechanical.

On the other hand, trailers are relatively simple affairs, especially those for smaller boats. After doing all this boatwork, there's no reason why most folks can't tackle a trailer as well. Parts are readily available, and all but the most rotten and rusted trailer can be re-welded and repaired.

There are several areas of trailer restoration that you should consider. These are:

- Bearing lubrication and replacement
- Axles
- Tires
- Lights
- Coupling and safety chains
- Bunks and chocks
- Winches and straps

Bearings

Let's start with the most commonly needed job: bearing lube and replacement. If your trailer has been sitting around for a few years, the grease in the bearings is probably dried out and no longer able to do its job. The bearings will need re-greasing. The only proper way to do this is to take apart the hub, clean off the old grease with solvent, massage new grease into the bearings by hand, and reassemble the hub. It's messy and somewhat intimidating the first time you do it, but you'll learn quickly. The job can be completed in an afternoon. Doing it right allows you to visually inspect the bearings and races. When the trailer is jacked and the wheels are free to turn, give them a spin. You shouldn't feel any roughness or play in the bearings, but they should turn smoothly. If they don't, plan on replacing the bearings. This is not a good place to take chances, as a bearing failure often causes the wheel to become separated from the trailer. The faster the bearing is going at the time, and the heavier its load, the more likely it is to fail. Thus, bearings most often fail when going down the freeway at high speed, with the boat on the trailer—an exciting event, to say the least.

Standard bearing sets often come with installation instructions, and you should follow these carefully. Bearings must be installed with both inner and outer races. The outer races are press-fit into the hubs. Of course, my old factory MacGregor trailer (from American Trailer Company, one of several vendors MacGregor used over the years) didn't use anything close to a standard bearing set. After removing a bad bearing, I set off in search of a new one. I tried three trailer supply dealers and one auto parts store, and I finally determined that an industrial bearing house was my only chance. One supplier had the bearing, a second had the race, but my hubs are unusual. One of the races seats against an internal snap ring. Of course, I didn't know this, and I broke the snap ring while driving out the bearing with a punch. The bearing dealer suggested another supplier that I'd never heard of for odd-size snap rings, and they had one. (It cost so little that the dealers gave it to me, no charge. A little embarrassing, but I finally had the parts I needed.)

The procedure for replacing bearings varies slightly with different hubs, but it's generally similar for all trailers. Block and jack the trailer so that the wheels are off the ground, and the trailer is stable. First, remove the grease cap. It's usually a friction fit and can be pried off with a flat-bladed screwdriver. Under the grease cap you'll find a large castle nut that is secured with a cotter pin. Remove the pin, then unscrew the large nut. This is the big nut that essentially keeps the wheel on the axle, via the bearings. It shouldn't be on too terribly tight; you may be able to free it with a large crescent wrench, but the preferred method is with a correctly-sized socket and a breaker bar. It helps keep things straight if you place the parts in a row, on a clean rag, in the order that they're removed. Once the nut is off, there should be a large washer, followed by the front bearing and cage. (There are two sets of bearings on each wheel—a front or outer set, which is on the outside edge of the wheel, and a rear or inner set, which is on the inside. Each set of bearings has a pair of races which the bearings roll against: an inner and an outer race. The inner race contacts the axle, while the outer race is press-fit into the hub.) You can get these off easily by pulling on the entire wheel, which should leave the inner bearing, washer, and grease seal (it looks like a cup-shaped washer with a rubber inner edge) on the hub. The grease seals are usually a friction fit and can be a little tight if they're correctly sized. I destroyed mine in the process of removing them, but the new ones went on and off by hand.

Getting the bearings and inner races off is relatively easy, but removing the outer races is more difficult because they need to be driven out with a punch or mild

The hubs after sandblasting. Take care not to get sand on the bearing surfaces.

steel bar. If you have one, use a brass punch. Before you can remove the races, you'll need to remove the grease seal. Carefully pry it out, then remove the rear bearing set. You should be left with a hub containing two races. Clean the old grease out of the inside of the hub and take a good look. If one of your bearing races rests against a snap ring, like mine did, then you should be able to see it. Be careful when you drive out the race, making sure you're driving the race and not the ring; otherwise you'll break it and spend an afternoon driving around town searching for a replacement.

Drive the bearings out carefully, so that you don't damage the hubs. Place the hubs flat on a piece of wood, and go around the edge of the race, driving a little at a time. Mine required some aggressive negotiation to get them out, but don't get too rough with them if you can help it. Of course, a hydraulic press is the professional way to get these out, but if you have one of those, you probably know more about bearings and press fitting than I do, and you can skip this section altogether.

Once the races are out, clean the surfaces of the hubs with fine emery paper to remove any scratches or corrosion. This will make installing the races slightly easier. The new races can be carefully driven in, or they can be pressed in by a trailer shop.

Once the outer races are installed in the hubs, the rest is easy. Just reverse the removal procedure, but stop when you get to the rollers—you need to grease them before you install them. Place a blob of grease in the palm of your hands, and then massage the grease into the rollers with your palms. It's messy, but it works. Complete the installation, greasing everything as you go. (Since you'll get grease all over your hands, you'll grease everything as you go whether you want to or not.)

After the bearings are greased and in the hubs, there's one additional step to take, and that's preloading the bearings. This is a fancy name for the way you should tighten the large castle nut in the center of the axle. Tighten the nut with your hands, as tight as you can. Then add another one-quarter turn with a wrench. Spin the hub a few times to distribute the grease. Then loosen the nut, retighten as far as you can by hand only, and then reinsert a new cotter pin. Replace the grease cap, and you're done.

Axles

If you have bad bearings and your hubs look nasty, you can replace the entire axle as a unit. For about $180, you can buy a new axle that allows you to grease the bearings without disassembly. These are available from Champion Trailer Supply, and probably other suppliers as well (see Appendix 7). They have a grease fitting in the center of the axle, and you just give each wheel a couple of pumps with a grease gun every now and again. It seems like it would be a very nice upgrade. Had I known of the difficulty I would experience finding replacement bearings for my trailer, I'd have done this at the outset and avoided the hassles.

Tires

There are two schools of thought about trailer tires. One school says that you must use special trailer tires, and the other says that, basically, any old tire will work as long as it isn't rotten. In truth, regular car tires will work, but they aren't the best choice if you need new tires on your trailer. Car tires, especially radials, are designed to maintain maximum traction on the road when you're turning, swerving, accelerating, or braking. To do this, they use flexible sidewalls. Trailer tires need rigid sidewalls to prevent sway. The only time they need traction is when braking, if the trailer is equipped with brakes. So the upshot is that while regular car tires will work in a pinch, real trailer tires are better. If you decide to pinch pennies and use car tires, be sure you have sufficient tongue weight to prevent sway (usually about ten percent of gross trailer weight). Hook up the boat, and put all the heavy stuff forward. Actually, this is good practice no matter what type of tires you use.

Lights

When I purchased my boat, there were no lights at all on my trailer. Lights are often neglected and nonfunctional on used trailers, but they're simple to fix. Most auto-supply stores carry submersible trailer light sets for around $25, but there are a few things you can do to extend the life of these systems.

One is to mount them up high. (Check your state trailering laws before you do this; there may be specific requirements about exactly where lights must be located on a trailer.) I bolted a pair of bent steel fence posts to the aft end of my trailer to make a pair of uprights. They serve two purposes: they make it easier to center the boat on the trailer when pulling the boat from the water, and they're a handy place to mount the lights where they won't be submerged. They also increase visibility a bit, because your brake lights will be at the eye level of drivers behind you.

The second improvement is to change the wiring a bit. Most manufacturers of aftermarket trailer lights will tell you to bolt the ground wire of your trailer to the trailer frame, which is standard practice in a car. A car isn't regularly submerged in water, though, so these ground connections in cars are rarely a problem. Many intermittent failures on boat trailers, however, can be traced to bad grounds, due to corrosion. Go to the hardware store and buy 50 feet of green wire and run a separate, isolated ground from your trailer electrical connector to each light. Solder and heat-shrink all connections, just as you did onboard. And support your wires well with a nylon cable clamp every 18 inches or so. This should greatly increase the reliability of your trailer lights.

Coupling and Safety Chains

Take a very close look at the trailer coupling. A little rust is OK, but make sure the bolt that secures the ball cap screws down tightly without binding. Chasing the threads with a tap and die set might clean things up enough to get a secure connection, but if it doesn't, you'll need a new coupling welded on. In other words, if you attach the trailer and it clunks when you tug up and down on the trailer tongue, there are problems. You shouldn't take it on the road until everything is tight and secure. Check your connection by pulling up and down as hard as you can once the trailer is connected to your hitch. If your ball cap screw is too loose, you'll be able to pop the trailer off the ball. This is especially bad at 55 mph.

Also examine the safety chains. Contrary to popular belief, these aren't cosmetic. They're your last chance if the hitch or coupling fails. If they have those silly little S-hooks on the end, go to the hardware store and buy a pair of screw-type chain couplers. Look over every link for thin spots. If the safety chains have been dragged, one of the links will probably be ground down to the thickness of a wire. Don't trust it. Buy a few feet of new chain and shackle it on. It's a simple and inexpensive fix that might prevent you from killing someone. And while you're at it, get a short length of chain and two screw shackles for the bow eye. Chain the bow eye to the trailer frame so that if the winch pawl fails, the boat will stay attached to the trailer.

Trailer Bunks and Chocks

The bunks are those long, carpeted wooden boards that support the bottom of your hull on the trailer. Better trailers have roller bunks, which can make launching and retrieving easier. Board bunks often come pre-rotted for you, so you can replace them with a trip to a building-supply house and a carpet store. I don't like using pressure-treated lumber because of the high amount of toxins involved, but it may be your only practical choice here unless you can get a pair of untreated yellow pine boards. (In my area of the country, the only commonly available yellow pine goes straight to the pressure-treating plant. Yellow pine is more rot-resistant than white pine, which is the other common choice.) You'll also need a long strip of indoor-outdoor carpet to cover the bunks. Using one continuous piece is better than patching together several scraps. There's some debate about carpet for your bunks; one camp says that you must use special "bunk carpet," which is available at marine chandleries. Your other option is plain-old indoor-outdoor carpet. I'm not sure that the difference is great enough to warrant any loss of sleep on your part. There is also a spray product called Liquid Rollers, which is a friction-reducing compound that's sprayed on the carpet. It's supposed to make launching and loading easier. I haven't tried it, but you might look into it if you plan on doing a lot of highway sailing. Your bunks might last longer with a coat of linseed oil applied before installing the carpet.

The chocks are big gray rubber blocks. My trailer has two—one for the bow and one for the keel. They can be replaced for about $7 each from a trailer-supply store.

Winches and Straps

If you have a questionable winch, it's usually best to replace the whole thing rather than attempting a fix. These are most commonly bolted on, which makes the job easier. If someone has welded on the winch, you'll have to grind the welds away.

When I bought my boat, I was amazed to find the original owner hadn't bothered to use a tie-down strap. The only thing keeping the boat on the trailer was gravity and hope. Ratcheting tie-down straps aren't too expensive, though they are prone to rusting and need replacing every few years. Don't leave home without them.

My trailer after sandblasting and painting. I'm still not entirely satisfied with the way the "uprights" turned out. Since I plan to replace those, they weren't painted. It still needs new carpet, a new winch, and new tires.

Sandblasting and Painting

Just about all that's left to do to your trailer is sandblast and paint. You can try a chemical rust treatment that's phosphoric-acid-based, but sandblasting does a better job of preparing a surface. I'd use a cold-galvanizing primer and an epoxy-based top-coat. I've heard of people spraying trailers with pickup bedliner material, but I can't imagine that would work too well.

Costs to Restore a 1972 MacGregor Venture 222

This list illustrates the range and scale of expenses that might be typical to restore a sailboat that is in poor condition, as mine was. This isn't meant to imply that this is what you should expect to spend if you decide to restore a boat. Instead, it's a real-world expense study for bringing a boat from poor to good condition. These costs reflect prices between 2000 and 2002.

A word about the sources: whenever I made a purchase from an unusual source, like eBay, I note that. Other boat chandlery items were mail-ordered, from suppliers like BoatU.S. or Defender. Items with no source noted were purchased locally, most from a good hardware store. Generally, if prices are close, I like to support smaller businesses rather than mega-retailers.

Used boat, purchase price	$500.00
Hose, TSP, sandpaper, miscellaneous cleaning	$34.86
Tarp	$8.00
Acetone, epoxy, masking tape	$7.50
Stainless fasteners	$3.62
DuraPly	$56.00
VHF radio (eBay)	$51.00
Sanding discs	$4.10
New halyard line (eBay)	$26.00
Epoxy and paint (from BoatU.S.)	$170.61
Fiberglass cloth	$19.00
Stainless screws, hose barbs, dado blade bushing	$14.63
Sanding disks	$4.10
Epoxy and polyurethane paint	$6.96
New battery switch (eBay)	$16.00
New Merriman genoa lead blocks, pair (eBay)	$40.00
Harken traveler car (eBay)	$47.37
VHF antenna (eBay)	$34.50
Anchor, portapotti, navigation lights, electric panel, mainsheet blocks (Defender)	$372.34

Outboard motor (eBay)	$450.00
Sandblaster and router bits (Harbor Freight)	$140.00
Fiberglass cloth (eBay)	$16.00
1½ gallon epoxy resin microballoons and pumps (from Raka)	$95.00
Sand for sandblaster	$7.00
Stainless bar, ¼ inch by 3 inches by 4 feet, rebuild winch support	$28.00
Bootop paint, through-hull fitting (not used), miscellaneous hardware (BoatU.S.)	$7.41
Gray Plexiglas sheet, 36 by 36 by ⁹⁄₁₆ inches	$27.06
Polyester resin for keel (should have used epoxy)	$25.00
Green upholstery fabric (eBay)	$30.46
SS fasteners, silicone for ports, gudgeons, motor-mount bolts	$30.00
SS fasteners, keel cable roller bolt, ports	$10.81
SS fasteners, ports	$2.81
SS fasteners, port washers, companionway slides	$9.10
SS fasteners, wire, varnish	$31.00
Stovetop cappuccino machine	$35.00
Propane camp stove	$19.00
Quart interior polyurethane paint	$8.65
Cable ties for wiring	$4.31
SS fasteners, winch mount bolts, electrical mounting screws	$7.35
SS fasteners, rudder bolts	$1.88
New compass ($27), two sections of T-track ($40) (from Minneys Yacht Surplus)	$67.00
SS bolts, wire (50 feet 12 gauge stranded), T-track mounting bolts, cable clamps	$19.75
SS fasteners (for forward mooring cleats, chainplate covers, wire for compass)	$11.25
SS fasteners, mast repair, install navigational lights	$6.91
New wire for masthead navigational light	$11.36
Hitch ball, plug for mast wiring	$12.52
Canvas for sun covers	$14.00
SS fasteners (traveler and halyard cleats) varnish	$8.65
SS for traveler mount	$4.35
Shroud adjuster, ⁵⁄₃₂ wire, thimbles (JSI)	$31.96
Grabrails, traveler track, fuel tank, clevis pins and rings, swage sleeves, battens and caps, T-track caps (Defender)	$190.17
Portable garage cover	$205.00

Battery, fuel line, fuel stabilizer	$36.00
Trim molding, interior halogen light, sheet foam for flotation	$45.00
PL 259 connector for VHF antenna	$4.86
SS Fasteners, heat-shrink tubing	$4.71
Dodger (eBay)	$76.00
Cushion foam	$123.00
Two packs brass grommets (for cushion cover lacing)	$5.72
Fuel connector (from BoatU.S.)	$18.71
Eyelets, 4200 caulk	$14.00
Snap fasteners, SSHardware	$15.10
Deck bimini hinges, fuel connector, long SS bolts for cam cleats	$26.00
SS fasteners	$1.70
New mainsail (from Sails East)	$320.63
Trailer lights, hardware	$31.00
Inner bearing and grease seal	$7.00
Ground wire, nuts for trailer	$5.00
Outer bearing and race	$9.00
Fenders, fire extinguisher, two storage bins	$39.00
Property taxes and registration fee	$42.75
Horn	$13.00
Screen for bags	$7.00
Epoxy, snaps for canvas	$20.00
SS boarding ladder (eBay)	$40.00
SS fasteners	$5.00
Depth sounder and speedo sending units, new (eBay)	$12.00
Depth sounder (eBay)	$18.00
Depth sounder and speed/log (eBay) (depth sounder doesn't work)	$18.00
New trailer winch, strap, and safety tie-down	$40.77

Subtotals

These subtotals aren't perfectly accurate, as I didn't break out every expense item. If a large order from BoatU.S. was mostly rigging related, it got recorded under rigging, though there may have been a fuel tank and a pint of paint in there. I believe that I captured most of the expenses, and the total should be pretty close. My expenses are ongoing—the line between a boat restoration expense and a boat ownership expense is blurry—and I'm always coming up with new little projects, but for the purposes of this book, I stopped recording the restoration expenses when we took our inaugural sail.

Boat (including delivery)	$500.00
Consumables (acetone, sandpaper, and so on)	$65.56
Tools (sandblaster, router bits; already had many tools)	$140.00
Cover (portable garage)	$205.00
Stainless steel hardware (bolts, screws, miscellaneous)	$242.62
Cushions and upholstery (includes canvas items used on deck, like grabrail covers and sailbags)	$214.18
Epoxy, paint, and fiberglass	$348.63
Electrical	$270.03
Wood and raw materials	$128.06
Rigging	$399.50
Sails (main, new, and 150, used)	$470.63
Motor (new tank and hoses)	$504.71
Taxes and registration	$42.75
Trailer	$105.29
Commissioning, miscellaneous interior equipment	$355.34
Miscellaneous deck equipment (dodger, swim ladder)	$116.00
Total	**$3,787.67**

Restoration Log

All jobs were rounded to the nearest 15 minutes. Some were undoubtedly not recorded, but I tried to keep a record of nearly everything I did.

April 2000

4/22/00 Purchased boat for $500 and delivered to the house. Pressure-washed it first, but it didn't help much.

4/23/00 Took out cabinet behind portapotti first. Then removed partial bulkhead. Wood screws along the top, 3¾-inch bolts along the bottom. Bolts were mild steel (rusty), need replacing with stainless. Removed seat bottom, secured with screws. (1 hour, 30 minutes)

4/25/00 Toe rails on foredeck were removed. Interior trim strips along the hull/deck joint were removed, secured with 1-inch SS oval-head wood screws. Table was secured by two ms bolts with wing nuts. Discovered winch support was very rotten after removing covering panel. Discarded a bunch of rotten stuff from winch area. (2 hours)

May 2000

5/2/00 Built sawhorses for the mast. (1 hour 30 minutes)

5/3/00 Finished sawhorses, stored mast level and off the ground. Removed four rusty carriage bolts that held outboard motor mount, need to be replaced with stainless. (1 hour)

5/7/00 Spent approximately 45 minutes removing the last two panels in the cabin. All the locker dividers will need limber holes at the bottoms. I then spent approximately 2 hours pressure-washing and draining the interior. I was hoping that this would leave the interior surface in paintable condition, but I don't think so. Needs sandblasting. (45 minutes)

5/11/00 Removed both portlights, took off some hardware and stripped some topsides paint. I still need to fabricate some kind of hood to control the dust from the angle grinder. (45 minutes) Found a source for Duraply: Brainerd Lumber, $27.50 per sheet.

5/14/00   Tried a razor scraper—it worked pretty well on the areas where the paint was still strong. Used it to peel the graphics and found it worked well on hull paint as well. Took off about 5 feet of paint from the stern quarter, took maybe 20 or 30 minutes, but made a big mess. (30 minutes)

5/15/00   Scraped hull today. Used a taped dropcloth to catch the chips, worked fairly well. (1 hour 30 minutes)

5/16/00   Worked a good bit on the boat today. Did a good bit of scraping, the starboard side is three-fourths finished. The yellow topcoat comes off fairly quickly, but the green beneath is more difficult to remove. Been collecting a lot of paint chips as I go. Also drilled some limber holes today—difficult to do but badly needed. Discovered quite a bit of stagnant water underneath one of the quarter berth lockers—a sealed area with no access. (4 hours)

5/17/00   Got a bit more done than I'd expected today. Got about one-third of the starboard side sanded and ready to paint! It looks good with all the crud off. I'm discovering a few areas of uncured or under-cured gelcoat—the scraper digs in and won't remove paint. Even paint remover doesn't seem to help. (1 hour)

5/18/00   Today I moved canvas and plastic forward and scraped the bow. Paint seems easier to remove—both layers—possibly because the bow is in the sunshine and was warmer. The green layer seemed more chalky; perhaps that's why it was easier to remove. At any rate, the starboard side is almost entirely scraped—there are still some spots and bits around the deadlight and waterline. (1 hour 30 minutes)

5/22/00   Did some scraping. Was more careful on this side (to scrape as much as possible off, and not leave any bits for the sander), since I've discovered scraping is a lot quicker than sanding. Got almost half of the port side scraped, and much of the starboard side sanded, but plenty remains along the sheer and bottom. (2 hours 30 minutes)

June 2000

6/6/00   Got a bunch of work done today, after a week off. No progress last week due to Nancy and Terry staying with us. Worked maybe 3 or 4 hours in 20-minute bits. Got almost all the hardware removed from the aft end, finished scraping transom, and scraped the stubborn spots on the starboard side. Started some sanding. Managed to remove the two deadlights in the forward section of the hull. Hope I can get them back in. (4 hours)

6/23/00   Haven't been keeping up with the log—lots of scraping, but only 30 minutes to 1 hour at a time. I'd guess I've put in 12 to 14 hours total over the past two weeks. The hull is almost ready to paint—100 percent scraped and only a little more to sand. I'm digging out some old repairs that were done with Bondo, refilling and repairing with epoxy. I've filled in all the holes from the toe rail, and still have some tough-to-get-at hardware to remove.

6/24/00   Worked a solid 4 hours today and got a bunch done. Trimmed down the anchor well, ground and sanded flush with the deck. Sealed it with epoxy, but it needs a layer of glass. Installed a drain (today is the first day I actually installed something) and an outlet for it. Now the anchor well won't collect stagnant water. Removed more hardware. All that remains are a few small hasps and hatch hinges. Did a little scraping, sanding, and vacuuming. (4 hours)

6/28/00   Worked about half an hour today (so far . . . might be able to sneak in a few more minutes later) and about half an hour yesterday. Finished sanding the hall, which is a bit of a milestone. Still have quite a bit left to do on the topside. I've been looking for a cheap VHF radio on eBay. I'm tracking a few auctions, but the boat equipment fund is pretty empty until I can sell off antiques, etc. I'm discovering that a stamp collection is practically worthless. (1 hour)

July 2000

7/5/00   Worked about two hours over the past week scraping the topsides. It's about three-fourths finished. Only some difficult spots remain. Quite a bit left to scrape in the cockpit, though. (2 hours)

7/11/00   Purchased two sheets of DuraPly, $53 total, to replace some settee tops and other rotted plywood parts. Sanded under sheerline a bit, hope to do some epoxying as well.

7/21/00   Scraped the cockpit. Scrape, sand, vacuum, scrape, sand, vacuum. . . . Still plenty to do. (1 hour 15 minutes)

7/23/00   Built a pair of stands to lift the boat in prep for keel removal. (2 hours)

7/25/00   Found some concrete blocks at a fill dirt site and brought them home to block up the hull. Going to wait until after Kyle's party to lift the boat.

August 2000

8/14/00   Worked about an hour on Sunday caulking the rubrail. Realized too late that I'd used the wrong stuff. I'd intended to use a polyurethane roof sealant, which behaves just like 5200. But I used a polyurethane construction adhesive (tube packaging is nearly identical), which doesn't appear as strong. It also reacted somehow and left lots of bubbles in the finished caulk line. It'll be OK on the underside, but I'm going to redo the top. Also worked an hour on Friday. Mixed up a little epoxy filler, and it worked extremely well. Filled the hull and most of the deck using a very small amount of epoxy. Sanded and primed part of the hull—a little more epoxy on the stern, then prime and sand the port side, and it'll be ready to paint. (2 hours)

Tonight I jacked up the hull and started removing the keel. This is a nerve-wracking, stressful job. I think it's pretty secure—I've got concrete blocks wedged in everywhere—but I'm still nervous. The boat seems awfully high up in the air. The keel, of course, is jammed in the slot. I've dropped it down about halfway, but I've run out of time for tonight. I'll have to finish tomorrow, then get the thing back on the trailer!

8/15/00   The keel is out and the boat is back on the trailer. It started to fall sideways as it was being lowered, but I managed to wedge some 2×4s against the hull before it went over. I need to come up with a better way to lift the boat when it's time to replace the keel—this way is much too hairy! (2 hours 30 minutes)

8/25/00   Sanded the port side of the interior and rolled on two coats of Kilz. Lots of work, but it looks good. Also started some preliminary work on the bridge deck repair. (5 hours)

September 2000

9/1/00   A bit more sanding. (1 hour 30 minutes)

9/2/00   Cut out rot and replaced with a new larger access hatch (locker lid).

9/6/00   Finished berth supports/side rails for the access hatch. Also expanded another access hatch just aft of the first (port side), and cut out a third with the jigsaw. Need to make DuraPly tops for these two; already finished a top for the first one.

9/14/00   Installed hose barbs to drain outboard well. Everything finished except installing hose and clamps (should have used larger size and more downward slope to the hose). (1 hour)

9/16/00   Blew off the AAC BG chapter meet (Appalachian Area Chapter blacksmithing group) and stayed home. Painted the hull instead. Looks beautiful, though not quite as nice as a spray job. Should have primed and sanded the entire hull, as there are lots of pinholes showing, especially on the port side. Still, a vast improvement! Used about ½ quart of paint. (2 hours)

9/17/00   Sanded and masked rubrail area, recaulked upper rubrail, did a little sanding and scraping of the deck area. Caulked the upper rubrail with the correct polyurethane roof patch. It seems to behave a lot like 5200, but it costs $3 per tube instead of $20. It's messy (just like 5200) so I masked the area off with masking tape.

It came out looking pretty good. (Note: Two years later it shows no sign of deteriorating or aging whatsoever.) (2 hours)

9/19/00 Spent maybe 1½ hours priming the topside. Most of this will get sanded off.

9/20/00 Did 1½ hours filling some holes with epoxy, miscellaneous cleaning, and trying to remove some T-track from the cockpit sole. Scraped the cockpit some.

9/21/00 Scraping. (45 minutes)

9/22/00 Scraping. (1 hour)

9/23/00 Last three days were spent on miscellaneous sanding and scraping, removed T-track in cockpit, removed stray bolts from pop-top, removed forward hatch. (45 minutes)

9/30/00 Relaminated and reinforced bridge deck. Repaired keel winch mounting holes and did some sanding, scraping, and cleaning in the cockpit. Almost ready for primer. Still need to get anchor well hatch relaminated and repaired. (2 hours, 30 minutes)

October 2000

10/1/00 Sanded and scraped the cockpit a little, then primed the deck and put a second coat of primer on the house. (2 hours, 30 minutes)

10/2/00 Sanded topsides primer. (30 minutes)

10/3/00 Built anchor well hatch, still needs to be laminated. (1 hour) Cut and mounted hatch stop rails into anchor well. (1 hour) Installed epoxy filler on hatch and anchor well. (1 hour) (Note: Made a mistake here. The new anchor well hatch is flush with the deck and designed to drain water directly overboard. As a result, the area for the anchor is a bit smaller, and the hatch wouldn't close with the anchor in place. Had to grind away a little of the hatch rails and re-epoxy so that it would close. It just barely fits. These boats are too small for forward anchor wells.)

10/4/00 Laminated anchor well with epoxy. (1 hour)

10/20/00 Prepared flotation (1 hour), incomplete. Repaired crack in the deck. (2 hours over several days)

10/30/00 Painted some of the topsides. (1 hour 30 minutes)

November 2000

11/28/00 Cleaned and sanded interior, primed V-berth. (2 hours)

December 2000

12/15/00 Ground and sanded headliner above V-berth. (2 hours 30 minutes)

12/29/00 Built heavy sawhorses for keel. (Note: Ended up using these for other jobs. The keel was so heavy, I was scared of what might happen if it got away from me and fell. I used a shipping pallet to elevate the keel a few inches off the ground and worked on my knees. That approach worked OK.) (1 hour 30 minutes)

12/30/00 Primed inside of locker, cut and painted cleat stock for locker lids. (1 hour 30 minutes)

12/31/00 Built locker hatch, installed remaining cleat stock. (2 hours 15 minutes)

January 2001

1/1/01 Primed three locker hatches, began restoration of tiller. (2 hours 45 minutes)

1/2/01 Sanded, oiled, and reglued tiller. (1 hour)

1/3/01 Removed starboard quarter berth top and sanded. (30 minutes)

1/5/01 Sanded and primed quarter berth tops. (1 hour)

1/6/01 Played hooky from work, rebuilt/repaired keel lockdown bolt hole. (1 hour 30 minutes)

Recoated and installed starboard berth tops and added flotation foam. (2 hours 30 minutes)

Miscellaneous cleaning and vacuuming.

1/7/01 Broken wrist!

1/28/01 Stripped keel. (1 hour)

1/29/01 Sanded and primed lazzarette hatch. (1 hour)

1/30/01 Painted hatch border, forward hatch, and lazarette hatch. (30 minutes)

February 2001

2/2/01 Cut trailing edge of keel from ¼ by 2 inches (mild steel) bar, still needs to be ground and shaped. (30 minutes)

Primed top and bottom of companionway hatch. (30 minutes)

2/4/01 Welded, wire-brushed, and treated both sides of keel with phosphoric acid compound (Must for Rust, from auto-parts store). (1 hour 30 minutes)

Painted companionway hatch and forward hatch. (1 hour)

Laminated two teak strips from tomato stakes to use as hatch slides, added two layers of extra glass to the chainplate area. (30 minutes)

Need to buy a ¾-inch drill bit to enlarge keel pivot. Also need more epoxy resin and fiberglass.

2/6/01 Drilled keel, second coat on hatches. (2 hours)

2/7/01 Painted nonskid area of hatches. Looks nice! (30 minutes)

2/8/01 Took old motor to Greyhound, picked up new one. Looks OK. (30 minutes)

Second coat of nonskid on hatches, removed pop-top hardware. (30 minutes)

Removed additional hardware and lifted pop-top from boat. (30 minutes)

2/11/01   Worked about 1½ hours. Sanded pop-top and filled all old bolt holes. Several were worn or drilled oversize. It appears that much of the core is damp, though the top isn't soft or spongy anywhere. Dug out old foredeck repair and filled with glass and epoxy. Much of the foredeck core is damp and delaminating.

2/12/01   Raining. Milled some of the strips for the hatch slides. Whatever wood this is, it's really pretty and should work well. (30 minutes)

2/16/01   Moved pop-top under carport. One week of solid rain. Scraped underside over last couple of days. (Approximately 2 hours total)

2/19/01   Finished scraping, epoxied holes, and primed the pop-top. (1 hour 30 minutes)

2/20/01   Epoxy fillet outboard edge of quarterberth. (2 hours)

2/21/01   Filled deck crack with epoxy.

2/23/01   Primed and painted underside of pop-top. (1 hour) Poured in a small amount of epoxy into deck crack. Attempted to glass underside of deck, but 3.1-oz. glass is too stiff.

2/25/01   Beautiful weather after a rainy Saturday night. Bailed, primed, and painted cockpit. Epoxied foredeck crack, wiped down most of the bottom to prep for bottom job. (3 hours 30 minutes)

2/26/01   Painted nonskid on most of deck and cockpit. Best results when compound was mixed with paint and then brushed on. (2 hours) Painted pop-top nonskid. (1 hour)

March 2001

3/11/01   Disassembled and cleaned keel winch. Still needs sandblasting. Pawl spring is broken and needs replacing, and friction washers could be replaced as well. Reassembled finger-tight with grease.

3/23/01   Finally received and assembled sandblaster yesterday. Borrowed larger compressor from Jack. Spent about an hour hooking up a "test blast" today. Initial impression is that it'll work, though it will be slow due to an undersized compressor. I'm guessing that the big one puts out maybe 6 cfm. I may try to T the small compressor into the line and use both at once to reduce the recycle time.

3/24/01   Sandblasted. (2 hours 30 minutes) It worked, but not as well as I'd hoped. Spent a lot of time unclogging the nozzle. Eventually had to dump an entire pot, screen the sand, and reload. Then even two compressors in tandem couldn't keep up. I may vacuum and blast the interior one more time to be sure the loose stuff is up, then sand a bit before painting and reinforcing. Several joints need fillets and glass; epoxy is ordered and on the way.

3/25/01   Primed the interior, quarter berth overhead and port side, brush.
          (2 hours)

3/26/01   Sandblasted and primed one side of keel. (1 hour 30 minutes)
          Flipped and prepped other side for sandblasting. Raka order ar-
          rived today—have plenty of epoxy now. Spent 1 hour applying
          epoxy compound to foredeck underside, using up the last of the
          Interlux—maybe one batch left. Still want to reinforce center-
          board trunk/hull joint and fix crack at transom motor mount pad,
          plus miscellaneous reinforcing here and there.

3/27/01   Finished up sandblasting today, keel is clean and primed on both
          sides. Did some sanding on the interior along joints to be "fillet-
          ted." Decided not to blast interior again. I'll spot sand the interior
          as needed. (2 hours)
          Did some additional grinding and epoxy work after Kyle went to
          bed. Used four batches of the new epoxy; the pumps make it easy
          to use. Made a radius board from stiff cardboard, it was just about
          right. The fillets look good, though I made one batch too thin—it
          sagged a bunch and will need another application. I also finished
          the chainplate reinforcing. (2 hours)

3/28/01   Applied several batches of epoxy, maybe 8 or 10. Fillet and fiber-
          glass both sides of centerboard trunk, applied second batch to
          transom. Still need to do the overhead, but there's plenty of epoxy.
          (2 hours)

April 2001

4/2/01   Epoxy work. (1 hour 30 minutes)

4/3/01   Epoxy work. (1 hour 30 minutes)

4/4/01   Epoxy work, deadlight filler pieces, and painted Kilz on starboard
          aft and overhead surfaces. (3 hours 30 minutes)

4/9/01   Epoxy- and fiberglass-laminated the filler piece in the deadlight.
          Seems to be working well, though I'll have some sanding to do to
          clean up the edges. Possibly will need a filler coat to smooth out
          the fiberglass weave. I wish I had made a paper pattern of the
          cutout before I wet out the plywood—would have made the job
          easier and neater. Used slow hardener, still very liquid after 2½ hrs
          at 74 degrees. (1 hour)
          Painted foredeck trim, but shouldn't have—moisture from the
          evening's dew caused the paint to dry flat. Not a real problem,
          since this needs a second coat anyway, but need to do the finish
          coat under cover (falling gunk from trees) early in the day.

4/10/01   Bought polyester resin for keel today, plus plexi for deadlights. Cut
          and fit quarter berth top foot section, but didn't install yet. Put
          filler on keel. (2 hours 30 minutes, not including travel time)

4/19/01 Laminate keel and turn over. (1 hour 30 minutes)

4/20/01 Primed interior. (2 hours)

4/25/01 Painted interior overhead and berth tops. Overhead with polyurethane, berth tops with latex. (3 hours)
Rolled the rest of the hull with oil-based polyurethane. I wish now that I had used oil-based poly throughout. I still have a lot of brushwork to do in the corners, top, and so on, but it looks vastly improved. Now I'll need to scramble to get the interior watertight.

4/28/01 Cut and drill starboard deadlights. (2 hours)

May 2001

5/4/01 Epoxy on keel. (30 minutes)

5/6/01 Paint under cockpit. (1 hour)

5/9/01 Installed one deadlight (to install the second will require the help of a second person) and one hull deadlight. Completed interior epoxy fairing in the bow section. Replaced one of the bolts in the motor mount. (5 hours)

5/27/01 Painted bottom. (1 hour 30 minutes)

5/28/01 Installed one cabin deadlight and one hull deadlight. Painted half the boottop; will need a second coat. Raining, so I didn't do the other side. (4 hours)

June 2001

6/9/01 Cut openings in panel to accommodate electrical panel, coated with epoxy. Also coated and sanded backing board for rudder pintles. Sanded the keel. Attempted to stand the keel up so I could work on the leading edge, but couldn't do it. I need to fabricate some metal levers to work on it. (1 hour 30 minutes)

6/10/01 Installed rudder pintles. (30 minutes)

6/11/01 Cut out and assembled replacement hatch cover (covers battery box). (2 hours)

6/12/01 Painted quarter berth overhead, second coat on electrical covering panel. (30 minutes)

6/13/01 Replaced bolts in outboard bracket, removed and oiled mount. This is the sort of thing that makes this job difficult—over an hour of work and over $12 just to replace four bolts! (1 hour)

6/15/01 Fabricated negative bus bar (cut from ⅛-inch-thick copper plate, drilled and tapped holes). Installed and labeled electrical panel, started making jumpers.

6/17/01 Father's Day. Painted replacement panel and lids—it's ready to install. Installed bow eye. Reinstalled all pop-top hardware. Finished fabricating companionway hatch slides, but one broke along the glue line. Repaired it. Varnished tiller and half bulkhead. (7 hours)

6/18/01   Sanded and varnished vertical hatch slides. (30 minutes)
Cut and painted second seat panel (the seat bottom). Installed first seat panel (the one over the battery). (45 minutes)
Painted seat panel and installed reinforcing cleat. One coat on the bottom, three coats on the top. Installed forward deadlight. Trimmed and varnished companionway slides. (2 hours)

6/19/01   Replaced forward seat bottom, replaced forward seat back (half bulkhead), except for the three bolts I can't find—I'll need new ones. Cleaned and oiled the head shelf unit, but I can't secure it until I replace the three bolts. Installed vertical companionway slides and located the electrical bulkhead. The outboard block of wood that secures the lower edge of the frame wasn't glued in the correct position—I'll have to add a new one later. (1 hour)
Pressure-washed the interior cushions. If they dry, they should be clean enough for a photograph. The two biggest jobs remaining are the wiring and the keel. (1 hour)

6/25/01   Glassed keel, used epoxy. (30 minutes)
Epoxied cleats for electrical bulkhead installation. (30 minutes)

6/28/01   Began dinette table rebuild. (1 hour)
Cut and bent stainless for winch bracket at shop. (1 hour)

6/29/01   More work on table. Cutout panels and glued up half. Discovered dresser tops were made of particleboard (!), but used them anyway. (2 hours)
Electrical work. Installed panel, secured bulkhead, installed battery switch. (1 hour 30 minutes)

6/30/01   Trimmed tabletop and glued up other sides. (30 minutes)
Finished winch bracket, welded on bottom section and buffed. Should've buffed all parts before welding. (45 minutes)
Prepared backing pads for the winch bracket, put another coat of varnish on tiller, installed keel cable rub bolt, painted interior, foredeck overhead, painted exterior foredeck trim. (3 hours)
Set up winch bracket—bolts too short, another trip to Ace for more stainless. (1 hour)
Installed and caulked winch bracket. (1 hour)
Sanded and stained dinette table. (3 hours)

July 2001

7/1/01   Epoxy-coated table. (1 hour)
Installed winch. It's out of position—entire thing needs to be ripped out and redone. (30 minutes)
Painted foredeck nonskid. (30 minutes)
Completed glasswork on keel, still need to sand and final coat. (2 hours 30 minutes)

Installed backstay chainplate and vent cover. (1 hour)

Fabricated forward navigational light bracket and installed, cleaned up a bit. (2 hours)

7/2/01   Installed anchor well hatch and hinges. (30 minutes)

Disassembled rudder. Ground off loose fiberglass on lower half; most is solid, some dry rot in both halves. Should be a fairly straightforward repair. (30 minutes)

7/3/01   Laminated rudder. (30 minutes)

7/4/01   Extra epoxy coat on rudder, finished keel and painted. (1 hour)

7/6/01   Discovered some delamination on opposite side of the rudder, so I ground this out. Laminated rudder, painted keel trailing edge. (45 minutes)

7/7/01   Reinstalled hardware on upper half of rudder, added another coat to bottom half. (1 hour)

Installed one mooring cleat. (1 hour)

Installed second mooring cleat. (15 minutes)

Installed both winches. (1 hour)

7/8/01   Ran wiring to bow light, started to secure with cable clamps. Need some shorter screws. Primer-coated bottom half of rudder. (1 hour)

7/14/01   Relocated winch. (1 hour)

7/15/01   Raised hull and blocked to work on keel. (1 hour)

7/16/01   Raised hull higher. Prepped for keel installation. (2 hours)

7/19/01   Rigged blocks and lines, dragged keel into position under boat. (30 minutes)

Connected keel cable and attempted to raise it into the slot. Going to need to elevate forward end. Jacked the boat a bit more, and made side supports to clamp to trailer. (1 hour)

7/20/01   More slow progress—it's almost there. The back end is all the way in, and I'm working on the forward end. A floor jack would be a huge help. (30 minutes)

7/21/01   Keel is installed, and boat is back on trailer! (4 hours)

7/29/01   Wiring installation. (30 minutes)

7/30/01   Installed aft quarter berth deadlight. It would be easier to fill them in. (1 hour)

August 2001

8/2/01   Installed hatch slides. (1 hour 30 minutes)

8/8/01   Worked on riser pads for turning blocks. Completed and oiled one, epoxied the second. I'll finish tomorrow. (1 hour)

8/9/01   Trimmed, oiled, and varnished both pads. Compass and T-track came in today. Perhaps can do some installing tomorrow. (45 minutes)

8/10/01   Varnished pads, need another coat on the end grain. Fabricated a mounting block for the compass from ipe. Looks very nice varnished. It's heavier than teak. Installed both sections of T-track. (2 hours)

8/11/01   Fabricated stainless standoff for stern light. (1 hour 30 minutes)

8/13/01   Wired and installed stern light. (30 minutes)

8/14/01   Installed fairing blocks. (1 hour)

8/15/01   Secured wiring for stern light. (30 minutes)

8/21/01   Installed final deadlight, still needs to be tightened. (1 hour) Wiring. (1 hour)

8/22/01   Installed outboard bracket. (30 minutes)
Installed the compass—looks shippy! (30 minutes)

8/25/01   Installed chainplate covering plates. (30 minutes)

8/26/01   Wired switch panel—it's pretty much complete. Still need to wire mast, attach plug, and mount VHF radio. Then all that will remain is buying a battery and hooking up the supply. (1 hour)

8/29/01   Installed forward hatch hinges—incomplete. (30 minutes)

September 2001

9/1/01   Filled holes in mast cap with epoxy, tapped mounting holes for machine screws (were pop rivets previously), fabricated mast steaming light bracket, drilled anchor light mounting holes. (1 hour 30 minutes)

9/2/01   Installed and tested anchor light and steaming light. (They work!) Still need to repair spreader and spreader bracket, and shorten the spreader bolt. Anchor light at masthead is especially vulnerable, I'd like to fabricate an SS bail to protect it. (1 hour 30 minutes)

9/5/01   Shortened spreader by ¾ inch and drilled heated and straightened spreader bracket. Epoxy filled holes on the mast, used JB Weld to fix. (1 hour)
Finished the mast, brought it back outside, shortened and reattached bolts responsible for chewing up inboard spreader end. Installed new hitch ball on the truck. Installed and assembled spreaders, but ran out of time for raising the mast. Did a little bit of wiring on the supply mains. (2 hours)

9/6/01   Wired in supply mains and battery switch. Navigational lights work. (30 minutes)

9/11/01   Miscellaneous small jobs. Completed hinge installation of forward hatch. (1 hour 30 minutes).
Stopped to watch the news when the World Trade Center was attacked.

9/12/01   Rolled the boat out and washed it. Worked some on a mast crutch to help raise and lower the mast. It got dark before I could do so, so I rolled it back in this morning. Ordered about $230 worth of stuff from Defender and SailNet. Should go a long way toward finishing. (1 hour 30 minutes)

9/13/01   Waxed hull and topsides. Didn't get to deck and cockpit. (30 minutes)

9/14/01   Finished cutting and trimming the companionway hatch boards. Gave the backsides and edges a coat of epoxy. (1 hour)

9/15/01   Sanded and fitted the hatch boards, gave them a coat of white undercoater. Order from Defender came in Saturday. (30 minutes)

9/16/01   Painted the hatchboards, sanded and varnished grabrails. (1 hour)

9/17/01   Second coat of varnish on grabrails, bought stainless to mount traveler and halyard cleats. (30 minutes)

9/26/01   Cut wood for traveler mounting and glued. (1 hour 30 minutes)

9/27/01   Varnished grabrails and tiller. (30 minutes)

9/28/01   Removed clamps from traveler base, trimmed and sanded. (30 minutes)
Installed grabrails and forward mooring cleats. (2 hours 30 minutes)

9/29/01   Added riser blocks to traveler base, painted backside of hatchboards. (1 hour)

9/30/01   Drilled and varnished traveler base. (1 hour)

October 2001

10/1/01   Put a third coat of varnish on the traveler base—only took ten minutes. Still waiting on backorder from Defender. Bought stainless hardware to mount traveler. (10 minutes)

10/2/01   Drilled the mounting holes in the traveler base and mounted the hardware. System seems to work great. (1 hour)

10/3/01   Got a lot accomplished today, worked about an hour in the afternoon and an hour in the evening. Attached the VHF antenna, mounted the traveler, secured the port halyard turning block, and soldered the electrical connections for the mast. Bought a battery and fuel line today. (2 hours)

10/8/01   Installed, stained, and varnished three out of four pieces of interior trim (over the last three days). (2 hours 30 minutes)

10/21/01 Raised the mast and rigged the boat, cut lines to length. (3 hours)

10/22/01 Lowered mast and backed the boat under the cover. (1 hour 30 minutes)

December 2001

12/18/01 Installed overhead light. (30 minutes)

12/27/01 Fabricated and installed bridge deck covering board. (1 hour)

12/29/01 Second coat of varnish on interior trim piece, began fabricating portapotti floor. (1 hour)

12/30/01 Attached companionway bracing. (30 minutes)

January 2002

1/1/02   New Year's resolution was to get the boat in the water before the year's end. (2 minutes)

1/10/02   Built and fit a cardboard mock-up of the new galley cabinet. (1 hour)

1/12/02   Finished portapotti floor, cut out galley cabinet, installed flex trim. (2 hours)

1/28/02   Stitched V-berth cushion, complete except for grommets and lacing. (4 hours, 30 minutes)

1/30/02   Stitched some of 2nd V-berth cushion, 7 yards of fabric left (out of 11). Five more cushions to go. (30 minutes)

1/31/02   Second V-berth cushion. (1 hour 30 minutes)

February 2002

2/3/02   Ironed and pinned the lacing strip. (30 minutes)
Finished second V-berth cushion, including laces. (1 hour 30 minutes)

2/6/02   Installed eyes into first cushion. (1 hour)

2/9/02   Worked on galley. Trimmed edges on table saw. (2 hours)

2/10/02   Sewing aft dinette seat cushion. (1 hour 30 minutes)

2/11/01   Aft dinette cushion. (1 hour 30 minutes)

2/16/02   Miscellaneous small jobs. Installed T-track ends, port halyard cleat, lazarette hinges. (1 hour 30 minutes)

2/18/02   Worked on galley cabinet, definitely taking shape now. (1 hour 30 minutes)

2/19/02   Cut and fit shelf bottoms in galley cabinet. (30 minutes)

March 2002

3/28/02   Assembled galley cabinet. (1 hour)
Sewing cushions. (1 hour 30 minutes)
Primed and painted galley cabinet. (1 hour)

April 2002

4/1/02   Cut L-shaped trim pieces from ipe for galley cabinet. (30 minutes)
Finished and epoxied four out of nine trim pieces on galley cabinet. (1 hour)
Finished another cushion cover—sewed in last panel, hand-stitched corners, installed eyelets, and laced it up. Only three more to go! (1 hour 30 minutes)

4/2/02   Trimmed, finished, and epoxied three more trim strips into galley. (1 hour 15 minutes)

4/11/02   Cleaned the boat (and killed the ants onboard). (30 minutes)

4/12/02   Cut access lid in half (where new galley cabinet covers) and finished the edges. Connected interior halogen light. (1 hour 30 minutes)

4/15/02   Bolted in galley cabinet. (1 hour 30 minutes)

4/16/02   Washed sail cover, cut new cushion foam, started hand-stitching sail cover. Also started sewing port forward seat cushion. It looks like I may just barely have enough fabric—maybe. (1 hour 30 minutes)

4/18/02   Restitched sail cover. Needs new zipper. (1 hour 30 minutes)

4/19/02   Worked on another cushion cover.

4/24/02   Completed cushion cover. (1 hour 30 minutes)

4/25/02   Hand-stitched corners and set grommets, finished lacing cushion. (1 hour 30 minutes)

4/29/02   Finished a pair of canvas handrail covers—turned out nice. (1 hour 30 minutes)

May 2002

5/13/02   Sewed a compass cover. (1 hour 30 minutes)

5/15/02   Started stainless sheet winch brackets. (1 hour)

5/19/02   Cut out and bent winch bracket, installed starboard winch. (1 hour 15 minutes)

5/20/02   Filled old winch mounting holes, cut riser pads for cam cleats. (1 hour)

June 2002

6/20/02   Fabricated second winch bracket and drill hull to mount, finished mounting winches. (1 hour 30 minutes)

6/23/02   Installed mast raising U-bolts, began bimini installation. (2 hours)

6/24/02   Installed bimini snaps. (2 hours)

6/25/02   Installed new lower shrouds. (1 hour 30 minutes)

6/28/02   Remove starboard trailer wheel, drive-out bearings, chase threads. (1 hour 30 minutes)

July 2002

7/2/02   Remove port trailer hub. (30 minutes)

7/4/02   Sandblasted and painted hubs. (30 minutes)

7/5/02   Reinstall port hub and tire. (30 minutes)

7/6/02   Installed flotation, caulked bimini mounts. (3 hours)
Completed bimini installation, installed bridge deck cover. (1 hour)
Began sewing settee cushions. (3 hours 30 minutes)

7/7/02   Finished sewing settee cushion—still needs eyelets. (2 hours 30 minutes)
Added snaps and eyelets to cushion. (2 hours 30 minutes)
Cleaned up, installed new seat cushions. (1 hour)
Finished eyelets and lacing on starboard aft seat bottoms. (1 hour)

7/9/02   Bent upright poles for trailer lights. (1 hour)

7/11/02   Finished upright poles, made U-bolts. (1 hours 30 minutes)
7/12/02   Installed poles and lights. Still need to wire. (30 minutes)
7/14/02   Completed trailer wiring, secured battery supply wires inside.
          (2 hours)
7/17/02   Installed new bearing, installed hub and tire on trailer. (1 hour)
7/19/02   Installed wiring harness on truck. (30 minutes)
          Tested outboard. (It works!) (30 minutes)
7/31/02   Sewed five net storage bags. (2 hours over several days)

August 2002

8/23/02   Fabricated and installed boarding ladder. (5 hours)
8/30/02   Installed padeyes to secure cooler, fire extinguisher bracket.
          (30 minutes)
8/31/02   Fixed anchor well, attached latch. (30 minutes)

September 2002

9/3/02   Loaded boat, launched, and motored to the new dock. (5 hours)

Time Summary to Date

Interior preparation	12 hours
Interior painting	16 hours
Exterior preparation	66 hours
Exterior painting	30 hours
Interior repairs (includes rewiring)	92 hours
Exterior repairs (includes re-rigging)	98 hours
Keel repairs	22 hours
Upholstery and canvas	33 hours
Trailer repairs (not including sandblasting and painting)	8 hours
Other miscellaneous work	15 hours
Total hours	**392 hours**

Note: There's always more to do. Remember, these times are approximate. Your results will certainly vary.

A Boat Restoration Photo Album

This is the complete photographic record of the restoration process of my boat. Many of the photos have been used in the text. I took a ton of pictures over the two years that I restored my boat—some may be useful for filling in gaps in the text, but the redundant ones are provided for continuity.

A look into the cockpit after the resurrection from the woods.

The port berth after some demolition. This is where the galley cabinet will eventually go.

The head area. Believe it or not, this is after a preliminary cleaning.

An evening photo after a day of removing and throwing away rotten stuff.

Another look at the boat in its new home.

The original anchor well was, in a word, ugly. It was basically a triangular wooden box fiberglassed into the foredeck.

Repairs here started by cutting the box flush with the deck. Instead of trying to keep the water out, which is pretty much impossible, the hatch will be designed to "leak" and drain overboard.

After cutting and grinding.

Installing cleats to the sides of the well. These boards pressed the cleat to the back while the epoxy cured.

The sides were easier to clamp.

Glassing the cleats. A coat of epoxy was brushed on, and then the glass was gently pressed into place.

Wetting out the glass is easier with a disposable chip bush. I used these by the case.

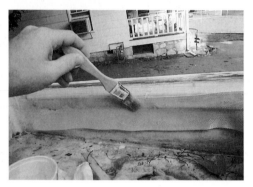

Wetting the glass. Getting it to stay in place took a little practice.

Finishing up the lamination.

The corners were especially tricky to laminate. The stiff glass doesn't like to be forced around corners.

A look at the finished cleats.

Another view of the cleats.

Marking the crown of the deck. This board will be used to curve the hatch.

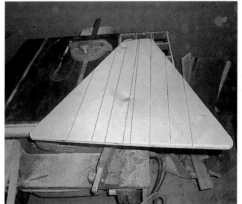

Some shallow saw cuts made the hatch more flexible.

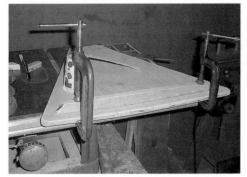

With the curved board installed, the hatch curves to match the deck.

The laminated anchor well hatch before painting.

Finished and in place, this is a much better-looking solution.

Another view of the anchor well and hatch. A 22-footer is really too small for this type of feature, as the resulting space is too small to hold anything of use.

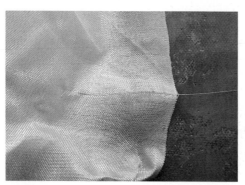

Here's a tip: when you need to cut a strip of fiberglass, pull out a single strand and cut along the resulting line.

Repairing the bridge deck. The keel winch bolts had pulled through. Small pieces of glass were epoxied on.

Next, two full layers were added.

The layers were saturated with epoxy.

After laminating, the new bridge deck is fairly strong. It will be further strengthened from below.

Repairing deck cracks. Polyester had failed, and water entered the deck. I dug out rotten plywood.

The crack was flooded with acetone and warmed with a lamp.

Fiberglass was stuffed into the groove, and epoxy was poured in. It took three layers to fill.

The keel trunk and lockdown area were damaged, so I filled it with compound . . .

. . . and then glassed over the bolt holes. Everything is stronger now.

A look at the transom joints, which were filleted and glassed. You can see the new motor well drains, too.

The companionway hatch after removal and cleaning.

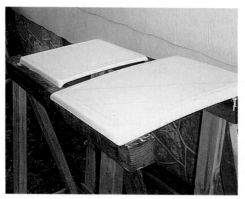

The forward hatch and after hatch being primed.

The completed hatches. It helps to paint these first to get a feel for the paint.

Tomato stakes of tropical hardwood. These are probably ipe (Brazilian walnut) or Brazilian cherry.

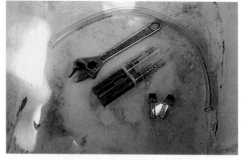

A cockpit drain installation kit. The key is the brass pipe nipples, available in hardware stores. These are actually too small; larger (at least ½") ones would drain faster and be less likely to clog.

A look at a pipe nipple from below.
It's bedded in epoxy and screwed in place.

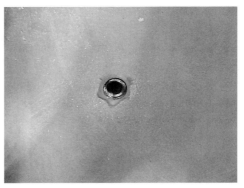

The same fitting from above, before sanding
smooth.

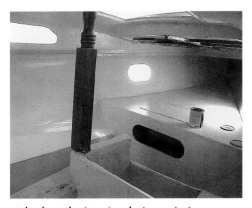

A look at the interior during painting..

A look at the inside. This is where the galley
was.

And this is where the dinette goes.
The panels for the seats were rotten
and replaced with new DuraPly.

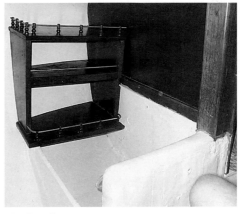

The head area.

More progress on the interior. Much of the interior has been replaced.

These are the parts for the dinette table. I thought that the tops were solid hardwood.

The table was pieced together using epoxy and contrasting hardwood.

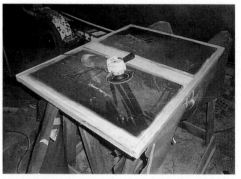

The trim hardwood was rough-sanded with the grinder, and then hand-sanded smooth. The angle grinder turned out to be a much-used tool.

After finishing, the cherry tops and ash edges didn't contrast as much as I'd hoped, but it still looks much better. The entire thing is sealed with epoxy.

Beginning to tackle the rudder. The lower half was fiberglassed using polyester and staples, which gave it a much tighter bond than plain resin. Still, some areas were lifting and rot was starting beneath, so these areas were peeled and ground back to solid wood.

Both halves of the rudder with a coat of epoxy resin.

Installing the hardware on the rudder. The stainless pintles were corroding the aluminum cheek plates, so I added a layer of tape between the two to insulate them.

New rudder with the hardware installed. The finish is varnish over epoxy—we'll see how it holds up.

I just had to see how it looked in place.

On to another project, a mini swim platform. It's barely big enough for your feet and mainly serves as a strong attachment point for the ladder.

The mini platform assembled.

Here's what it looks like installed. The finish is just a few coats of linseed oil, another experiment to see how this wood holds up.

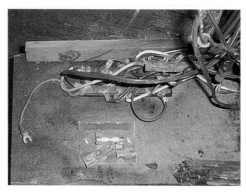

What's left of the electrical "system," which was woefully inadequate when brand-new.

After a few years, a few owners, and a generous helping of neglect, this is an obvious case for redesign and replacement.

New mast lights by AquaSignal. These earned high marks from Practical Sailor, and so far work quite well.

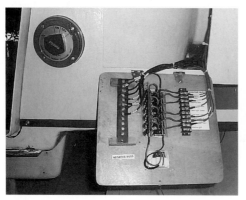

The new electrical panel opened for servicing.

Tracing the registration numbers. I printed them out on the computer and cut them out.

The paper was used as a pattern to trace the letters onto the hull with a permanent marker.

The resulting outline was painted in using topsides enamel and an artist's brush.

Launch day. Once we made it to its new home, we had to see what it looked like with the sails up.

And before you knew it, we were off sailing, even though the wind was pretty much non-existent.

We managed a little sailing but mostly drifted about.

Several other MacGregor owners came up to help me celebrate the launching of my boat. One of the fringe benefits of sailing is the wonderful people you meet.

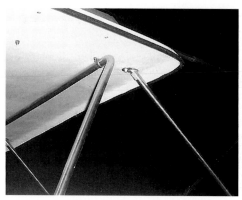

Some Mac owners have e-mailed me about the pop-top supports and how they attach to the boat. Here's a look.

My boat came with a second set of pop-top poles that were shorter than the stock poles, at about 24 inches. Notice the rust under the paint.

My new boat at the summer mooring.

Well worth it: a good-looking, well-found boat. You can do it, too!

Restoration Resources

Internet Resources

The Internet can be an incredibly useful source of information for sailboat restorers, but there are a few downsides. The most important is its volatility and changeable nature. I almost hate to give URLs, because it's certain that many links will be inactive by the time you read this. When you do come across a dead link, search for the Web page title in one of the search engines, since pages are often moved rather than deleted. You'll often find newer and possibly better pages that way as well. Also, take Internet information with a grain of salt. Information published by individuals on the Internet can often be highly opinionated and, in some cases, incorrect.

Web Pages

Here are a few for starters:

- http://www.access.gpo.gov/nara/cfr/waisidx_99/33cfr183_99.html (USCG mandatory requirements for electrical systems)
- http://www.bluesea.com/abyc.htm (electrical and wiring information)
- http://www.boats.com/content/default_detail.jsp?contentid=1326
- http://boatbuilding.com/content/rot.html ("Chemotherapy for Rot" by Dave Carnell) http://www.boatbuilding.com/ (more boatbuilding resources)
- http://www.boatforsale.org/value/ (*Boat For Sale* magazine's list of boat prices)
- http://www.boatsafe.com/nauticalknowhow/radio.htm#ch (VHF radio tips for boaters)
- http://www.boattraderonline.com/newadsearch.html (Boat Trader On-Line classified listings)
- http://www.bookfinder.com/ (the source for out-of-print sailing books)
- http://www.bucvalu.com/ (BUC boat values online)
- http://www.glen-l.com/wood-plywood/bb-chap5.html. (Boatbuilding with Plywood by Glen-L Marine)
- http://www.goodoldboat.com/ (*Good Old Boat* magazine for sailboat owners)
- http://home.clara.net/gmatkin/design.htm (boat design resources)
- http://isbn.nu (out-of-print book source)
- http://www.iSealife.com/ (general cruising site)

- http://www.macgregor-boats.com/ (MacGregor boats)
- http://www.MacGregorOwners.com/index.htm (MacGregor boats)
- http://members.cox.net/sholley1/electric.htm (using a trolling motor as a sailboat auxiliary)
- http://www.nadaguides.com/MarineHome.aspx? (click on "Boats" for NADA values)
- http://www.nauticaltrader.net/index.html (used and surplus boat parts)
- http://www.oldmercs.com/basics.html/ Read "Digging In: Some Tips on Evaluating and Fixing Up and Old Merc"
- http://www.paracay.com/ (online nautical bookstore)
- http://www.practical-sailor.com (*Practical Sailor Magazine* online)
- http://www.sailboatlistings.com/cgi-bin/saildata/db.cgi (more classified ads)
- http://www.sailingtexas.com/ (lots of boats for sale—free ads, inexpensive boats)
- http://www.sailrite.com
- http://www.simplicityboats.com/index.html (building simple boats)
- http://www.woodenboat.com/ (*WoodenBoat* Magazine's website)
- http://www.yachtworld.com/boats/index.html.en (YachtWorld.com's classified listings)

Suppliers

This listing isn't meant to be any kind of endorsement of a particular company, nor should it be considered a complete or definitive list. For example, there are many, many more sail lofts besides Sails East, but I mention that particular loft in the text because I've ordered from them and they gave me good service. I've ordered from many, but not all of these suppliers.

Tools

- Harbor Freight, www.harborfreight.com, (805) 388-2000
- Enco Tool, www.use-enco.com, (800) USE-ENCO
- Wholesale Tool, www.wttool.com, (800) 521-3420
- Northern Tool and Hydraulics, www.northerntool.com, (800) 221-0516

Trailer Parts

- Champion Trailer, www.championtrailers.com, (800) 229-6690

Marine Supplies

- BoatU.S. (Boat Owners Association of the United States), www.BoatUS.com, (800) 395-2628
- Defender, www.defenderus.com, (800) 628-8225
- Jamestown Distributors, www.jamestowndistributors.com, (800) 423-0030
- JSI/SailNet, www.jsisail.com, www.sailnet.com, (800) 234-3220
- Raka, Inc. (epoxies and boatbuilding supplies), www.raka.com, (772) 489-4070

- Rigging Only, www.riggingonly.com, (504) 992-0434, e-mail: sail@riggingonly.com
- SailRite, www.sailrite.com, (800) 348-2769, e-mail: sailrite@sailrite.com
- Sails East, www.sailseast.com, (718) 478-0025
- West Marine, www.westmarine.com, (800) BOATING

Bibliography

Note: A number of very good books listed below are out-of-print. To buy them, try an internet used book service . . . two that I use are http://www.bookfinder.com and http://isbn.nu.

Boat Restoration and Upgrading

Butler, Paul, and Myra Butler. *Fine Boat Finishes.* Camden, ME: International Marine, 1992.

Butler, Paul, and Myra Butler. *Upgrading and Repairing your Small Sailboat for Cruising.* Camden, ME: International Marine, 1988.

Casey, Don. *This Old Boat.* Camden, ME: International Marine, 1991.

Maté, Ferenc. *The Finely Fitted Yacht.* New York: W. W. Norton, 2005.

Maté, Ferenc. *From a Bare Hull.* New York: W. W. Norton, 1995.

Spurr, Daniel. *Spurr's Boatbook: Upgrading the Cruising Sailboat*, 2nd ed. Camden, ME: International Marine, 1993.

Fiberglass Work

Hankinson, Ken. *Fiberglass Boatbuilding for Amateurs.* Bellflower, CA: Glen-L Marine Designs, 1982.

Vaitses, Allan. *The Fiberglass Boat Repair Manual.* Camden, ME: International Marine, 1988.

Interior Yacht Joinery

Bingham, Fred. *Boat Joinery and Cabinetmaking Simplified.* Camden, ME: International Marine, 1993.

Naujok, Michael. *Boat Interior Construction.* New York: Sheridan House, 2002.

Spurr, Dan. *Yacht Style: Design and Décor Ideas for Your Boat.* Camden, ME: International Marine, 1997.

Marine Canvaswork, Marlinspike Seamanship

Carr, Lisa. *Practical Boat Canvas Work.* Great Falls, VA: Waterline Books, 1995.

Casey, Don. *Canvaswork and Sail Repair.* Camden, ME: International Marine, 1996.

Grant, Jim. *The Complete Canvasworker's Guide.* Camden, ME: International Marine, 1992.

Lipe, Karen. *The Big Book of Boat Canvas.* Camden, ME: International Marine, 1991.

Rosenow, Frank. *Canvas and Ropecraft for the Practical Boatowner*. New York: Norton & Co, 1987.

Smith, Hervey Garrett. *The Arts of the Sailor*. New York: Van Nostrand, 1953.

Williams, Jeremy H. *Canvas Work*. New York: Sheridan House, 1993.

Marine Electrical Work

Barre, Harold. *Managing 12 Volts*, 2nd ed. Redwood City, CA: Summer Breeze Publishing, 2002.

Beyn, Edgar J. *The 12 Volt Doctor's Practical Handbook*, 5th ed. Annapolis, MD: Spa Creek Instrument Co., 1998.

Calder, Nigel. *Boatowner's Mechanical and Electrical Manual,* 3rd ed. Camden, ME: International Marine, 2005.

Casey, Don. *Sailboat Electrics Simplified*. Camden, ME: International Marine, 1999.

Myatt, John. *Simple Boat Electrics*. London: Fernhurst Books, 1998.

Payne, John. *The Marine Electrical and Electronics Bible*, 2nd ed. New York: Sheridan House, 1998.

Wing, Charlie. *Boatowner's Illustrated Handbook of Wiring*. Camden, ME: International Marine, 1993.

Marine Surveying

Casey, Don. *Inspecting the Aging Sailboat*. Camden, ME: International Marine, 2005.

Mustin, Henry. *Surveying Fiberglass Sailboats*. Camden, ME: International Marine, 1994.

Nicholson, Ian. *Surveying Small Craft*. London: Coles, 1974.

Practical Boat Buying, Volume 1, 6th ed. Riverside, CT: Englander Communications, 2003.

Warren, Nigel. *Metal Corrosion in Boats*. London: Stanford Maritime, 1980.

Outboards

Sherman, Ed. *Outboard Engines: Troubleshooting, Maintenance, and Repair*. Camden, ME: International Marine, 1997.

Sails and Rigging

Marino, Emiliano. *The Sailmaker's Apprentice*. Camden, ME: International Marine, 1994.

Pardey, Lin, and Larry Pardey. *The Capable Cruiser*. New York: Norton, 1987.

Pardey, Lin, and Larry Pardey. *The Cost-Conscious Cruiser*. Arcata, CA: Pardey Books, 1998.

Pardey, Lin, and Larry Pardey. *Cruising in Seraffyn*, rev. ed. Arcata, CA: Pardey Books, 2001.

Pardey, Lin, and Larry Pardey. *Seraffyn's European Adventure*. Arcata, CA: Pardey Books, 1998.

Toss, Brion. *The Complete Rigger's Apprentice*. Camden, ME: International Marine, 1998.

Setting Up Shops
Landis, Scott. *The Workshop Book*. Newtown, CT: Taunton Press, 1998.
The Small Workshop: Best of Fine Woodworking Magazine. Newtown, CT: Taunton Press, n.d.

Woodworking Resources
Bingham, Fred. *Practical Yacht Joinery*. Camden, ME: International Marine, 1993.
Maté, Ferenc. *The Finely Fitted Yacht*. London: Albatross Publishing, 1994.
Saunders, Mike. *Yacht Joinery and Fitting*. Camden, ME: International Marine, 1981.
Spurr, Dan. *Yacht Style*. Camden, ME: International Marine, 1997.

Trailers
Henkel, Steve. *Boat Trailers and Tow Vehicles: A Users Guide*. Camden, ME: International Marine, 1994.
Witt, Glen L. *How to Build Boat Trailers*, 2nd ed. Bellflower, CA: Glen-L Marine Designs, 1996.

INDEX

Numbers in **bold** refer to pages with illustrations